Women,
Nazis,
and
Universities

Women,
Nazis,
and
Universities

_Female University Students
in the Third Reich,
1933–1945_

JACQUES R. PAUWELS

Contributions in Women's Studies, Number 50

Greenwood Press
Westport, Connecticut • London, England

Library of Congress Cataloging in Publication Data

Pauwels, Jacques R.
  Women, Nazis, and universities.

  (Contributions in women's studies, ISSN 0147-104X ; no. 50)
  Bibliography: p.
  Includes index.
  1. National socialism and education. 2. Higher
education of women—Germany—History. 3. Women college
students—Germany—History. I. Title. II. Series.
LA721.81.P39   1984   378'.1982   83-20161
ISBN 0-313-24203-8 (lib. bdg.)

Library of Congress Catalog Card Number: 83-20161
ISBN: 0-313-24203-8
ISSN: 0147-104X

First published in 1984

Greenwood Press
A division of Congressional Information Service, Inc.
88 Post Road West
Westport, Connecticut 06881

Printed in the United States of America

10 9 8 7 6 5 4 3 2 1

For Danielle

Contents

Figures

Acknowledgments

More than ten years have elapsed since I started the research that led to publication of this study. During that time, an inestimable number of individuals and institutions graciously provided expert advice, valuable suggestions, constructive criticism, encouragement, financial help, and many other forms of assistance. I am grateful to all, but to some I owe a very special debt.

First of all, I wish to express my appreciation for the financial support I received from the German Academic Exchange Service in Bonn and from the Interuniversity Centre for European Studies in Montreal.

Dr. Hans D. Oppel, the former archivist of the *Archiv der ehemaligen RSF und des NSDStB* in Würzburg, deserves to be cited for the incredible goodwill he never ceased to display towards the young researcher for whom—undoubtedly in an unguarded moment—he had once opened the doors of the little-known but truly remarkable institution of which he was then in charge.

The obviously ungrateful task of introducing an ingenuous outsider to the intricacies of the historiography of the Third Reich, and of administering the medicine of scholarly discipline to a reluctant but needy patient, fell to Professor Michael H. Kater of York University in Toronto. In sending him a disciple of dubious caliber, academic fate may not have been kind to him, but I am grateful indeed to have had such a masterful mentor, without whom this study would never have been started, let alone completed.

Finally, for her unwavering support and wonderful patience during all these years, I owe a unique debt of gratitude to my wife, Danielle, to whom this work is dedicated.

Abbreviations

AHR	*American Historical Review*
ANSt	*Arbeitsgemeinschaft Nationalsozialistischer Studentinnen* (Working Community of National Socialist Women Students)
ARNW	*Archiv der ehemaligen Reichsstudentenführung und des NSDStB* (Archives of the Former Reich Student Leadership and of the NSDStB) (Würzburg)
BA	*Bundesarchiv* (Federal Archives) (Koblenz)
BDM	*Bund Deutscher Mädel* (League of German Girls)
BRD	*Bundesrepublik Deutschland* (German Federal Republic)
CEH	*Central European History*
DAF	*Deutsche Arbeitsfront* (German Labor Front)
DB	*Die Bewegung* ("The Movement")
DCSB	*Deutsche Christliche Studentinnenbewegung* (German Christian Women Students' Movement)
DSt	*Deutsche Studentenschaft* (German Student Federation)
DStZ	*Deutsche Studenten-Zeitung* ("German Student Newspaper")
FAD	*Frauenarbeitsdienst* (Labor Service for Women)
GBA	*Generalbevollmächtigter für den Arbeitseinsatz* (Plenipotentiary for Labor Mobilization)
GLAK	*Generallandesarchiv* (General State Archive of Baden) (Karlsruhe)
HGdF	*Hochschulgemeinschaft deutscher Frauen* (University Community of German Women)
HIS	Hoover Institution on War, Revolution, and Peace (Stanford, California)

HJ	*Hitlerjugend* (Hitler Youth)
HZ	*Historische Zeitschrift* ("Historical Journal")
IZG	*Institut für Zeitgeschichte* (Institute for Contemporary History) (Munich)
JCH	*Journal for Contemporary History*
JMH	*Journal of Modern History*
JSH	*Journal of Social History*
KHD	*Kriegshilfsdienst* (War Aid Service)
MuK	*Mutter und Kind* (Mother and Child Project)
NAW	National Archives (Washington)
NSDAP	*Nationalsozialistische Deutsche Arbeiterpartei* (National Socialist German Workers' Party)
NSDStB	*Nationalsozialistischer Deutscher Studentenbund* (National Socialist German Student League)
NSF	*Nationalsozialistische Frauenschaft* (National Socialist Women's League)
NSK	*Nationalsozialistische Partei-Korrespondenz* ("National Socialist Party Correspondence")
NSLB	*Nationalsozialistischer Lehrerbund* (National Socialist Teachers' Association)
NSV	*Nationalsozialistische Volkswohlfahrt* (National Socialist People's Welfare Organization)
PO	*Politische Organisation* (Political Organization of the NSDAP)
RBWK	*Reichsberufswettkampf* (Reich Vocational Contest)
REM	*Reichserziehungsminister* or *Reichserziehungsministerium* (Reich Education Minister or Reich Ministry of Education)
RJF	*Reichsjugendführung* (Reich Youth Leadership)
RKF or RKFDV	*Reichskommissar für die Festigung deutschen Volkstums* (Reich Commissar for the Strengthening of German Folkdom)
RLB	*Reichsluftschutzbund* (Reich League for Air Protection)
RMdI	*Reichsministerium des Innern* (Reich Ministry of the Interior)
RSF	*Reichsstudentenführung* (Reich Student Leadership)
SA	*Sturmabteilung* (Storm Troopers)
SD	*Sicherheitsdienst* (Security Service)
SIPO	*Sicherheitspolizei* (Security Police)
SS	*Schutzstaffel* (Protection Guard) or *Sommersemester* (summer semester [in figures only])
StPD	*Studenten-Pressedienst* ("Student Press Service")
TeNo	*Technische Nothilfe* (Technical Emergency Aid Organization)
TH	*Technische Hochschule* (Technical University)
TR	Trimester
VB	*Völkischer Beobachter* ("Folkish Observer")

VKDST	*Verband Katholischer Deutscher Studentinnenvereine* (Federation of Catholic German Organizations for Women Students)
VSWG	*Vierteljahrschrift für Sozial- und Wirtschaftsgeschichte* (''Quarterly for Social and Economic History'')
VZG	*Vierteljahrshefte für Zeitgeschichte* (''Quarterly for Contemporary History'')
WHW	*Winterhilfswerk* (Winter Aid Organization)
WS	*Wintersemester* (winter semester)

Women,
Nazis,
and
Universities

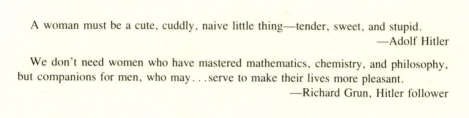

A woman must be a cute, cuddly, naive little thing—tender, sweet, and stupid.

—Adolf Hitler

We don't need women who have mastered mathematics, chemistry, and philosophy, but companions for men, who may...serve to make their lives more pleasant.

—Richard Grun, Hitler follower

Introduction

Today's student of that relatively short period in German history commonly referred to as the Third Reich cannot help but experience a faint feeling of guilt in presenting the printed results of his or her historical research to the public. After all, more than 50,000 biographies, diaries, source editions, monographs, and other serious studies have already been published on the topic of Hitler, the NSDAP (*Nationalsozialistische Deutsche Arbeiterpartei*—National Socialist German Workers' Party), and the Nazi state.[1] Every five or six years, moreover, a new "Hitler wave" seems to flood Europe and North America, leaving behind a bewildering (if fascinating) jetsam of popular histories of dubious value and taste, sensational articles on Hitler's sex life, counterfeit SS (*Schutzstaffel*—Protection Guard) or *Wehrmacht* regalia and Hitler diaries, television documentaries, and lavish Hollywood productions.[2]

But the pendulum of public interest can also swing the other way. We frequently hear suggestions that too much has already been written about Hitler and that we know virtually all there is to know about the Third Reich. In Germany there is an understandable desire to bury the past, to close the books on an inglorious episode of that nation's stormy annals. And anti-fascists everywhere, fearful of the political dangers of a too often uncritical fascination with the Nazi adventure, deplore "the revival of numerous Hitler legends and the glut of publications which mystify Hitler and glorify Nazism."[3] For the sake of objectives as different from each other as respect for German national sensitivity and international antifascist vigilance, then, a moratorium on further publications on National Socialism might appear desirable.

But silence on the subject breeds equally dangerous ignorance. The Germans learned this lesson not so long ago, when an inquiry revealed the grotesque misconceptions about Hitler that had taken root in the minds of their teenagers

as a result of deficient history instruction in the classrooms of the Federal Republic.[4] Furthermore, the gargantuan output of studies on the Third Reich not-
withstanding, only a relatively limited number of themes of its history have been
adequately dealt with. The analysis of the careers of the *Führer* and the other
major actors in the Nazi drama is a good example.[5] Ever since the Nuremberg
Trials, moreover, the foreign policy of the Third Reich and the events leading
up to the outbreak of the Second World War have been closely scrutinized, as
have the military campaigns of the war itself.[6] In addition, the magnitude of the
crimes perpetrated on Jews in Germany and in the occupied territories could not
fail to stimulate research in that field and focus attention on the sinister instruments of Nazi terror, specifically the SS.[7] Finally, historians have not neglected
to examine the roots and nature of National Socialist ideology in the context of
peculiarly German traditions or within the more general framework of European
Fascism.[8]

Although we have thus undeniably learned a great deal about Hitler, his party,
and his state, many questions remain to be answered and much remains to be
understood. In particular, we still know relatively little about the "average"
German in National Socialist society. What did this hypothetical person really
think about the *Führer* and the Nazi regime, how did this man or woman adapt
to the everyday realities of life during those difficult years of regimentation,
terror, war, and defeat? These are important questions, but the answers are far
from clear. It is encouraging, therefore, that small but growing numbers of
historians have recently been turning away from the conventional themes of the
history of the Third Reich in order to cultivate the fallow field of the social
history of Nazism and Nazi Germany.

A pioneering work in this respect was David Schoenbaum's *Hitler's Social
Revolution: Class and Status in Nazi Germany, 1933–1939*, first published in
1966. The author analyzed the impact of the National Socialist "revolution" on
various "constituent groups" of German society, such as farmers, civil servants,
industrial workers, and women, and came to the startling conclusion that Nazism,
an intrinsically reactionary regime, actually functioned as a "locomotive" of
some form of social progress. As Schoenbaum saw it, the Nazi "revolution"
may not have been a genuine revolution, but it produced revolutionary results
in that it acted as a catalyst of modernization and social change in a Germany
that in this respect had lagged behind Western Europe. In order to confirm or
refute Schoenbaum's fascinating thesis, it was clear that the role of his "constituent groups" would have to be studied in much greater detail than he had
been able to do.

In the 1970s considerable progress was made in this direction. Research on
labor in the Third Reich, for instance, produced a veritable *magnum opus* as
early as 1975 in the form of T. W. Mason's *Arbeiterklasse und Volksgemeinschaft*. Moreover, a surprisingly large number of young historians both in Germany and in North America focused their attention on the peculiar relationship
between German university students and National Socialism in the Weimar Re-

public as well as in the Third Reich itself. The National Socialist Student League was thus dealt with by Ursula Dibner, Anselm Faust, Manfred Franze, and Geoffrey Giles, to mention but a few; the aspirations and frustrations of Weimar students were dealt with by Michael Steinberg and Michael Kater. The present study, then, is conceived in part as a contribution to the continuing investigation into the role played by university students—in this case by female students—in Hitler's movement and state.

In comparison with workers and students, women of the Nazi era had virtually been ignored by historians (including social historians) of the Third Reich until the mid-1970s. This deplorable situation was particularly difficult to understand since women were one of the few "constituent groups" of Nazi society whose plight had been investigated in great detail by a foreign sociologist as early as 1938, when Clifford Kirkpatrick published *Nazi Germany, Its Women and Family Life*. This book may not be without its shortcomings, but it constitutes a treasure chest of social data, and it really should have inspired an historical study about women in the Third Reich as soon as Clio turned her attention to the social history of Hitler's state. As it turned out, the theme of women under National Socialism was not to attract historical investigators for another decade, that is, until the mid-1970s. It is true that David Schoenbaum dedicated a chapter of his book to "The Third Reich and Women" and that Joachim Fest did the same in his masterful collection of portraits of Nazi leaders, *The Face of the Third Reich* (1970). Both treatments were meritorious, but far too brief to be satisfactory in any way. Much the same could be said about Hans-Peter Bleuel's reflections on "Das Frauenbild des Nationalsozialismus" in his study of sex in Nazi Germany, *Das Saubere Reich*,[9] and about the chapter on women in Richard Grunberger's *The 12-Year Reich* (1971), a book that claims to be "a social history of Nazi Germany" but offers little more than a collection of vignettes and anecdotes.

In recent years, however, this situation has changed entirely. The activities of the women's movement provided a powerful impetus for the development of women's studies in general at universities and institutes from Los Angeles to Berlin. Specifically, it stimulated historical research into the position of women in the Nazi state. Even at this early stage, the results are quite impressive. The role of women in the Third Reich in general, and their regimentation by the Nazis in particular, have been treated by Jill Stephenson in *Women in Nazi Society* and *The Nazi Organisation of Women*, published in 1975 and 1981, respectively. Claudia Koonz has examined the role of female NSDAP members prior to 1933 as well as the alteration of Nazi policies with regard to women after that fateful year. The position of female labor in the economy of Hitler's state is analyzed impressively in Dörte Winkler's *Frauenarbeit im "Dritten Reich"* (1977) and Stefan Bajohr's *Die Hälfte der Fabrik* (1979). As for the war years, we have Leila Rupp's comparative study of German and American propaganda efforts directed at women, *Mobilizing Women for War* (1978). And just recently three more general treatments of the role of women in the Third Reich have come off the press: Dorothee Klinksiek's *Die Frau im NS-Staat*

(1982), a collection of essays prepared by the *Frauengruppe Faschismusfor-schung* and entitled *Mutterkreuz und Arbeitsbuch* (1981), and Rita Thalmann's *Etre Femme sous le IIIe Reich* (1982). This list is far from complete; it contains only a few examples of the excellent work in this field.

The present study focuses on women university students (*Studentinnen*) in the Third Reich. The theme is not entirely new; it was briefly touched on by Kristine von Soden and Gaby Zipfel in *70 Jahre Frauenstudium: Frauen in der Wissen-schaft* (1979), and it had been examined in greater detail by Jill Stephenson in a short chapter of her first book.[10] Stephenson's *Women in Nazi Society* (1975) was an important pioneering work, the first global study of women in the National Socialist state. Its author offered interesting viewpoints and reached sound con-clusions on a broad range of issues, including birth control, marriage and moth-erhood, emancipation, and female employment. The wide scope of Stephenson's interest, however, precluded the kind of in-depth research that most of these themes deserve. It is now time for us, as Renate Bridenthal put it, "to refine the valuable ore Stephenson has extracted."[11] Just as Dörte Winkler has recently investigated the status of female labor in the Third Reich in much greater detail than Jill Stephenson could possibly have done, I now present a study that is intended not to supersede but to complement her work on women students in Nazi society. Having had the opportunity to search the massive (if chaotic) records of the National Socialist organizations for women students, for instance, I was able not only to retrace their history but also to learn a great deal about the background, aspirations, and attitude towards National Socialism of women students at the universities of the Third Reich. And the discovery of a considerable number of important wartime documents of the former Reich Ministry of Edu-cation in the Koblenz *Bundesarchiv* made it possible to expand the scope of this study to include the war years, about which Stephenson remains silent, and to analyze critical issues such as the role of female students in "war service" and resistance.

This book deals with women university students, but not *only* with women university students. The first part focuses on *Nazi policies* with regard to female academic aspirations. It is also true that certain questions with regard to women students of the Third Reich are not answered here; for example, those interested in the private lives of Germany's young female academics in the 1930s and 1940s will be disappointed, since little will be said about that admittedly fas-cinating topic. This book, then, is not a genuine feminist study; it does not deal with women, but with *women in a world of men*, more specifically in a world of *antifeminist men*, as a reviewer of the manuscript pointed out. Two factors may be cited to explain this. First, the author's bias as a male student of Nazi social and educational policies, and second, the nature of the sources—mainly official documents—at his disposal. (Private letters and diaries, for example, which may serve to throw light on the personal experiences of individual women students under National Socialism, are extremely rare. Perhaps a fortunate his-torian will some day be able to locate sufficient numbers of them to undertake a study of those aspects of the role of women students in the Third Reich which could not be dealt with on these pages.) In spite of its obvious shortcomings from the feminist point of view, however, it is hoped that this work may be considered a bona fide addition to the growing number of investigations into the role of women in the Third Reich.

Two final remarks concern terminological problems. First, in this context, "universities" and "university studies" refer to the German *Hochschulen*—institutions of higher learning in general—and *Hochschulstudium*. This includes universities proper (*Universitäten*); technical universities (*technische Hochschulen*); higher commercial institutes (*Handelschochschulen*); colleges of agriculture, veterinary science, forestry, and mining (*landwirtschaftliche, tierärztliche, forstliche Hochschulen*, and *Bergakademien*); training colleges for teachers (*Hochschulen für Lehrerbildung*); theological seminars (*philosophisch-theologische Hochschulen*); and certain special medical schools such as the medical academy (*medizinische Akademie*) in Düsseldorf. Higher technical institutes (*Fachschulen*), however, were not considered. Second, the German term *Frauenstudium*, which refers to higher education for women, is not easily translated into English. "Female academic aspirations" or "women's academic studies" come to mind, but do not do justice to the German expression's combination of formal elegance and conceptual complexity. Consequently, while English translations will be offered whenever possible, the German term *Frauenstudium* alone will be used frequently, especially in those cases where no English term seems adequate.

PART 1

National Socialism and Women in Higher Education: Theory, Policy, Consequences

1

National Socialism and the Academic Aspirations of German Women: Theoretical Foundations

In a popular tract on National Socialist ideology, published with a keen sense of political as well as commercial timing in 1933, the Nazi takeover, eulogized as the "German resurrection," was characterized as "a male event" (*ein männ-liches Ereignis*).[1] This was not just a metaphor inspired by the spectacle of endless columns of storm troopers marching triumphantly through the streets of Berlin, but a rather accurate description of reality. The Nazi "revolution" *was* a male achievement in the sense that it produced a state that was, and wanted to be, an intrinsically antifeminist "state of men" (*Männerstaat*).[2] Moreover, by contemporary as well as modern criteria, the Nazi party itself was unques-tionably a bastion of male chauvinism and misogyny.[3] Joseph Goebbels and less prominent authorities on National Socialism called the NSDAP a pure "mas-culine movement" (*Männerbewegung*).[4] Particularly in its early stages, before it developed into a mass organization, the Nazi party cultivated the aura of a "male league" or *Männerbund*, an all-male order of soldierly leaders welded together by the presumably masculine virtues of loyalty, patriotism, and courage. According to the controversial protagonist and theoretician of the *Männerbund* phenomenon, Hans Blüher, the male league was typified by homo-erotic over-tones, even though not every member, nor for that matter the majority, had to be homosexual. As Blüher saw it, the *Männerbund* was the product of the "male-male eros," just as the family was the fruit of the "male-female eros." In Germany, the *Männerbund* idea had been greatly fostered by the experiences of life at the front during the Great War and by the adventures of the Free Corps in the years thereafter, but it was also inspired by what were regarded as historical precedents, such as ancient Sparta, the Teutonic Order, and the Knights Templar.[5]

The early Nazi party, then, was modelled on this *Männerbund* pattern. A contemporary American sociologist, Clifford Kirkpatrick, drew attention to "the latent homo-erotic character'' of the NSDAP,[6] and political opponents of Nazism likewise recognized the trend,[7] as did women, both in Germany and abroad.[8] Blüher himself wrote after the Second World War that "the Hitler movement was a male league, subject to the laws of the male bond, to a hair."[9] And one of the most authoritative voices in the field of anthropological research on the male bond today, Lionel Tiger, refers to the circle of Nazi stalwarts around Hitler as "that very special male bond of senior Nazis."[10] Finally, the fact that women were scrupulously excluded from all posts of any importance within the party, and the prominence of a number of overt homosexuals (such as Ernst Röhm and Rudolf Hess) within the NSDAP's inner sanctum, has not escaped the attention of historians. They too have concluded that the Nazi party originated as an elitist *Männerbund* of sorts.[11]

One of the most typical exponents of Nazi *Männerbund* mythology and its most prolific purveyor was the Nazi party philosopher Alfred Rosenberg; but the bulwark of National Socialist masculine mystique was the SA (*Sturmabteilung*—storm troopers).[12] Homosexuality proper was less widespread among the rank and file of the storm troopers than has hitherto been believed, but *Männerbund* ethics as well as homo-erotic relationships definitely characterized the SA's top leadership, exemplified by men like Edmund Heines and Röhm.[13] Speculation that Hitler himself may have been an active homosexual has recently been discounted, but psychohistorians such as Robert Waite and Helm Stierlin attribute to him latent homosexual tendencies, which it is said he sought to suppress.[14] Hans Blüher shared this opinion and claimed to have recognized in Hitler the typical "male hero" (*Männerheld*) for whom "the male was destiny."[15] The *Führer* had read Blüher's treatise on the *Männerbund* and was fascinated by his exotic theories of homosexual superiority and his visions of "a new Hellas peopled by strong, naked, but chaste men, inspired by heroism and capable of leadership."[16] Hitler thus sought to sublimate his own homosexual leanings within the framework of a pure (i.e., strictly male exclusionist) Nazi *Männerbund*, capable of rejuvenating Germany in the image of the heroic, soldierly, and patriarchal societies evoked by Blüher.

The *Führer*, furthermore, had other reasons for excluding women from his Nazi male league. It is generally known that his personality and manners radiated a certain femininity.[17] He himself was aware of this, worried a great deal about it, and had doubts about his own masculinity. Waite tells us that this is the reason Hitler went to great lengths to emphasize his hardness and brutality, qualities he associated with masculinity. "His protestations of masculinity (as he defined it) [were] so strident, as to suggest that he was . . . defending against fears about his own masculinity. He was determined that no one would ever suspect him of sexual inadequacy, femininity, or homosexuality."[18] Toughness and brutality, Hitler's criteria for manliness, thus became a "normative value" in the *Führer*'s world, in the Third Reich, and most of all in the Nazi party. A rugged, brutal style of masculinity was the celebrated trademark of "all Nazi Führers from the idealized leader at the top down through all the echelons of his society. The district leaders of the Party, the leaders of youth, cultural, educational, athletic, literary, and medical societies—all cultivated the toughness, brutality, and compensatory masculinity of their master.''[19] But Hitler was not content to exorcize his own suspected femininity by an impressive display of tough manliness alone. He also went to great lengths to dissociate himself from everything feminine, and from women in particular. He may have professed to revere women and exhibited an awkward, old-fashioned style of chivalry in their presence, but in reality he despised, feared, disliked, and mistrusted them, and considered them inferior to men.[20] It is clear that the last word has not yet been spoken on the intriguing topics of the Nazi *Männerbund* and Hitler's ambivalent attitude to women. But there can be no doubt that male exclusionism and its corollary, misogyny, were essential characteristics of the National Socialist movement and strongly colored the Nazis' views of women in German society.

For the cultural and intellectual ambitions of women, members of the Nazi *Männerbund* had nothing but contempt.[21] In particular, they were convinced that women were unfit for studies at university level. Hitler himself developed a rudimentary epistemology of sorts, which held that man arrived at knowledge through intellect, woman through feeling, instinct, and faith. Since this was declared to be the natural state of things, he condemned women's intellectual aspirations as "intellectualism of the worst sort.''[22] Alfred Rosenberg was another stalwart believer in the intellectual inferiority of women. In his *Mythus*, he claimed that women were characterized by a certain "lack of [intellectual] capacity" (*Fähigkeitslosigkeit*), that they were incapable of grasping major problems in their entirety in what he called an "architectonic" fashion. Women, he averred, could only think "lyrically," an undefined but supposedly inferior mode of thought.[23] Other Nazis echoed Hitler's and Rosenberg's misgivings about female academic aspirations. One Georg Lange, for instance, was convinced that women could not possibly grasp abstractions or understand history, and a certain Josef Rompel predicted not only degeneration of the German "race" but "emasculation of our continent" if women were allowed to continue to dabble in intellectual affairs.[24] Elsewhere women were said to lack the capacity for the kind of "technical-constructive" and "purely intellectual" thinking required for the study of such disciplines as law or chemistry. Others claimed that a lack of creativity made women unfit for university studies.[25] The Nazi press contributed regularly to the diffusion of these misogynic prejudices. In October 1926 the *Völkischer Beobachter* published an article endorsing the views of the Danish scholar Knud A. Wieth-Knudsen, one of the best-known proponents of the theory of women's intellectual inferiority.[26] As for irrefutable cases of highly successful female students or significant scholarly achievements by women, they were generally brushed aside as exceptions to the rule or as *Bienenfleiss*, the result of sheer hard work without intellectual substance.[27]

The myth of women's intellectual inferiority did not have to be invented by the Nazis. Here, as in so many other aspects of their ideology, they were simply echoing an old bourgeois prejudice. Professor Ernst Bumm, in a famous lecture at the University of Berlin in 1917, had already enumerated some of the prevailing popular beliefs in this respect, notably the notion that woman's brain was smaller than that of man and that women had an aversion to abstract thinking.[28]

The arrogant assertion that only men were endowed with the intellect required for university studies was cynically paraphrased by one woman student, who wrote, "Intelligence is a part of the male sexual apparatus" (*Intelligenz ist ein Stück Geschlechtsapparat des Mannes*).[29] But this belief was only one of many characteristically male exclusionist prejudices against the *Frauenstudium*. Another one was the assertion that women were not really interested in university studies and that academic careers could not possibly bring them happiness. The *Führer* himself stated on one occasion that education, intellect, and cultivation were unimportant to women, that their sole concern in life was simply to be admired by men.[30] From such premises it followed logically that women could not take a genuine interest and could not find happiness in academic pursuits. Theodor Friedrich thus ventured the opinion that studying violated the female nature and that by attending college young women forfeited the happiness they could easily have found in love, marriage, and motherhood.[31] The fact that increasing numbers of women did flock to institutions of higher learning was sometimes rationalized as the result of the whim of status-seeking bourgeois parents; more frequently, however, it was interpreted as plain husband-hunting. Josef Rompel, the Nazi author of a rabidly antifeminist pamphlet, bemoaned the rapid degeneration of the German universities into "marriage markets" (*Heiratsmärkte*) ever since the admission of the first women to academe. He cited an allegation to the effect that one-quarter of all female students abandoned their studies as soon as they had found a suitable partner, thereby wasting "a considerable investment on the part of their family and of the state."[32] Such an explanation evidently gratified the male ego and was therefore extremely popular among Nazi professors and students.

According to the Nazi male-supremacist gospel, women were intellectually unfit for higher studies and in any case not genuinely interested in such studies. Moreover, most Nazis sincerely believed that women did not need the knowledge that results from a higher education. After all, women's allegedly predestined role in nature and society, in the Nazi view, was to bear children, and that was supposed to be a simple task. Modern-day critic Hans-Peter Bleuel has effectively paraphrased this attitude in the slogan "A minimum of intellect is sufficient to give birth" (*Ein Minimum an Intellekt genügt zum Gebären*).[33] The Nazis thus cynically arrogated for themselves the right to decide what women needed. In making this decision, they were guided solely by their own interests, and these were the interests of the "petty bourgeois patriarch who looks down upon women, yet needs them for his pleasure and propagation."[34] For this purpose, women obviously did not require much of an education. As one of Hitler's followers had it: "We don't need women who have mastered mathematics, chemistry, and philosophy, but companions for men, who may . . . serve to make their lives more pleasant."[35]

Nazi male exclusionists firmly believed that the university had always been, and ought to be, an institution for men, and for men alone, just like the army. Consequently, women were looked down on as unwelcome intruders, and their presence at the institutions of higher learning was interpreted as a symptom of decadence.[36] A modern sociologist, Wolfgang Nitsch, has pointed out that the German university has remained until the present in practice what it had been until the beginning of the century in law, "not only a male prerogative, but men's own institution, defending their cause against the other sex." Others, notably Hannelore Gerstein and Helge Pross, cite the traditional "male outlook" (männliche Prägung) of the German university.[37] While there can therefore be no doubt about the continuity of this type of male exclusionist prejudice, it is also a fact that it was unusually widespread among the Nazis, if only because they—and the SA men in particular—used to look on the university as a sort of army training camp, a Spartan or Prussian semimilitary institution for young soldiers. The Nazi student leader Andreas Feickert, for instance, regarded higher education as a "battle experience" (Kampferlebnis) and the university as a battlefield or a camp for physical and political training. Alfred Baeumler, a professor in Berlin, promoted similar ideas and proposed to transform the German university into an authoritarian "home of men" (Männerhaus) that would have no place for what he termed the "feminine-democratic" element.[38]

The Nazis' opposition to women's academic aspirations was obviously determined by the intrinsically male exclusionist nature of their movement, but it was further reinforced by eugenic considerations. As the Nazis saw it, the influx of women at the universities compounded an issue that alarmed them greatly, namely, the decline of German fertility. They expected that women's elimination from the temples of learning would bring about a reversal of this decline and would thus help to safeguard the future of the German people.

A few figures may serve to illustrate the decline of German fertility in the years after the First World War. The average number of live births per 1,000 Germans, which stood at 40 in the late 1800s and at 29.8 in 1910, dropped drastically to 25.9 in the year 1920, to 19.6 in 1926, and to 14.7 in 1933.[39] The overall fertility rate of the population of the Reich, if we use the constant 100 for the year 1871, declined to 47 in the year 1925. This meant that German fertility was threatening to fall below the level required for adequate replacement of the existing population and that it was lower than in any other European nation, with the exception of Austria.[40]

Many Germans were greatly concerned about this development, particularly since a number of authorities in the demographic field conjured up images of "a dying people" (Volkstod).[41] More distressed than anybody else were the Nazis, since the specter of a decreasing population jeopardized Hitler's plans for conquest[42] and even threatened to bring about a political and military dwarfing of Germany. But a ready explanation, and a handy scapegoat, were soon found. Curt Rosten, author of a popular tract on Hitlerite ideology, flatly stated that "when a race degenerates, it is the fault of women."[43] As Rosten and other Nazis saw it, women had been neglecting their "natural" duties to "the race"— marriage and motherhood. They had yielded to the siren call of the emancipation movement and were increasingly involving themselves in such "unfeminine" activities as employment outside the home and university studies. Women's "intellectual pretension" (der weibliche Bildungswahn) was seen as eugenically unsound, as "one of the worst dangers for the biological future of the race," as National Socialist Wilhelm Hartnacke asserted in a speech in Munich in 1932.[44]

Such, in great lines, was the Nazis' eugenic case against the Frauenstudium. In addition, it was claimed that women's constitutions could not sustain the great mental and physical efforts that university studies required. Ignoring this would have catastrophic consequences, since it would turn women into nervous wrecks and "defeminize" them, thus making them "spiritually and physically unfit for motherhood." Such creatures, it was argued, were simply no longer women but second-class men, and could therefore not be expected to fulfill woman's role within marriage.[45] The Nazis claimed, furthermore, that higher studies could seriously impair and even permanently damage the procreative capacities of women. It was not an uncommon belief that intellectual pursuits might lead to functional disorders of the genitals or that the pressure associated with such pursuits, and even the need to remain seated for long periods of time, might lead to menstrual disturbances, to a sort of academic amenorrhea.[46]

Tales such as these were often accompanied by impressive but unsubstantiated statistics. Without referring to the source of his information, a Nazi physician from Düsseldorf wrote, ostensibly in all seriousness: "Eighty percent of all our female university graduates are permanently sterile; the few who do get children are 'blessed' with one or two usually weak children . . . the firstborn dies in most cases."[47] This state of things loomed all the more tragic to the Nazis since they also believed that precisely the "racially most valuable" women tended to take up university studies and therefore to become sterile on account of "intellectual overexertion." The best elements were thus lost for the procreation of "the race" and the result, as the Nazis saw it, was that the law of natural selection was sabotaged. With only mediocre and inferior women left to participate in the procreation process, the average intelligence of Germans was said to be degenerating. Instead of the desired Darwinian selection of the best, a "counterselection" (Gegenauslese) allegedly occurred which spelled catastrophe for "the race."[48]

With all this the repertory of the Nazis' eugenic case against the Frauenstudium was far from depleted. University studies were also held to lead to a highly individualistic and egotistic attitude in young women, to a sense of superiority that bred contempt for household work and motherhood. Why men were not similarly affected by academic work was not explained by the Nazi educational experts. In any event, through some mysterious process university studies presumably caused women to look on children as a needless source of aggravation. But this dereliction of their procreative duties did not go unpunished; as "their intellect repudiated what their instinct longed for," such women were said to suffer, albeit unconsciously, from acute schizophrenia (*seelische Zwiespalt*).[49] The Nazis were also convinced that it was nearly impossible for female university graduates to find a marriage partner. Not only did they have to compete with younger and therefore presumably more attractive women for the relatively few men who were available on the marriage market of postwar Germany,[50] but their own criteria were now also much higher. Many therefore chose to remain single, and the result was once again a loss of "valuable hereditary stock." Even if they did marry, prospects for large and healthy offspring were presumably dim, for the best years of these women's childbearing period were said to be over.[51] In any event, women graduates were believed to make poor wives and mothers since they had never had the time for adequate training in cooking, child care, and homemaking in general. Theodor Friedrich lamented:

The academic woman has become twenty-four and even twenty-five years old, yet not even once has she been active coherently in the household like her sisters in the days of old. . . . Indeed, there are now girls and young women who, after ten or thirteen years of schooling and an additional four or five years of university, have not even the slightest inkling of household work, particularly of cooking and child care.[52]

Evidence for all this was supplied in the form of more statistics that purported to demonstrate the low marriage rate of women graduates and the prevalence of the one- or two-children system, or even the "no-children system" (*Keinkindersystem*), among the married ones. The average fertility of academic women was estimated at only 0.8 children per capita.[53]

The eugenic argument against women's academic aspirations was summarized by one Dr. Richard Grün from Düsseldorf. Higher education, he asserted, was tantamount to a "castration of our women," and consequently the doors of the German institutions of higher learning had to be closed to them. If not, Grün prophesied darkly, "the German people will perish for the sake of a false educational ideal, which transforms women into second-class men and thereby jeopardizes their femininity."[54]

Purely male exclusionist delusions and eugenic phobias inspired by the decline of German fertility were two significant determinants of the Nazis' negative attitude towards women's academic aspirations. A third factor, and one of at least equal importance, consisted in considerations of an economic nature. Women's employment was regarded by the Nazis as a cause of men's unemployment, and the *Frauenstudium* was condemned because it yielded steadily increasing numbers of female job-seekers in the academic professions, a field already ravaged by unemployment. The Nazis argued that unemployment, which plagued Germany's economy more or less consistently throughout the 1920s and early

1930s, was caused primarily by the increase of female employment in the wake of the First World War. Compared to the prewar years, women's share of the Reich's labor force had indeed grown considerably. The fact, too, that female labor suffered less from unemployment caused resentment, and women's work thus became the scapegoat for male unemployment.[55] Sending women back to the home became part of Hitler's "secret recipe" (Patentlösung),[56] as a cynical political commentator called it, for solving the unemployment crisis.

In the years after the First World War, women had made impressive inroads into the area of the academic professions. As of July 11, 1922, for instance, women were admitted to the practice of law throughout the Reich, and the number of female lawyers quintupled between 1925 and 1933. Women flocked to the teaching profession, mainly at the level of elementary and secondary schools but also at the universities; the first female university lecturer made her appearance in Munich in 1919, and a woman earned an appointment as full professor for the first time in 1923. The number of women physicians mushroomed, rising from 195 in 1907 to 2,572 in 1925 and 4,395 in 1933. Comparable gains were made in dentistry.[57]

But all this occurred during years when the academic professions were devastated by unemployment. Academic unemployment plagued Weimar Germany from the very moment of its birth; it was triggered by such factors as the "migration of intellectuals from areas lost to the Reich as a result of the Treaty of Versailles" and limitations on the size of Germany's army, which "closed an important avenue of comparable social prestige for many."[58] The overcrowding of the universities and the plight of the jobless "intellectual proletariat," to which prominent Nazis like Joseph Goebbels belonged, was a hot issue throughout the 1920s and even more so in the early 1930s, when prospects for a career in the academic professions decreased further as a result of the Great Depression. In 1933, for instance, vacancies in all academic professions combined were estimated at only 11 to 12,000, while the surplus number of university graduates was reported to approach 50,000.[59] Many Germans therefore came to look on women's progress in the academic job market with great misgivings and resentment,[60] even though only small numbers of women were involved in proportion to their share of the total population of the Reich.[61] In the 1920s, women flocked to the universities in growing numbers. The total number of female students grew from 8,186 in 1920 to 19,394 in 1931, and women's share of the student population rose from 9.4 percent to 17.9 percent over the same period.[62] To the Nazis this seemed an extravagant development that unduly heightened the tensions on the academic labor market. In their eyes, the "normal" proportion of women within the student body was the one of the prewar years, for instance of 1913, when women had accounted for 4.3 percent of all university students, or even 1911, when it had been 3.3 percent.[63] As the Nazis saw it, the rapid growth of the Frauenstudium in the 1920s was one of the main causes of academic unemployment, and they drew the conclusion that "a restriction of the higher education of women" was imperative if "a rational and just partition of the academic living space" was to be brought about.[64] The NSDAP thus proposed to solve the problem of academic unemployment at the expense of women students, just as unemployment in general was to be solved at the expense of working women. Undoubtedly this may help explain the early success of Hitler's movement among male students, who were naturally keenly aware of the women's competition. There was an analogy in this respect with the Nazi students' demand for a *numerus clausus*—a restricted number of new matriculations—for Jews at the universities, voiced as early as 1926, a demand that was likewise inspired (or at least reinforced) by a desire to reduce the number of competitors for the few opportunities available in the professional field.[65]

The Nazis, then, opposed the presence of women at German institutions of higher learning for three basic reasons. First, the NSDAP displayed many features of a misogynic *Männerbund*, and male exclusionist attitudes were rife among its membership. Many of Hitler's followers firmly believed that women were unfit for higher studies, that they could not possibly take a genuine interest in intellectual matters, and that they should be barred from the university, which was regarded as a male sanctuary like the army. Second, National Socialist dogma held that intellectual ambitions necessarily detracted from women's "natural" eugenic vocation—marriage and motherhood—and contributed to the catastrophic decline (from their viewpoint) of German fertility. Third, the Nazis had economic misgivings about the *Frauenstudium*, for they viewed the influx of young women at the universities as the chief cause of academic unemployment. It came as a surprise to nobody, then, when Hitler's government proceeded to implement these misogynic views in the wake of the *Machtergreifung* (Hitler's "advent to power"; literally, "grabbing of power") of early 1933. What is remarkable, however, is that the Nazi campaign against the *Frauenstudium* turned out to be a tame and ineffectual affair, strangely out of proportion to the fury of the invective they had been heaping on women who cherished academic aspirations.

2

The Nazi Campaign Against Female Academic Aspirations, 1933–1935

The pièce de résistance of the Nazi regime's campaign against women's academic ambitions consisted in the introduction on December 28, 1933, of a *numerus clausus* that was to limit women in the future to a mere 10 percent of the new matriculations at all institutions of higher learning of the Reich. Officially at least, this measure did not discriminate against women; Wilhelm Frick, Reich minister of the interior, who was responsible for higher education at that time, based the executive order that established the *numerus clausus* on the "Law against the *Overcrowding* of German Schools and Universities" of April 25 of that same year, and restrictions on the number of male freshmen were likewise introduced. Even so, the *numerus clausus* clearly did discriminate against women. Female students were to be limited to 10 percent of the maximum of 15,000 new registrations that would be permitted in 1934.[1] But ever since the late 1920s, women had accounted for at least 19 percent and as much as 25 percent of all first-year students. And at Easter 1933 there had been 11,919 females in a crop of 43,162 high school graduates, representing approximately 25 percent of the total.[2] This clearly illustrates that the new Hitler government had its mind set on a drastic reduction of the number of female students in the Reich. And yet the importance of the *numerus clausus* should not be overestimated. At the start of the summer semester of 1934, instead of 1,500 girls being allowed to register for the first time, as had been planned, 1,699 were admitted, representing 12.5 percent of all newcomers rather than the officially projected 10 percent.[3] In reality, Frick's decree remained a dead letter.

Other measures proved even less impressive. The Nazi authorities instructed offices of vocational counselling (*Berufsberatungsstellen*) to discourage female high school graduates from pursuing academic studies and instead to try to interest them in careers in "housekeeping and agriculture" (*Haus- und Landwirtschaft*).[4]

But no coercion was used, so that women who were determined to study likely did so regardless of the advice they received. Indeed, it was no secret that of the few who were thus persuaded not to attend university, many nevertheless matriculated after a time.[5] The Study Foundation of the German People (*Studienstiftung des Deutschen Volkes*), which administered all state scholarships, was taken over by the Nazis shortly after the *Machtergreifung* and duly embarked on a strikingly misogynic policy.[6] Its new director, Hanns Streit, believed that women's academic aspirations ought to be "drastically limited" and that withholding scholarships was a perfectly appropriate means to achieve that objective.[7] Shortly before Christmas 1933, new "Basic Principles Governing Scholarships for German Students," which reflected Streit's views, were issued. Women students, it was declared, ought to be supported only "in those disciplines that lead to careers open to women, and only in proportion to the number of women required in the corresponding profession."[8] This statement may not have sounded entirely unreasonable were it not that nearly all disciplines and professions were considered either "unfeminine" or "overcrowded."[9] Consequently, women's share of all official grants dwindled from 11 percent in 1932 to 7 percent in 1934,[10] much to the satisfaction of the Nazi educational authorities, who described this development euphemistically as a "readjustment" or "normalization," a reduction of the number of scholarships for girls to its "natural" level.[11] But the results of this restriction were relatively insignificant. One has to keep in mind that, even before Hitler's advent to power, only an extremely small number of women students benefited from such grants. In the summer of 1932, for instance, only slightly more than 2 percent of all female university students had received a public scholarship. After the *Machtergreifung*, this ratio remained basically the same.[12] A woman's prospects for a grant in the Third Reich were thus neither better nor worse than in the last years of the Weimar Republic; both before and after 1933 they were extremely slim. In any event, it is clear that although this restriction may have resulted in a considerable amount of hardship and suffering in individual cases,[13] its overall impact was very limited, as only a tiny fraction of the female student population was affected by it.

On February 23, 1934, the Nazis introduced a compulsory six-month "labor service" for female high school graduates planning to take up academic studies (*Arbeitsdienst der Abiturientinnen mit Studiumsabsicht*). As of Easter of that year, no female was allowed to matriculate for the first time at a German university unless she could produce evidence that she had fulfilled this obligation.[14] The *Arbeitsdienst* was hailed by Nazi educators and officials as a great new educational and social experiment that, among other things, would teach Germany's future "academic women" (*Akademikerinnen*) respect for manual labor and thus provide them with an antidote to the overdose of intellectualism to which they would presumably be exposed at the university.[15] Such rhetoric, however, hardly obscured the fact that the pre-university "labor service" was intended primarily as an obstacle that would curb, or at least delay, women's enrollments at the institutions of higher learning. The introduction of the *Ar-*

beitsdienst served to lengthen the period of time before a woman could graduate and find employment, thus increasing the considerable financial sacrifice associated with university studies and disheartening those for whom such studies already loomed as an inordinately long and difficult proposition. Moreover, the life of the "labor maids" (*Arbeitsmaiden*) in the camps was far from pleasant, although Nazi publications invariably depicted it as idyllic and rewarding. The prospect of six months in a Spartan labor camp far from home, of hard work in the fields, inexorable discipline, and minimal comfort,[16] was undoubtedly a powerful deterrent to many young women who would normally have embarked on an academic career. Rumors of sexual permissiveness in the camps, which allegedly received frequent nocturnal visits from Hitler Youth members, alarmed many parents, who must have wondered whether exposing their daughters to the risk of an untimely pregnancy was not too high a price to pay for the right to study.[17] The *Arbeitsdienst* also served as a pre-university selective mechanism in a more formal way. Each woman's performance was assessed by her leaders at the end of her turn of service, and even a "satisfactory" (*genügend*) mark disqualified the recipient from taking up higher studies, since this result presumably demonstrated that "her general human conduct does not measure up to the standards prospective women students ought to meet."[18] In theory, therefore, the *Arbeitsdienst* was a formidable obstacle on a female's path to academe, but a closer examination reveals that its actual effects were not nearly as drastic as one might think.

Enforcement of the "labor service" regulations, for one thing, met with unforeseen difficulties from the very start. Sufficient space was simply not available for "academic women" in the camps of the organization of the Labor Service for Women (*Frauenarbeitsdienst*), which was primarily concerned with unemployed young women.[19] As a result, not all *Abiturientinnen* (female high school graduates) of Easter 1934 could be accommodated in the *Arbeitsdienst* in the summer of that year, and some four hundred had to be allowed to register at the universities in the fall without having performed their service.[20] A year later, in 1935, the space problem persisted, so it was decided to have the women serve thirteen weeks, or only half the prescribed six months.[21] Even so, it remained impossible to accommodate all candidates. In southwestern Germany, for instance, only 45 of a total of 240 *Abiturientinnen* could be accepted.[22] Throughout the Reich, 140 high school graduates fulfilled their "labor service" duty by performing a so-called "compensatory service" (*Ausgleichsdienst*), which consisted mainly of light office work within the Nazi welfare organizations and was normally reserved for young women who, because of health or physical handicaps, were deemed unfit for the heavy work in the labor camps.[23] But the majority of the *Abiturientinnen* for whom no place could be found were simply absolved of their *Arbeitsdienst* duty and could present themselves to be registered forthwith at the university of their choice.[24] In 1934/35, many aspiring female university students thus escaped all or part of the "labor service" obligations. As for those who did serve, there is no evidence that any were denied admission to the university on account of an inadequate or even simply "satisfactory" performance. Prior to 1936, therefore, when a start was finally made with the more-or-less consistent enforcement of its regulations, the *Arbeitsdienst* could hardly be regarded as a serious obstacle on the road to a higher education, as historians interested in the scheme have tended to do.[25]

In order to achieve their antifeminist objectives in the academic field, the Nazi rulers also resorted to cynical manipulations of the professional job market. By excluding women from a variety of professions that were proclaimed "unfeminine," for instance, or by simply threatening such measures, they hoped to deter females from taking up the studies that led to these careers. In December 1933 the head of the Reich Association of Physicians (*Reichsärztebund*) publicly declared that it was the goal of the NSDAP gradually to rid Germany of all women doctors.[26] What seemed like a first step in this direction was taken shortly thereafter, in the beginning of 1934, when married women physicians whose husbands had an adequate income were barred from panel practice (*Kassenpraxis*), that is, from working for official health insurance organizations.[27] But only 115 female panel doctors (*Kassenärztinnen*) were affected by this measure, instead of the estimated 600 to 700.[28] Since well over 4,000 German women were practicing medicine at that time,[29] it would be an exaggeration to say that women's place in that profession was jeopardized. Moreover, the position of female physicians was not challenged again, at least partly as a result of the spirited opposition put up by the association of women doctors, led by a Dr. Thimme.[30] In reality, women were effectively barred only from the careers of judge, state attorney (*Staatsanwalt*), and lawyer (*Rechtsanwalt*), de facto from as early as 1933, de jure as of January 10, 1936, the date of a decree to that effect issued by the Reich justice minister.[31] But even this flagrant discrimination was unlikely to drive women from Germany's law schools and turn law into an exclusively male discipline. It should be kept in mind that also before the *Machtergreifung* only a very small number of women had access to such careers.[32] In 1933 there were only 251 women lawyers in the entire Reich, and of a total of 10,441 German judges only 36 (one-third of 1 percent) were women.[33] The steadily increasing numbers of women who had graduated with a law degree before 1933 had clearly opted for other careers in such fields as social work, private industry, and the civil service, many of which remained open to them after the Nazi takeover.[34] As a matter of fact, new career opportunities were to open up for female law graduates after 1933, including that of legal advisor in the rapidly growing Nazi women's organizations.[35] Consequently, it is evident that the embargo on the legal profession was by itself unlikely to have more than a marginal effect on enrollments of females in Germany's law schools, since sufficient alternative careers remained open to women who graduated with a law degree.

It was an integral part of the Nazi offensive against the *Frauenstudium*, finally, that male exclusionist bigotry took the German universities by storm in the months following Hitler's appointment as Reich chancellor. Misogynic professors were nothing new,[36] but in 1933 they were given carte blanche to air their views without any inhibitions, and some of the most rabid were promoted to positions of influence and power.[37] The attitude of the male students was perhaps even worse than that of the faculty. Here too there was an old tradition of *Männerbund* mystique and misogyny, dating as far back as the early nineteenth century[38] and culminating in the Third Reich. The tone was set by the Nazi Student League, which had become a kind of satellite of the notoriously male exclusionist SA, and whose leaders were eager to emulate the macho manners of Röhm and his cronies. Oskar Stäbel, for instance, who became *Führer* of the Nazi students on February 2, 1933, was a high-ranking SA officer and was appointed by Röhm on March 23 of that year as "academic expert" (*Hochschulreferent*) within the SA leadership.[39] In a recent study of the subject, further attention is drawn to the "close organizational and personal ties between the SA and the Nazi Student League" at that time.[40]

The influence of the SA at the universities reached its zenith on September 18, 1933, with the creation of a special "SA university office" (*SA-Hochschulamt*), which purported to provide all German students with paramilitary training in the storm trooper spirit.[41] The fanatical male exclusionism of the SA thus permeated the Nazi Student League, and many reports document the hostility displayed by male students towards their female counterparts.[42] A female student in Dresden complained, "We girls hear all too often that women don't belong in politics, and that therefore we don't belong at the present political university either."[43] And in Berlin a Nazi student leader wrote in an article that women were only tolerated at the schools of higher learning as "guests," implying that this was merely a temporary favor that could be revoked at men's discretion.[44] Most Nazi student leaders found it opportune to insult female students from time to time, perhaps believing that their superiors might interpret such feats as signs of wit, manliness, and National Socialist reliability. A certain Lattermann, a student leader in Leipzig, made the following announcement in February 1934: "In order to implement the will of our *Führer* Adolf Hitler also here at the university, I will present a gift worth forty marks to every woman student who will abandon her studies for a marriage. Such women may personally select their gift."[45] The eruption of male exclusionist fanaticism among male students and professors undoubtedly turned the German universities into an inhospitable and unpleasant environment for female students. But whether considerable numbers of women decided to leave or stay away from these institutions of higher learning is a different question. There is no evidence that incidents such as those described above often caused women to discontinue their studies; instead, they may well have strengthened their determination to go on with their work. After all, a successful graduation was the most effective refutation of the male exclusionist gospel.

When the Nazis came to power, many women feared that the *Frauenstudium* was in jeopardy,[46] but the balance sheet of the measures that have been described did not at all resemble the kind of embargo that had been anticipated. In fact, the entire effort amounted to no more than a halfhearted amalgam of an ineffective *numerus clausus*, vocational guidance wavering between blackmail and supplication, financial pressure affecting only a handful of individuals, virtually unenforceable "labor service" obligations, a ban on careers that had never been open to women anyway, and the harassment of women students, which served primarily to gratify the male exclusionist ego of male students and professors. This series of measures could never have achieved the Nazis' objective of curbing the academic aspirations of women. Had they wanted to, Germany's National Socialist rulers could certainly have taken much more drastic and more effective steps against the *Frauenstudium*. But perhaps they had calculated that a total restriction of the academic activities of women was unnecessary, that young women would recognize the signs of the changing times and gradually abandon their intellectual and professional ambitions of their own accord. As early as 1935 it was clear that this expectation was not being fulfilled, since women continued to attend the German universities, albeit in decreasing numbers. It was not yet too late for a radical restriction that might put an end to this, but the Nazis were now no longer interested in such a solution, for in the mid-1930s their attitude towards the *Frauenstudium* was changing dramatically.

3

The Change in the Nazi Attitude Towards Women University Students, 1935–1939

Already in 1934, statistics suggested that the long decline of German fertility was coming to an end. The birthrate recovered from its all-time low of the previous year, jumping from 14.7 to 18.0 live births per 1,000 Germans. Over 200,000 more babies were born in the Reich in 1934 compared with 1933, and the concomitant increase of the number of marriages from 638,000 to 740,000 raised hope that this demographic revival could be sustained in the years to come. The upward trend did in fact continue in the second half of the 1930s, so that in the year of the outbreak of the Second World War the birthrate stood at 20.4, the absolute number of births at 1.4 million, and the number of marriages, at 770,000.[1]

Whatever the causes of this rise in fertility may have been,[2] its consequences are of greater importance in the context of this study. It became gradually obvious that the pessimistic forecasts of a few years earlier about the impending extinction of the German people had been grossly exaggerated. And the Nazi rulers could breathe more easily now that "the biological future of the race," as they called it, appeared secured after all.[3] Scapegoats were no longer needed, and the accusation that women neglected their "biological duties" lost its credibility. Now that statistical evidence indicated that "the race" was no longer in danger, it was pointless to argue that the *Frauenstudium* constituted "one of the worst threats to the biological future of the race," as the Nazi pamphleteer Wilhelm Hartnacke had done for so long. The eugenic argument against women's academic activities consequently lost much of its urgency.[4]

The Nazi attitude towards women's presence at the university was even more decisively affected by important changes in the realm of the Reich's economy. Reasonably soon after its advent to power, the Nazi regime registered significant successes in the battle against unemployment. Signs of improvement appeared as early as 1935, but the real turning point came in 1936, when "something approaching full employment existed [again] in Germany."[5] What is more, the end of the unemployment crisis was soon followed by a labor shortage. This has been attributed to the demands of the Four-Year Plan (*Vierjahresplan*), which aimed to prepare Germany for war by achieving economic self-sufficiency (*Autarkie*) and which therefore called for an effort to exploit the Reich's available labor force to the fullest.[6] Labor thus emerged in the mid-1930s from a "position of servitude to that of a scarce commodity."[7] Consequently there were no longer any rewards to be reaped from squeezing women out of the labor force. Instead, the pressures on the German labor market henceforth dictated full exploitation of women's labor potential.[8] Women's work was no longer frowned on but suddenly found itself in great demand, and female skills were once again appreciated. A female student, writing in March 1937, aptly illustrated this new attitude: "The great creative work of the *Führer* demands the active cooperation of each and every German. In particular, he cannot forego the energies of half the German people, those of German women."[9]

The restrictions imposed on female employment during the first years of the Third Reich were either relaxed, left unenforced, or entirely abolished.[10] Women's share of the German labor force, which had declined from 35.36 percent in 1933 to 31.20 percent in 1937, was to increase again in the late 1930s, to 31.35 percent in 1938 and to 32.77 percent in 1939. On the eve of the Second World War, there would be 6.8 million working women in the Reich, nearly 2 million more than in 1933.[11]

In the academic professions, too, the battle against unemployment was crowned with success in the mid-1930s, and already in 1935 warnings were sounded that a serious shortage of university-trained professionals might soon occur.[12] In many faculties the number of graduates was falling so rapidly (for reasons that will be discussed later) that adequate replenishment of the ranks of the corresponding professions seemed in immediate jeopardy.[13] Moreover, this shortage threatened precisely at a moment when the Four-Year Plan was generating a greater demand for all kinds of academically trained specialists, particularly in technical and scientific subjects but also in every other field.[14] The problem was exacerbated by the wholesale elimination from the professions of "non-Aryans," Social Democrats, Republicans, and other real or imaginary enemies of National Socialism.[15] But if the Nazis had hoped to replenish the dwindling ranks of professionals with young *men*, they were sorely disappointed. The contempt that Hitler and his cronies tended to display for intellectual and academic achievements had devalued the prestige that professional careers had traditionally commanded in Germany. Talented and ambitious male adolescents were therefore attracted to the alternative avenues of social prestige opening up in the new army and in the SS.[16] The introduction of compulsory military service in March 1935, in particular, had a depressing effect on new enrollments of men at the institutions of higher learning. In 1935 there were still nearly 11,000 new registrations by men, but one year later this number fell to 7,700.[17] As a result, the Nazi authorities had to rely increasingly on *women* to keep Germany supplied with sufficient numbers of university-trained specialists. The end of academic unemployment thus created precisely those conditions which, as a German feminist had predicted in 1932, would dissipate the objections against women's intellectual ambitions: "The sting of the opposition to the *Frauenstudium* will be dulled and weakened from the moment the pressures on the academic labor market are removed."[18] This prediction proved to be correct. The shortage of academically trained specialists and the failure of Germany's young men to provide the required supply (*Nachwuchs*) of new recruits forced the Nazi leadership to turn to women for this purpose. Within a few years, between 1935 and 1937, all restrictions on the *Frauenstudium* were removed, and female high school graduates were actively encouraged to take up university studies. The *numerus clausus* that in theory at least had limited females to 10 percent of all new matriculations was lifted as early as February 9, 1935, after "it had been in force for [only] a little more than a year and effective only for the 1934 intake of students."[19] Women who had been victimized by the *numerus clausus* and who had subsequently registered as auditors (*Hörer*) were now given full retroactive credit for the courses they had taken.[20] But the Nazi attitude towards the *Frauenstudium* changed most dramatically in 1936/37, when the shortage of university-trained specialists became more acute and when it had become obvious that young men alone could not provide an adequate supply of graduates. The vocational counselling of female high school graduates, for instance, completely changed its tune in those years. Whereas young women had previously been discouraged from taking up university studies and thus from eventually entering a profession, precisely the opposite was true from approximately 1936 on. Even such supposedly unfeminine disciplines as law were henceforth recommended to them, as women's cooperation in the field of jurisprudence was suddenly discovered to be "not only desirable, but actually indispensable."[21] Early in 1937 the Reich minister of education publicly endorsed the new course in vocational counselling for girls. In a speech in Hannover he declared that "university inflation" (*Hochschulinflation*) had been checked, and he called on *Abiturientinnen* to take up higher studies.[22] His appeal was widely echoed in women's magazines, newspapers, and even National Socialist party publications.[23] In order to promote the academic and professional aspirations of German women, there was founded in June 1937 an organization that purported to unite all women, university graduates or others, who took an interest in the *Frauenstudium* and who were willing to support it actively. This was the University Community of German Women (*Hochschulgemeinschaft deutscher Frauen—HGdF*).[24] Although this *Hochschulgemeinschaft* was never to be a going concern, merely the fact that such an association— a *Frauenstudium* lobby—was allowed to exist was a clear symptom of the changed Nazi view of women's role in the academic field.

This change was also reflected in the policies of the Study Foundation (*Studienstiftung*). Invoking the "growing need for professionally and academically trained women in nearly all professions," the foundation reversed its misogynic attitude and proceeded to award more (although still very few) scholarships to female students. Women's share of all its grants subsequently increased, from 6.3 percent in 1937 to 10.7 percent in 1938.[25] "On account of considerations of population policy," it was also decided to support female students in another form. From 1937 onwards, a fifty-mark "delivery allowance" (*Entbindungshilfe*) was paid to every female student, married or not, who gave birth to a child. In order not to offend bourgeois sensibilities, though, it was carefully (if somewhat sheepishly) stipulated that this measure "was not intended to promote illegitimate births."[26] Unfortunately, we do not know how many women took advantage of this sample of largesse on the part of the Study Foundation.

If the about-face in the Nazi attitude towards women's academic activities could occur as smoothly as it did, this was largely due to the concomitant purge of the most fanatic misogynists from the National Socialist party and state. The "*Röhm Putsch*" of June 30, 1934, had resulted in the liquidation of most of the SA leaders, the outstanding proponents of a male exclusionist ideology within the NSDAP. And although Hitler had ordered the bloodbath for purely Machiavellian reasons, he justified it hypocritically (and for lack of a more plausible excuse) by means of the "corrupt morals," meaning the homophile tendencies, of the SA leadership.[27] The *Führer*'s words discredited not only homosexuality but, by association, male exclusionism and misogyny in general, all of which had so obviously characterized the now defamed *Männerbund* of the storm troopers.[28] Even Alfred Rosenberg, Nazi male exclusionist par excellence, found it opportune to change the rabidly antifeminist tune he had hitherto struck in his speeches and writings. In a speech delivered on Mother's Day 1935, he made a vague but unmistakable plea for better educational chances for women.[29] The SA itself, formerly the bulwark of Nazi machismo, was emasculated and humiliated and became the "*bête noire* of the Nazi family."[30] The storm troopers' ascendancy over the Nazi Student League was terminated as early as July 1934, and all vestiges of SA influence at the universities were radically eliminated, culminating in the dissolution of the *SA-Hochschulamt*.[31] Professors and male students no longer found it opportune to identify themselves with the misogynic SA spirit. Henceforth they were careful to suppress whatever male exclusionist notions they may have cherished. Of incidents such as those that occurred so frequently in 1933–1934, hardly a trace is to be found in the following years. Flexing macho muscle had suddenly gone out of style. Female students, formerly regarded as unwelcome "guests" at the universities, were now actually declared full-fledged "comrades" (*Kameradinnen*) of their National Socialist male colleagues. It was a sign of the changing times that in June 1937, at the annual student rally in Heidelberg, the Nazi women students' leader could openly announce that the place of women at the German universities was secure in spite of the opposition that had been mounted against it. The audience, predominantly male students in brownshirt, did not boo her down, as would certainly have been the case in 1933 or early 1934, but responded with a rousing ovation.[32] Nazi misogyny may not have been eradicated as a result of the events of the summer of 1934, but it was muzzled and was henceforth unable to poison the atmosphere at the German institutions of higher learning, as it had done in the first years of the Nazi regime.

By the end of the decade, it was obvious to all that the National Socialist regime encouraged women to study at the Reich's universities, and in whatever field might strike their fancy. The idea of limiting the number of female students was no longer discussed, not even in disciplines that had formerly been deemed unfeminine. Anna Kottenhoff, leader of the Nazi women students' organization, did not exaggerate when she wrote in 1939 that all German universities and all faculties welcomed any woman with the necessary intellectual qualifications and that "the crisis of the *Frauenstudium*" was over.[33] And yet the situation was not quite as idyllic as these words may imply, because in the wake of the Nazi *Machtergreifung* and throughout the remainder of the 1930s an unprecedented decline occurred in the enrollments of women at Germany's degree-granting institutions.

4

The Decline of Women's Enrollments at the German Universities, 1933–1939: Result of Nazi Antifeminism?

In the years that followed Hitler's accession to the chancellorship of the Reich, the total number of female students at all German universities declined rapidly (see figure 1). Already between the summer semesters of 1933 and 1935, within a mere two years, it fell by over 40 percent, from 17,685 to 10,190, but the nadir was reached in summer 1938, when only 6,337 women remained at all German institutions of higher learning. This meant that of every three studying women in 1933, only one was left five years later.[1] The average number of female students at a German university, which had stood at 793 in 1932, was reduced to less than half that figure (to precisely 367) by 1936. During the second half of the 1930s, women almost disappeared from a number of German colleges. In the summer of 1936, for instance, Halle had only 111 female students left, Erlangen 90, and Giessen a mere 50.[2] Certain faculties were virtually abandoned by women. In 1932, Germany had counted not less than 1,137 female students of law; by 1938 only 42 remained. The number of female students of natural sciences fell from 3,010 in 1932 to 482 in 1938, a decline of 84 percent.[3] In all disciplines combined, new matriculations of women dropped from 4,618 in 1932/33 to 1,511 in 1937/38 (see figure 2), and from 18.4 to 12.3 percent of the total number of first registrations.[4] This numerical decline of the German female student population finally levelled off in 1938/39. On the eve of the Second World War, the absolute number of female university students stabilized around 6,500, and their share of Germany's entire student body was approximately 11.5 percent.[5] In the academic year 1938/39, also, new registrations of young women rose to 1,898, 20 percent more than the figure of the previous year.[6]

It has been widely assumed that this decline in the number of female university students in the Third Reich was the direct result of Nazi misogyny in general and of Nazi opposition to women's academic ambitions in particular. For in-

Figure 1.
Women's Enrollments at the German Institutions of Higher Learning, 1933-1939

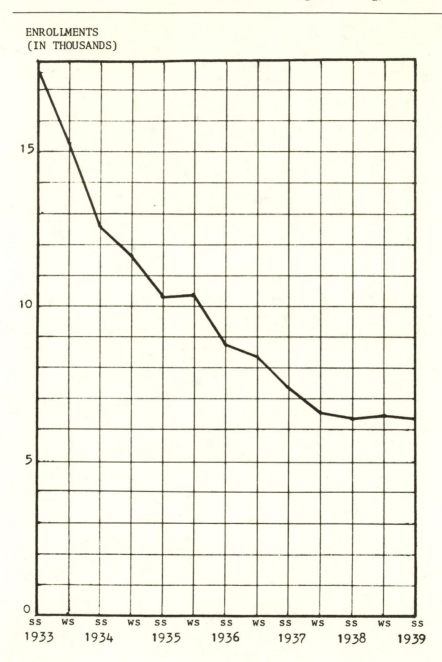

ENROLLMENTS
(IN THOUSANDS)

Figure 2.
**New Matriculations of Women at the German Institutions of Higher Learning,
1932–1939**

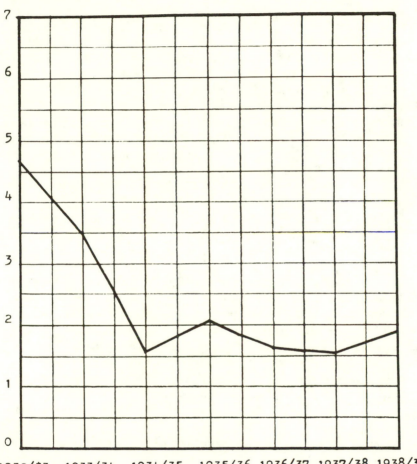

NEW MATRICULATIONS
(IN THOUSANDS)

WINTER SEMESTER

stance, the British sociologist Walter Kotschnig wrote in 1937: "The decrease in numbers of women students [in Germany] since the arrival of Hitler speaks for the effectiveness of the [antifeminist] ideas of the regime."[7] In Germany statistician Charlotte Lorenz voiced the same opinion a few years later. Somewhat euphemistically she attributed the decline of the *Frauenstudium* to the educational, propagandistic, and labor policies of the National Socialist government in favor of men, in other words, to its antifeminist bias.[8] Such beliefs have persisted to the present day. The author of a study of Nazi educational policies claims that the Nazis had deliberately planned to oust women from studies in general and that the decline of the number of female students in the Third Reich was primarily due to the introduction of Frick's *numerus clausus*.[9] A recent sociological analysis of the *Frauenstudium* in the Federal German Republic likewise identifies the *numerus clausus* as the major culprit in its brief treatment of the decline of women's matriculations in the Third Reich.[10] This conventional wisdom also found its way into a West German history of the *Frauenstudium*, published in 1979 on the occasion of the seventieth anniversary of the admission of women to the Prussian universities,[11] into the two latest studies of the role of women in the German resistance against Nazism,[12] and into a new French book on women in the Third Reich.[13]

But we have seen that the actual measures taken by the National Socialist authorities against women's studies in 1933–1934, including the widely publicized *numerus clausus*, were too ineffective to account for such a drastic decline, which lasted almost to the end of the decade. We also remember that the Nazi attitude towards the *Frauenstudium* changed in the mid-1930s from one of opposition to one of benevolence and that female high school graduates were subsequently encouraged to take up university studies. If Nazi interference had been the decisive factor in the development of female matriculations, the number of women university students in Germany should have increased in the second half of the 1930s and not decreased, as was the case. Additional evidence suggests that the numerical decline of the female student body in the Third Reich may not have been the result of Nazi prejudices with regard to the *Frauenstudium*. First, the number of male students also dropped sharply between 1933 and 1938, specifically from 95,562 to 48,536, a decline of nearly 50 percent.[14] Since this development can hardly be explained in terms of Nazi antifeminism, it must be assumed that other factors were at work and that these may also have played a role in the decline of women's enrollments. Second, the numbers of both male and female university students had started to dwindle *before* the Nazi takeover, which suggests that the main causes of the decline must not be sought in National Socialist policies. Indeed, after a period of sustained growth in the 1920s,[15] the number of university students in Germany had reached an unprecedented high in the summer semester of 1931, when the Reich counted 109,812 male and 21,074 female students. After that, however, a decline had set in which reduced the overall number from 130,886 to 126,381 in the summer semester of 1932 and to 119,702 in the winter semester 1932/33.[16]

What were the real causes of this decline? Already during the late 1930s social historians and sociologists outside Germany, such as Edward Hartshorne and Charlotte Luetkens, had suggested that the answer could be found in demographic and economic factors. Hartshorne emphasized the importance of *demographic* conditions, more particularly the "cut in the university age-groups in the [German] population because of the fall in the war birth rate just eighteen years before."[17] And Luetkens pointed out that the numerical drop in the German student population in the 1930s was above all the natural result of a sudden decline of "the number of persons approaching university age." Between 1925 and 1933, she claimed, the number of Germans in the age-group of eighteen to twenty had dropped from 2,570,135 to 2,117,077, and their share of the entire German population had dropped from 4.1 to 3.2 percent.[18] Neither Hartshorne nor Luetkens elaborated further on this demographic factor, so it it necessary to deal with it here in greater detail.

During the First World War, the annual number of live births in Germany had declined drastically, from 1.8 million on the eve of the war, in 1913, to just over 912,000, or almost precisely half that figure, in 1917. A slight improvement occurred in 1918, when 926,000 births were recorded, but it was only in 1919 that, with 1.2 million, the number was again anywhere near the prewar annual average.[19] *The inordinately small size of the age-groups born during the First World War predetermined the volume of university attendance eighteen to nineteen years later.*[20] The fact that the annual number of births had dropped by 50 percent between 1913 and 1917/18 halved the supply of potential university students for a period of five to six years from approximately 1932 onwards. Only a drastic increase of that percentage of all eighteen- to nineteen-year-olds who did normally realize this potential and actually pursue higher studies could have prevented university enrollments in Germany from imitating in the 1930s the downward trend displayed by the birthrate during the First World War. In the depression-ridden third decade of the twentieth century, however, not *more* but *fewer* families than before found themselves economically in a position to carry the burden of long and expensive academic studies.[21] It is not surprising, then, that the German student population declined by even more than 50 percent in the 1930s, from about 130,800 in 1931 to 54,800 in 1938.[22]

This demographic factor also provides an explanation for the continuing and accelerating decline of the number of female students in the second half of the 1930s, in a period when the Nazi government was actively *encouraging* female academic ambitions. In these years the last numerous prewar age-groups were graduating, while more and more representatives of the war cohort were beginning their studies. The nadir was reached in 1938, when the war cohort virtually monopolized the universities: the prewar age-groups had all graduated; the again more numerous postwar age-groups had yet to begin their studies. Similarly, the end of the decline in 1938/39, when women's enrollments increased from 6,337 to 6,587 and new matriculations of young women rose from 1,511 to 1,898,[23] reflected the coming to university age of the representatives of the more numerous postwar age-groups.

Both Hartshorne and Luetkens also attached much importance to the *economic* causes of the decline of the number of university students in the Third Reich. The role of the Great Depression in this respect can hardly be overestimated. Widespread academic unemployment and the emergence of an "intellectual and professional proletariat" (Luetkens) made university studies an unattractive enterprise and a luxury fewer and fewer people could afford. Since a degree was no longer the key to a prosperous and prestigious career, young people understandably became less eager to take up long and difficult academic studies.[24]

The inordinately small size of the cohort born in the period from 1914 to 1919, which came to university age in the 1930s, together with the effects of the Great Depression must rank as the prime factors behind the decline of the German student population, both male and female, from 1932 onwards. A contributory determinant, Nazi antiintellectualism, began to play a role in 1933. It is no secret that Hitler and his followers looked down on intellectuals and academic pursuits and that irrationality was one of the trademarks of National Socialism.[25] The prestige traditionally associated with university studies and professional careers thus declined considerably in Germany after the *Machtergreifung*, and this too affected university attendance negatively during those years.[26]

The decline of women's enrollments at the universities of the Third Reich was a function of the overall decline of Germany's student population in the 1930s, and this overall decline was caused mainly by demographic and economic factors: the small size of the cohort born during the First World War, and the Great Depression. A third factor, the sinking prestige of academic studies and careers in the antiintellectual atmosphere of Hitler's state, likewise played a role, albeit a marginal one, but only from 1933 onwards, when the decline was already well under way. It is evident, therefore, that the numerical decline of the female student body in the Third Reich should not be attributed to Nazi misogyny in general and to Nazi prejudices with regard to the *Frauenstudium* in particular.

But the drop in enrollments of women was more rapid and ultimately greater than that of men. Can this divergence be ascribed to Nazi efforts to implement their objections to women's academic aspirations? Between 1931 and 1933 the number of female students declined by an average of 5.5 percent per semester, for a total drop of 70 percent. The number of male students, on the other hand, fell by only 4.9 percent per semester, for an overall decline of 44 percent over the same period. It was practically only in the summer of 1935 that the rate of decline of men's enrollments was greater than that of women, and that was the result of the introduction of compulsory military service in March of that year.[27] Consequently, women's share of the total German student body fell consistently, again with the sole exception of the summer of 1935, throughout the 1930s, from 16.1 percent to 11.2 percent between the summer semesters of 1931 and 1939.[28]

Here too, however, one must be careful not to overestimate the importance of Nazi misogynic policies, as Dörte Winkler does in her otherwise excellent monograph on women's labor in the Third Reich, and Harald Focke and Uwe

Reimer do in their study of everyday life in the Third Reich. Describing the *numerus clausus* as the cornerstone of Nazi misogynic policies in the field of higher education, these authors credit it, and it alone, with having caused the decline of women's share of the total student population from 15.8 percent in 1932 to 11.2 percent in 1939.[29] A number of factors suggest that this view is totally mistaken. For one thing, the differentiation between the decline in the number of students of both sexes was already in evidence before the *Machtergreifung* gave the Nazis an opportunity to implement their antifeminist prejudices. In comparing the figures for the winter semester 1932/33 with those of the summer semester 1931, we observe that the number of women students fell by 10.8 percent, that of male students by only 8.2 percent. Women's share of the total student population was already on the decline at this early stage, dropping from 16.1 percent to 15.7 percent between 1931 and 1932/33. Moreover, the rate of decline of the number of female students was more rapid in 1932/33 than in all but four of the thirteen semesters between the Nazi takeover and the outbreak of the Second World War.[30] All this suggests that even the differentiation between the numerical decline of male and female students in the Third Reich was not of Nazi making, that here too other factors must have been at work.

The real causes of this differentiation were of social-psychological nature. Since it had always seemed a less astute investment and a somewhat extravagant luxury to let a daughter study at the university, as compared to a son, it was only natural that the *Frauenstudium* suffered more once hard times—the Great Depression—dictated austerity and retrenchment. In her book *Krisis des Frauenstudiums*, published in 1932, feminist Gertrud Bäumer pointed out that university enrollments necessarily suffered from the general pauperization of the population and from the resulting reluctance "to finance expensive studies, [an investment] with uncertain dividends." This concern, she added, "affects [the studies of] girls much more than boys, as is already evident at the present time [1932]."[31] One of Bäumer's colleagues in the German women's emancipation movement, Gertrud Meissner, described this attitude even more effectively: "The studies of a son are a safer investment in the eyes of the parents than those of a daughter, who may be looked after with a good marriage."[32] It is important in this respect that in the Third Reich, as well as in the Weimar Republic, university students were recruited predominantly from the lower middle class,[33] which displayed an unmistakable tendency to favor sons studying over daughters studying.[34] In Prussia in the 1920s, for instance, families of "intermediate civil servants" (*mittlere Beamte*) yielded six male students for every female student.[35] This ratio was even more lopsided in favor of a son in the depression-ridden 1930s—9.6 to 1 in the winter semester 1933/34, 7.3 to 1 a year later, and 8.8 to 1 in the summer semester of 1938.[36] It was this social-psychological factor, and not Nazi antifeminism, that accounted for the differentiation between the drop in the number of students of both sexes in the 1930s. At most, the Nazi opposition to the *Frauenstudium* may have played a role in the slight intensification of this differentiation after 1933 (see figure 3).

Figure 3.
Number of Male and Female Students in Germany, 1932-1939

BASED ON SS   1931-100

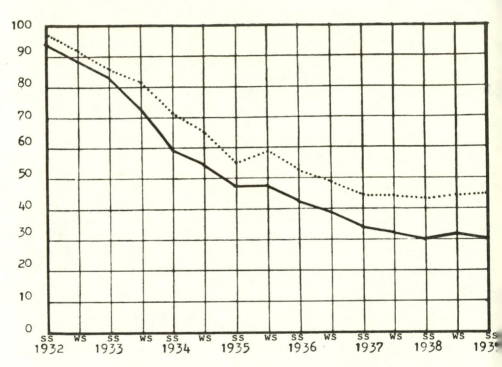

Male Students:_____   Female Students:..........

40

The possibility remains, finally, that Nazi prejudices with regard to women may have been effective in another respect, namely, in that they may at least have caused women's retreat from certain faculties and disciplines. According to this hypothesis, female university students in the Third Reich were prevailed on to abandon faculties leading to careers deemed unfeminine by the Nazis; a proportionately larger share of all female students, on the other hand, supposedly opted for disciplines leading to professions that, in the words of Wilhelm Frick, "correspond to the female nature."[37]

Professions considered particularly unfeminine were those demanding "purely intellectual" or "technical" skills and talents, such as the practice of law and all careers in the natural and technical sciences.[38] Some professions, however, were declared to be suitable fields of feminine activity, particularly for those women who could not depend on a husband for their livelihood.[39] Hitler himself vaguely defined these careers as those involving "aiding, healing, and educa-tion."[40] His oracular pronouncement was generally construed to sanction wom-en's professional aspirations in social work, medicine and related activities, and education, notably the education of young children and especially of girls.[41] The teaching profession appeared in the Nazi mind to be extremely well suited for women, since it supposedly afforded opportunities for "spiritual motherhood" to Germany's numerous unmarried women.[42] In view of this, one could indeed speculate that in the Third Reich, female students might have flocked to faculties that prepare for careers in medicine, education, and social work, while staying away from those that lead to presumably unfeminine occupations, such as the practice of law. A superficial glance at the statistics of faculty enrollments in the 1930s may even serve to confirm this conjecture. But the hypothesis that Nazi notions about feminine and unfeminine professions constituted the prime determinant in the coeds' choice of faculty is largely a myth unable to stand the test of closer scrutiny.

Let us consider the case of medical studies, which prepare for a profession involving healing and which were therefore considered acceptable for women. Between 1933 and 1939 the percentage of all women studying medicine increased from 28.9 percent to 41.3 percent, a net gain of 12.4 percent. This development caused medicine to overtake the humanities as the most popular discipline for women. For all medical studies combined, that is, general medicine as well as pharmacy, dentistry, and veterinary science, the net increase amounted to 13 percent over the same period.[43] It would nevertheless be premature to conclude that Nazi benevolence towards women's ambitions in the medical field was the prime cause of this increase, since the percentage of female students of general medicine had already risen from 14.9 percent in the summer of 1928 to 26.1 percent in the winter semester 1932/33, and since the share of all medical studies combined had increased from about 19 percent to more than 39 percent between the summers of 1928 and 1933.[44] These data imply that the growing popularity of medical studies among German women in the 1930s had little or nothing to do with Nazi attitudes. Strengthening this suspicion is the fact that in the Third

Reich increasing numbers of *men* were also attracted by the study of medicine.[45] Consequently, women's share of all medical student enrollment declined after 1933, from 20.2 percent in the summer of that year to 15.9 percent in the spring semester 1939, and this decline occurred after a period of virtually uninterrupted growth between 1919 and 1933.[46]

The true causes of the growing popularity of medical studies among young women of the Third Reich must be sought in certain aspects of the medical profession which made this career increasingly attractive in this period. Important in this respect, according to Luetkens, were "the improved economic opportunities for physicians, following the wholesale exclusion of Jews and other 'non-Aryans' from the training and practice of medicine . . . [and] further, the medical demands of the new army, and the stress laid on physical fitness, sport, etc."[47] Another important factor was the trend towards specialization in the medical profession, which is believed to have stimulated the influx of women into fields such as gynecology and pediatrics.[48] Finally, more opportunities were created for women in the medical profession by the departure of great numbers of male physicians who opted for a career in the SS rather than in private practice.[49]

The hypothesis that Nazi notions about the professional role of women were not very important in this matter, but marginal at best, is further corroborated by the fact that the influx of women into medicine in 1933–1939 flowed not from "unfeminine" tributary disciplines such as law but from the humanities (*Kulturwissenschaften*), which usually led to a teaching career, an acceptable profession for women in the eyes of the Nazis. Between 1933 and 1939 the percentage of all female students in the humanities dropped from 31.9 percent to 24.9 percent. Within this group, even such supposedly favored disciplines as German language and literature (*Germanistik*) lost ground. Only physical education deviated from the general downward trend, registering an increase from 1 percent to 4.6 percent in its enrollments.[50]

There is one last reason why the increasing popularity of medical studies among female students of the Third Reich should not be ascribed to Nazi attitudes. Although the Nazis' notion of medicine as an acceptable profession for women may have given them some ground to look kindly on female aspirations in this field, they had even more reason to oppose them. During the first year of the regime, for instance, the medical profession was considered "overcrowded," and Gerhard Wagner, the leader of the Reich League of Physicians, proposed to exclude women from medical studies. If Nazi attitudes towards female ambitions in the medical profession had really been decisive, women's enrollments in the faculties of medicine should have suffered. Instead, the percentage of all women who studied medicine actually rose from 28.9 percent in 1933 to 37.9 percent in 1935 (see figure 4).

Equally instructive is the case of women's enrollments in the faculties of law. Here too a superficial glance at the statistics may lead to false conclusions. Between 1933 and 1938 the percentage of women studying law dropped con-

Figure 4.
All Women Students in Various Academic Disciplines, 1928-1939

PERCENTAGE

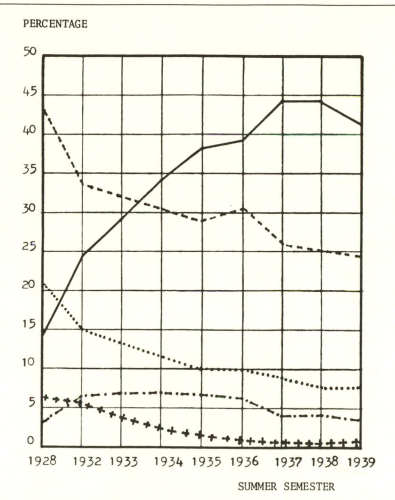

SUMMER SEMESTER

Medicine:_____   Humanities:_ _ _ _ _

Dentistry:_._._.   Law:++++

Natural Sciences:........

43

sistently, from 4.2 percent to 0.6 percent of all female university students. But
it would be wrong to theorize that this reflected the Nazis' view of jurisprudence
as an "unfeminine" occupation. Two facts suggest that other factors were at
work. First, the number of *male* students of law likewise declined significantly
between 1933 and 1939, from 15 percent to 8.9 percent of all male university
students.[51] Second, women's retreat from the faculties of law had started before
the Nazi takeover; whereas in the summer of 1928 some 6 percent of all women
students were taking law, this share declined to 5.2 percent as early as the winter
semester of 1932/33.[52] Among male students, too, law had already lost popularity
before the *Machtergreifung*.[53] The decrease in the number of female law students
in the Third Reich must also be seen as the continuation of a trend that had
started in the Weimar Republic and as part of an overall decline in the popularity
of law studies among both male and female students. As to the causes of this
trend, it has recently been suggested that the diminishing attractiveness of law
studies since the mid-1920s reflected shrinking career opportunities for law graduates in the administration and the judiciary.[54] Similar factors may have played
a role in the Third Reich when the civil service, traditionally the destination of
many law graduates, lost a great deal of its former appeal.[55]

There is yet another indication that Nazi notions about the "unfemininity"
of jurisprudence had little or nothing to do with women's dwindling enrollments
in the law faculties of the Third Reich. Around 1936–1937 a complete about-
face occurred in the Nazi attitude towards women's role in the legal profession:
henceforth women were actively and openly encouraged to study law and to
become *Juristinnen*.[56] But the exodus of women from the law faculties continued.
Within the female student body the share of students of law dropped further,
from 1.3 percent in 1936 to 0.9 percent in 1937 and 0.6 percent in 1938. A
slight improvement took place on the eve of the Second World War, but women
students of law remained a tiny minority that in the spring of 1939 represented
only 0.9 percent of the female student population.[57]

A close look at women's enrollments in the faculties of natural and technical
sciences likewise reveals the irrelevance of Nazi antifeminist attitudes. In the
first years of the regime these disciplines were considered particularly "unfeminine," but in the second half of the 1930s this objection was dropped, and
women were openly encouraged to opt for careers in mathematics, engineering,
architecture, chemistry, and the like. However, women's enrollments in the
faculties of technical and natural sciences failed to reflect the changing Nazi
attitude. The popularity of natural sciences among women students declined
consistently in the 1930s, from 13.6 percent of the female student population in
1933 to 7.7 percent in 1939.[58] Natural sciences also lost popularity among male
students during this period,[59] and this overall trend had started long before the
Nazi takeover.[60] This suggests that the decline of women's enrollments in this
faculty had very little to do with Nazi attitudes towards female professional
aspirations in the field of natural sciences. The same conclusion may be reached
for the faculty of technical sciences. Women's ambitions in this area were

strongly condemned at first on account of the alleged unfemininity of such professions, but they were encouraged after 1936 in view of the great need for university-trained specialists in such areas as electronics, engineering, and architecture. The evolution of women's enrollments in this faculty was compatible with the Nazi attitude in 1936–1939, when the number of women studying technical sciences increased from 0.8 percent to 1.1 percent of the entire female student population. In the period before 1936, however, technical sciences had also gained in popularity among female university students. Between the summer semester of 1933 and the winter semester of 1935/36, the percentage of women in this discipline had risen from 0.7 percent to 1.1 percent, and this occurred in spite of Nazi objections. The irrelevance of Nazi attitudes was perhaps most clearly demonstrated by the decline of women's enrollments in the faculty of technical sciences between the winter of 1935/36 (1 percent) and the summer of 1937 (0.7 percent), precisely in the years when the Nazi authorities, concerned with the labor needs of the Four-Year Plan, were vociferously encouraging young women to take up such studies.[61]

Statistics indicate only too clearly that the decline in the number of female university students in the Third Reich was not caused by Nazi antifeminism in general and by Nazi opposition to the *Frauenstudium* in particular. This decline was part of an overall contraction of the German student population which had started in 1931, well before the Nazis came to power, and which was caused primarily by demographic and economic factors, namely, the inordinately small size of the age-groups born during the First World War and the Great Depression. A third factor, Nazi antiintellectualism, played a contributory role from 1933 onwards. Even the differentiation between the decline of university enrollments of men and women was not caused by misogynic Nazi policies but was determined by social-psychological factors that had nothing to do with National Socialism. Finally, even the increasing or decreasing popularity of certain disciplines among female students of the Third Reich cannot be said to reflect Nazi endorsement or disapprobation of women's professional aspirations in these fields.

Although the Nazi campaign against the *Frauenstudium* did not cause the decline of women's university matriculations in Germany in the 1930s, it did have an important nefarious effect in that it contributed greatly to the socially selective character of this decline. From 1933 onwards, female students were to be recruited increasingly from what is best referred to as the "upper middle class" or *Oberschicht* ("higher level") of German society. This sociological category includes the upper class of Imperial Germany, the landed aristocracy whose members remained an upper class in the narrow sense after 1918, as well as wealthy industrialists and other members of the middle-class elite, a group that is often called the *haute bourgeoisie* in other European countries and which in Germany had been unable before 1918 to acquire social prestige and political power commensurate with its economic strength. After Hitler's advent to power, then, young upper-middle-class women made numerical progress at the German universities at the expense of the female representatives of the "lower middle class" (*Mittelstand* or *Mittelschicht*)—the *moyenne* and *petite bourgeoisie*, as this category would be called in France—and of the working class (*Arbeiterschaft* or *Unterschicht*).[62] This phenomenon was all the more striking since precisely these last two groups had greatly increased their share of the entire German student body in the time between the end of the First World War and the Nazi *Machtergreifung*.[63] *Under the Nazi regime, the decisive criteria for a woman's admission to the university were not so much her intellectual qualifications as her family's wealth and social rank.*[64] The statistical material on the social background of female students may not be abundant,[65] but it is certainly sufficient to bear this out. Between the summer semester of 1932 and the winter trimester of 1941, for example, women from the upper middle class increased their share of the entire female student body from 44.9 percent to 48.5 percent, while women from the lower middle class and the working class fell back from 50.4 percent to 46 percent and from 2.7 percent to 2.3 percent respectively.[66] Within the first group, the greatest gains were made by daughters of high-ranking civil servants (*höhere Beamte*), who advanced from 21.1 percent to 23.1 percent of all women students. On the other hand, intermediate civil servants (*mittlere Beamte*), the most important segment of the second group, saw their share decline considerably, from 26.3 percent to 21.8 percent, while daughters of independent craftsmen and small businessmen fell back from 14.7 percent to 11.5 percent.

The changing social structure of the *Frauenstudium* in the Third Reich is even better revealed by the more plentiful statistical information on new matriculations (*Neuimmatrikulationen*) of female university students. Women from upper-middle-class families accounted for 45.4 percent of all new registrations of females in the summer semester 1933, but for 50.3 percent in the summer of 1939. They clearly achieved these gains at the expense of their counterparts from the *Mittelstand*, who fell back from 50.8 percent to 44.5 percent during the same period. Here too the biggest losers were the intermediate civil servants (from 27.7 percent to 21.8 percent) as well as the independent craftsmen and small businessmen (14.4 percent to 9.8 percent). The share of workers' daughters, meanwhile, was halved, dropping from an unimpressive 2.4 percent to a paltry 1.2 percent.[67]

Commenting on this development in an article in the 1937/38 volume of the journal *Die Frau*, an observer concluded that "the social structure of the *Frauenstudium* was losing its equilibrium."[68] This was basically correct, although "equilibrium" was clearly an overly euphemistic term to characterize the situation prior to 1933.[69] As for the causes of the post-1933 trend towards monopolization of university studies by daughters of upper-middle-class families, this tendency reflected the relative immunity of the economically strong *Oberschicht* to the effects of the Great Depression. In the years after the *Machtergreifung*, the universities ceased to be the "arenas of social struggles of conquest" and "vehicles for social ascent" to which representatives of the lower middle and working classes had been attracted in the Weimar Republic.[70] Because of lingering academic unemployment and Nazi antiintellectualism, a university degree no longer offered prospects of social advancement by means of prestigious and well-paid professional careers. In the case of women, furthermore, the regime's official antifeminist policies of the years 1933–1935 made such advancement all but unthinkable. Consequently, academic studies lost precisely those powers by means of which they had hitherto hypnotized ambitious young members of *Mittelstand* and even, although to a much lesser extent, the working class. For the upper middle class, on the other hand, the universities remained useful "instruments to preserve their social-economic status."[71] The *jeunesse dorée* of this class had never embarked on academic studies simply because a university degree afforded a measure of prosperity and prestige; they possessed both in abundance, even without academic titles. For them, a degree served primarily to sanction and uphold the social rank of their family, and it continued to serve this purpose after Hitler's accession to power. In light of this objective, it was a matter of marginal importance whether a son or daughter acquired academic credentials. If anything, preference was probably more often given to a daughter's studies. Since to outsiders student daughters must have seemed a more extravagant luxury, particularly in the depression-ridden 1930s, they were more likely to achieve the purpose of publicly ratifying the family's wealth and status. This factor, too, helps explain why female representatives of the upper middle class considerably strengthened their position at the universities in comparison with girls from other social groups, and accounted for no less than half of all new matriculations of women by the summer semester of 1939.

Women from lower-middle-class and working-class families might have maintained a better representation in the female student body in the Third Reich had they not been deprived of an expedient that had enabled many of them to attend university in the Weimar era, namely, the opportunity to help finance their studies through part-time work (*Werkstudententum*).[72] In the summer semester of 1928, for example, 6.3 percent of all women students had been such "work students"; in the winter semester 1929/30, they accounted for 5.1 percent, representing approximately 760 individuals in each of these two cases.[73] After 1933, however, the phenomenon of the female working student seems to have disappeared completely from Germany, as neither records nor contemporary literary sources reveal the slightest trace of its existence.[74] The causes of this disappearance must probably be sought in the effects of the Great Depression, notably unemployment, which drastically curtailed students' opportunities for part-time work.[75] Contributory factors may have been the ideological objections against paid employment of women in general and the public misgivings about the "spiritual dangers" (*seelische Gefährdung*) to which young working women supposedly were exposed.[76]

After the *Machtergreifung*, female representatives of the economically weaker strata of German society also lost the few scholarships that had hitherto enabled at least some of them to take up academic studies. Finally, we should not underestimate the role of the "labor service" in this respect. As it served to lengthen the period of time before a woman could graduate and find employment, and since travel to and from the camps was often an expensive affair,[77] the "labor service" constituted an additional financial burden that many lower-middle-class and working-class families could ill afford. Although it was celebrated as the "ultimate manifestation of 'German Socialism' and *Kameradschaft* ['comradeship'], the irresistible solvent of existing class differences,"[78] the "labor service" thus contributed to make higher education a virtual monopoly of the upper middle class of German society.

It would be a mistake, however, to think of this change in the social structure of the *Frauenstudium* after 1933 as a mere historical accident. The fact that in the domain of higher education for women Germany's upper middle class *did* prosper under National Socialism (as it did in many other fields), while the lower middle class and working class *did not* (as indeed these classes did not in most other fields), reflects the class character of Hitler's regime. In spite of the humble origins of many of its leaders (including the *Führer* himself) and in spite of its "socialist" rhetoric and token concessions in the realm of social policy, the Third Reich consistently served the interests of Germany's traditional *Oberschicht* elites, including large landowners, powerful industrialists, wealthy professionals and businessmen, and high-ranking members of the civil service and army. In this sense, the term *Männerstaat*, which was used earlier to describe Hitler's state, is misleadingly crude. The Third Reich did not cater to the interests of *all* men but to those of an upper-class *minority* of men, and it trampled on the rights of the male working masses. *In its misogyny, then, the Nazi state was as socially selective as it was in its androcentrism.* Just as the Third Reich did not indiscriminately favor all men, it did not indiscriminately discriminate against all women, or for that matter against all women students. That women in general lost ground at the German universities in the 1930s was something National Socialism had little or nothing to do with; but that, in the process, the academic interests of working-class and lower-middle-class women were ruthlessly violated while upper-middle-class women virtually monopolized the *Frauenstudium* was something for which the Nazis must be held responsible.

PART 2

Women University Students in the Nazi "State of Men"

5

Women's Academic Franchise in Danger: The Reaction of German Women and Women Students

The Nazis' inveterate opposition to the *Frauenstudium* and their actual campaign against it in the years 1933–1934 yielded a great deal of invective but little effective action. Consequently, the Nazi attitude was not a factor of much importance in the concomitant decline of women's enrollments at the institutions of higher learning of the Reich. The combination of violent rhetoric and ostensibly draconian measures, such as the highly overrated *numerus clausus*, however, could not fail to create a widespread impression that the place of women at the German university was seriously threatened by Nazi misogynic ideas and policy. Understandably, Germany's women were greatly alarmed. Determined to defend the "academic franchise" (*akademische Bürgerrecht*) they had won only recently and after such a long struggle,[1] they decided to meet the challenge. The German "women's emancipation movement" (*Frauenbewegung*) itself had been denounced by the Nazis as the agent of a "Jewish conspiracy to undermine the German race" and was neutralized at the time of the *Machtergreifung*.[2] But some of its former leaders, including Lenore Kühn and Gertrud Bäumer, held right-wing views that were not at all incompatible with National Socialism, and they fervently hoped that a place in the Nazi sun would be available for at least an elite of German women. (Because of this, Kühn and Bäumer are sometimes referred to as "Nazi feminists," a confusing and misleading term.)[3] These women remained in a position to defend women's rights, and they did so primarily in articles in journals like *Die Frau*.[4] They did not challenge National Socialism itself, but merely criticized some of the assumptions on which the Nazi objections to female academic aspirations were based.

As early as February 1933 an attempt was made to convince Hitler himself that the eugenic case against the *Frauenstudium* was totally untenable. In an open letter to the *Führer*, one Irmgard Reichenau argued ingeniously that women's intellectual ambitions did not constitute a biological danger to "the race," but that precisely the opposite was true: to deny intellectually gifted women the fulfillment of their academic aspirations, she claimed, could only degrade and disillusion them and would thus necessarily stultify their feminine and maternal instincts.[5] Other women followed Reichenau's example in challenging the validity of the eugenic argument against the *Frauenstudium*. Some pointed out that female university graduates married just as frequently and had as many children as those who had not studied.[6] Others went one step further to assert that university studies were racially and eugenically beneficial since they resulted in a better understanding of women's tasks in society and instilled in women such values as punctuality, order, and sense of duty.[7] The economic argument against women as students was likewise publicly questioned. The president of the League of Women Physicians pointed out that women's representation in most professions was so insignificant that even to eliminate them completely would not create much relief on the overcrowded academic labor market.[8] Ready answers were also found to the male exclusionist objections to the *Frauenstudium*. To give but one example, it was retorted that women in general, and German women in particular, displayed an excellent record of intellectual and artistic achievement. Contrary to Alfred Rosenberg's contentions, German history was said to have reached unprecedented heights precisely when women played a central role in society, and the very exclusion of women from the nation's cultural life was alleged to have ushered in eras of decadence and decline.[9] Women also sought to turn the Nazis' anti-Semitic prejudices and Francophobia to their advantage; not without a good dose of disregard for historical truth, they argued that it was "only among Romanic and Oriental peoples that women played a subordinate role."[10] Furthermore, a shrewd appeal was made to the Nazi predilection for social-Darwinian principles. One woman thus wrote that the Third Reich had to be constructed on the foundation of "natural aristocracy," whereby the sole criterion ought to be talent, not sex.[11] More than one forcible *argumentum ad hominem* was used to refute the male exclusionists. Here, too, Irmgard Reichenau set the tone. The truly strong male, she suggested, did not need to convince himself that women are weak and intellectually inferior.[12] Other women continued in the same vein. "The more militarily minded the men are, the more cultivated women ought to be" was the message proclaimed in an article in *Die Frau* of January 1934.[13] The myth of women's intellectual inferiority was also undermined by the revelation of some hard facts. Gertrud Bäumer thus pointed out that only 15.7 percent of all women who had taken part in the Prussian barrister's examination in the period before 1931 had failed, compared to 24.7 percent of all male candidates.[14]

Women of the older generation, often members of the former women's emancipation movement and active in one of the academic professions, sought to discredit the theoretical basis of Nazi opposition to female intellectual aspirations. But such a strategy was not likely to make a great impact in the irrational atmosphere that prevailed in Hitler's Germany. Their association with the now-defamed women's emancipation movement and their bourgeois background, moreover, obviously undermined the authority women like Gertrud Bäumer had previously commanded, and decimated their following. In any event, all they could hope for was that the new regime would somehow tolerate the presence at the universities and the continued professional activity of no more than a very small number of women. A more ambitious program, however, was put forth by the leaders of the small Nazi association for women students. They proposed to make the *Frauenstudium* palatable to the Reich's new rulers, not by the force of logical argumentation but by nothing less than creation of a new type of German woman student, who like themselves would wholeheartedly embrace National Socialism itself. The very emergence of this new type of women students would radically change the character of the *Frauenstudium*, or so they believed, and make it an asset rather than a liability to the National Socialist state.

In contrast to her precursor of the Weimar era, typecast as the unintelligent, unfeminine, and antisocial "bluestocking" (*Blaustrumpf*) who had jeopardized the reputation of the entire *Frauenstudium*,[15] the new type of woman student was to be a monument of personal integrity and social consciousness, a true scholar, a virtuous young German lady, and last but not least a champion of the National Socialist cause. In the words of one of the leaders of the Nazi women students:

The National Socialist woman student has nothing in common with the pale, psycholog-ically perverted bookworm or with the decadent "luxury coed" [*Luxusstudentin*] of days gone by. We want spiritual breadth and trained logical thinking, but also comradeship and discipline, physical and spiritual deportment, straightforwardness and health, deep and rich femininity full of vitality. We want to mature to the great responsibility of the German woman....[16]

The alpha and omega of this new, National Socialist type of woman student was to be the "performance principle" (*Leistungsprinzip*). Feminine, social, political, intellectual, and athletic as well as cultural performance was to char-acterize the female student of the Third Reich and thus, in the opinion of her Nazi leaders at least, provide "the most important basis for a total vindication of the *Frauenstudium*."[17] The female university student of the National Socialist state would excel most in womanly performance. Keenly aware of her respon-sibilities as a German woman and future mother, she would be a worthy partner for the "soldierly male of the new Germany," a woman with "a strong heart," a genuine German "mistress" (*Herrin*). It was a matter of course for her that marriage and motherhood would follow immediately or soon after her graduation:

In this respect the *Frauenstudium* is no longer an issue...since marriage follows auto-matically on studies and employment. The years spent on studies and a professional career are useful years of apprenticeship and travel for the developing personality of the German woman student. They are followed by marriage, in which woman's mastery [*Meister-schaft*] is put to the test.[18]

In addition to this womanly performance, which was to minimize or entirely obliterate whatever eugenically harmful effects academic studies might have on young women, the female university student of the Third Reich was also to be characterized by what was referred to as "socialistic performance" in the service of the racial community, the *Volksgemeinschaft*, by genuine intellectual and scholarly achievement, by athletic and artistic performance, and of course by unconditional and enthusiastic service to the cause of National Socialism itself.

To mold this new generation of women students, to achieve this metamorphosis that would change the character of the *Frauenstudium* once and for all—this was the ambitious dream of the leaders of the Nazi women students' league. They regarded themselves as a vanguard, a "shock troop" (*Stosstrupp*) capable of providing the leadership, organization, and National Socialist inspiration required for this task. And in 1933 they eagerly welcomed the opportunity to create the new type of woman student who would be "worthy of the National Socialist university and the National Socialist state."[19] As we will see, however, they were to be sorely disappointed. Germany's women students were simply not interested in the grandiose schemes of their Nazi leaders, in the *Leistungsprinzip*, or in National Socialism itself. Not that this lack of interest mattered a great deal; if the Nazis never did withdraw the "academic franchise" of German women, it was not because they were impressed by the virtues, activism, and National Socialist integrity of women students but because they realized all too soon that they could not achieve their long-range economic, political, and even military goals without an adequate supply of female professionals. And in the late 1930s, when acute labor shortages occurred in virtually all professions, they would gladly have hired even the most repulsive "bluestocking" graduate imaginable to the fertile minds of Nazi women student leaders. The latter could thus have spared themselves the frustration and disappointment of a fruitless and, as it turned out, totally needless search for the new type of German woman student, the one who, in their minds at least, was to have redeemed the *Frauenstudium* in the Third Reich. But the efforts of the self-appointed Nazi "shock troop" of Germany's women students deserve our attention because they reveal a great deal about the mentality and mood of the young women who studied at the universities of the Third Reich, about their ambitions, interests, concerns, and their attitude towards National Socialism and the Nazi regime.

6

The "Working Community of National Socialist Women Students"

In reality, if not always in theory, the Nazi women students' association was a subdivision of the National Socialist German Student League (*Nationalsozialistischer Deutscher Studentenbund*—NSDStB), which had been founded on February 20, 1926.[1] The NSDStB had no special department for women in the early years of its existence, although it did welcome small numbers of women students into its ranks. But Baldur von Schirach, who became Nazi student leader in July 1928, deemed it opportune to create a special section for women students. In doing so, he hoped to keep women out of student politics, thus conforming to the orthodox NSDAP party line with regard to women's role in political matters in general and retaining full control over National Socialist women students while granting them some token autonomy. The Working Community of National Socialist Women Students (*Arbeitsgemeinschaft Nationalsozialistischer Studentinnen*—ANSt), founded in this manner on August 12, 1930, ostensibly as an independent organization for female university students with Nazi sympathies, was in fact a mere "appendix" (Faust) of the NSDStB.[2] In spite of this, the ANSt turned out to be relatively successful in the recruitment of new members as well as in the cultivation of a National Socialist esprit de corps among its rank and file.[3] Still, only a tiny proportion of Germany's women students proved susceptible to Nazi proselytizing, for by September 1, 1932, on the eve of the *Machtergreifung*, the ANSt, by its own admission, counted no more than 704 followers among nearly 19,000 female university students.[4] Then, on January 30, 1933, Adolf Hitler took office as chancellor of the Reich, and National Socialism carried the day. This turn of events permitted the ANSt to move out of the doldrums and for the first time play a significant role in the affairs of Germany's women university students.

Towards the end of June 1933, ANSt Reich Leader (*Reichsführerin*) Gisela Brettschneider instructed her local leaders to organize all women studying at their respective universities into a special department of the local student union for purposes of National Socialist "political education" as well as physical training. This was intended as a first step in the direction of the implementation of the "performance principle" and the creation of a new, National Socialist type of woman student. It was considered a matter of the greatest importance that the leadership of these new "offices for women students," which were to be amalgamated at the national level by the Main Office VI (*Hauptamt* VI) of the German Student Federation (*Deutsche Studentenschaft*—DSt), be in the hands of reliable ANSt members, just as the DSt itself was to be controlled by the NSDStB (see figure 5).[5] In the summer of 1933, however, the ANSt was hardly in a position to provide firm, National Socialist leadership. In the wake of the *Machtergreifung*, thousands of opportunists had flocked into the Nazi party formations, and even the unprestigious ANSt had profited from this phenomenon. In fact, its membership had suddenly mushroomed, but the quality of the new-comers left much to be desired from the National Socialist point of view. Local leaders thus reported many instances of disobedience, failure to pay membership dues, gossip, intrigues, negative criticism, "frivolous behavior and immoral conduct" including flirting with "non-Aryans," smoking, and other violations of Nazi dogma and discipline. In short, the ANSt was simply swamped with "opportunists" (*Konjunkturhelden*), who were not genuinely interested in the cause of Adolph Hitler.[6] On the other hand, a good many convinced Nazi women students chose to stay aloof from the ANSt, most likely on account of this opportunism. Since it was clear that the ANSt itself had to be transformed into a true elite of fanatic women students before anything else could be accomplished, Gisela Brettschneider ordered a ruthless membership purge, introduced much stricter criteria for the admission of new members, and obtained the release of a party directive to the effect that all studying female NSDAP members were to join the ANSt forthwith.[7] Under those circumstances, it could be expected with a reasonable amount of confidence that the Nazi coeds' association might at last be able to yield a sufficient number of reliable prospective leaders, whose task it would be to control the organization of the new "offices for women students" within the local student unions (*Studentenschaften*) and to educate their members in the ways of National Socialism.

At the start of the winter semester 1933/1934, the ANSt was thus ready to embark on its grandiose scheme of reeducation of Germany's women students. "Offices for women students," embracing all female members of the *Studentenschaften*, had been created in each university city and were duly controlled by the leaders of the local ANSt section, just as each student union had been subordinated to the local NSDStB. This ascendancy of the Nazi Student League over the federation of student unions was formally sanctioned on the highest level by the appointment of NSDStB leader Oskar Stäbel as president of the

Figure 5.
The National Socialist Student Organizations in Spring and Summer 1933

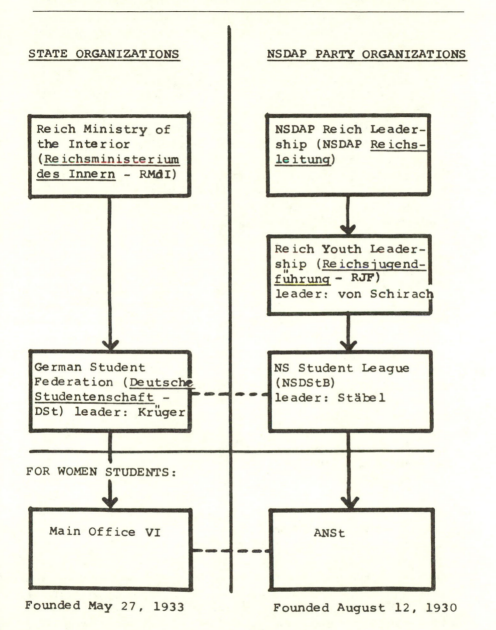

STATE ORGANIZATIONS

Reich Ministry of the Interior (Reichsministerium des Innern - RMdI)

German Student Federation (Deutsche Studentenschaft - DSt) leader: Krüger

FOR WOMEN STUDENTS:

Main Office VI

Founded May 27, 1933

NSDAP PARTY ORGANIZATIONS

NSDAP Reich Leader-ship (NSDAP Reichs-leitung)

Reich Youth Leader-ship (Reichsjugend-führung - RJF) leader: von Schirach

NS Student League (NSDStB) leader: Stäbel

ANSt

Founded August 12, 1930

Deutsche Studentenschaft[8] and of ANSt leader Gisela Brettschneider as head of the DSt's Main Office VI in September 1933.[9]

A wide range of extracurricular activities was now introduced, which were henceforth to be compulsory for all women students. In early November detailed instructions worked out by Brettschneider's staff reached the local sections of the "office for women students." Extracurricular physical education was to be compulsory for all women in the first four semesters. In addition, all women of the first six semesters had to follow special courses in "women's service" (*Frauendienst*), dealing with air protection (*Luftschutz*), communications (*Nachrichtendienst*), and health instruction (*Sanitätskurs*), and had to serve from time to time in the Nazi charity organizations. Women students of the first three semesters were told to participate in what was described as "community service" (*Gemeinschaftspflege*) and consisted in the cultivation of folklore, folk songs, traditional dances, and the like.[10] Proof of participation in these activities was to be entered into a special "duty pass" (*Pflichtenheft*).[11]

On paper at least, this ambitious scheme looked impressive. But implementing it was another matter. In fact, surviving reports indicate that the instructions were carried out in very few places, and even then often only partially.[12] In important university cities such as Leipzig and Halle, nothing at all was accomplished.[13] The reason for this fiasco was simply that most women students decided they had better things to do during their leisure time, and they ignored the instructions of their Nazi leaders. They were able to do so with impunity because Main Office VI lacked the power to enforce its own decrees. The ministries of education of the various German states (*Länder*) had been approached no sooner than the end of November with the request that the obligatory character of the new extracurricular activities be acknowledged, and most of them took their time to respond.[14] The many women students who shirked the initiatives of Main Office VI, meanwhile, could not easily be punished. Furthermore, in the absence of ministerial instructions, faculty deans and university rectors proved reluctant to cooperate with the Nazi women student leaders, and so did the local NSDStB personnel. Intoxicated as we have seen them to be with the male exclusionist spirit of the SA, the Nazi students had nothing but contempt for the plans of their female colleagues, and quite frequently they cynically sabotaged their activities.[15] Gisela Brettschneider herself held no influence at all with the Reich leadership of the NSDStB and the DSt, and all she could suggest to her frustrated representatives was the adoption of a tactic of "diplomacy and amiability" in the face of such affronts.[16] The women in charge of the local offices for women students nevertheless issued a collective protest against the intolerable attitude of the NSDStB and the DSt. They complained in particular about the censorship of their correspondence, the lack of financial support, and the arbitrary dismissal of dedicated ANSt staff members in such places as Greifswald, Tübingen, and Cologne.[17] Their hopes for at least a measure of sympathy and cooperation were disappointed, however, when Nazi student boss Stäbel reacted to their initiative on November 28, 1933, by unceremoniously demoting a number of dissatisfied

ANSt leaders, dissolving all but two of the eleven departments within Main Office VI, and curtailing the relative autonomy of the ANSt and Main Office VI by means of a closer integration into the NSDStB and the DSt.[18] Stäbel even contemplated liquidating the ANSt altogether, but changed his mind in the nick of time—an order had already been published in the Nazi student paper—after Brettschneider and her colleagues had lodged a last, desperate protest.[19]

These incidents naturally eroded whatever prestige and authority the Nazi women student leaders had ever enjoyed among Germany's women students and thus jeopardized the important tasks ANSt leaders had set for themselves. No wonder, then, that female students continued to display more interest in the familiar, established, and usually denominational coeds' associations, which offered sociability without regimentation and coercion. In comparison to giants such as the Federation of Catholic German Organizations for Women Students (*Verband Katholischer Deutscher Studentinnenvereine*—VKDSt) or the protestant German Christian Women Students' Movement (*Deutsche Christliche Studentinnenbewegung*—DCSB), the ANSt was and remained, for the time being at least, a dwarf. The Nazi student leaders could not even dream of "coordinating" (*gleichschalten*), that is, Nazifying, these federations, which between them commanded the support of the great majority of Germany's women students and which, in the case of the VKDSt at least, enjoyed the protection granted Catholic associations under the terms of the newly signed Concordat between Hitler's Reich and the Vatican. It was only much later, in July 1938, that the VKDSt and the DCSB were dissolved by order of none other than the Nazi grand inquisitor, SS Reich Leader (*Reichsführer*) Heinrich Himmler.[20] Until then, however, both organizations continued to wield considerable influence over female university students at the expense of the ANSt and Main Office VI. The independence of these denominational federations and their relative immunity to National Socialism were dramatically illustrated by the public refusal of the DCSB membership, assembled at a convention in Hannover on November 25 and 26, 1933, to adopt the "Aryan paragraph" (*Arierparagraph*), cornerstone of Nazi anti-Semitic policies at the universities. Adding insult to injury, this decision was defiantly communicated to the DSt in formal fashion.[21] The weakness of the ANSt and Main Office VI was reflected not only in their tacit acceptance of this affront but also in their toleration of dual membership in the ANSt and the DCSB,[22] an uncharacteristic sample of National Socialist pluralist goodwill, undoubtedly inspired by the knowledge that, given only one choice, women students were more likely to opt for the DCSB than the ANSt. In any event, it was only through such pliancy and compromise, which obviously did little to promote its National Socialist integrity in the public eye, that the ANSt could hope to recruit significant numbers of new members, including potential leaders, from the ranks of the denominational coeds' associations and among unaffiliated women students (*Freistudentinnen*).[23]

By watering down its own National Socialist principles in order to accommodate the unconvinced, the unenthusiastic, and the indifferent, or whatever opportunist who fancied to join, the ANSt forfeited its intended role as a Nazi elite formation that was to create the new, National Socialist type of woman student of the Third Reich. This too contributed greatly to the failure of the grandiose program of compulsory extracurricular activities organized by Main Office VI in the fall of 1933. The plans of the previous summer, to screen applicants strictly and limit the number of new members in order to safeguard the elitist character of the ANSt and transform it into a true Nazi vanguard, were never implemented, as a quick glance at some membership figures may confirm. In Göttingen, for instance, the ANSt section increased its enrollments from 20 in February 1933 to 88 one year later. The Technical University of Dresden counted 15 ANSt members in February 1933 and 60 (four times as many) in November 1933. The ANSt section at Munich University had a following of 40 members early in 1933, 85 in August 1933, and a stunning 450 in the early spring of 1934.[24] Figures for the total ANSt membership in the Reich are not available, but on the basis of the above figures, we may speculate that by the end of 1933 it stood three or four times higher than on the eve of the *Machtergreifung*, when it had been approximately 700.[25] As a result, the ANSt, its ranks swamped with unreliable or at best inexperienced novices, hardly found itself in a position to provide the effective and inspired National Socialist leadership that had been expected. Consequently, in the spring of 1934 a fresh attempt was made to purge the Nazi coeds' league of the opportunists within its ranks. A new "membership embargo" (*Mitgliedssperre*) went into effect, aimed at limiting the ANSt in future to a maximum of one thousand members. Notice was served that only the brightest and the best—from the National Socialist viewpoint, of course—would stand a chance of being retained or admitted.[26] That these new guidelines were indeed implemented, at least at some universities, appears from the case of Munich University, where the ANSt section duly cut its enrollment from 450 to 230.[27]

The effort to turn the ANSt into an efficient "leadership organization" (*Führerorganisation*) also included the introduction of a vigorous training program for the benefit of women who were selected to act as group leaders and instructors for the activities of Main Office VI during the coming summer semester. A series of special "training camps" (*Führungslager*) were organized for that purpose in the spring of 1934. Participating women were subjected to sessions in political indoctrination, briefed on general questions of organization and leadership, and acquainted with the significance of the extracurricular activities they would soon be supervising.[28] As for these activities, the fiasco of the previous winter had brought home to the Nazi women student leaders the impracticability of their extravagant program. Since the lack of cooperation on the part of the authorities of state, university, and even the DSt and the NSDStB had left Main Office VI without any means to enforce its own decrees, other methods had to be found to overcome the apathy of women students. It was decided to rely more on the carrot than on the stick in the future. The new instructions of Main Office VI, issued on May 18, 1934, not only called for considerably fewer obligatory activities but also made it abundantly clear that "the recalcitrant and the untalented" would under no circumstances be coerced to comply. Shrewdly speculating not only on the coeds' pride but also on the students' traditional infatuation with diplomas of any kind, Main Office VI also offered to deliver certificates to women who would report of their own volition.[29]

In spite of all this, success once again eluded the planners of the ANSt and Main Office VI. Reports indicate that their exhortations and incentives failed to engender much enthusiasm and that their modest instructions were often only partially, and sometimes not at all, implemented.[30] For one thing, the problem of the lack of ministerial recognition continued to bedevil the scheme of the Nazi women student leaders. A single Reich Ministry of Education (*Reichser-ziehungsministerium*—REM), with jurisdiction over Germany in its entirety, had just been created in May 1934 and had been placed under Bernhard Rust, who in December of the previous year, as Prussian minister of education, had led all his colleagues in formally recognizing the compulsory nature of the extracurricular activities of Main Office VI.[31] Still, the matter of ministerial approval in the various states was not settled until at least a full year later. In the meantime, university rectors or faculty deans with little sympathy and even less respect for the Nazi coeds' plans continued to hinder their work. A good example was Kiel University, where the rector refused to cooperate in any way, explaining hypocritically that he had never received word from the ministry about "duty passes" for women students and feigning concern about overburdening them with this proposed extracurricular work. He betrayed the blatantly male exclusionist motives for his recalcitrance, however, by adding that he would negotiate such matters only with the (male) leaders of the DSt, not with Main Office VI.[32]

Incidents like this may explain why women students could not be compelled to take part in the extracurricular activities organized by their Nazi leaders, but they do not suggest why women students would not participate of their own free will. In any event, their susceptibility to the incentives and propaganda of Main Office VI was never fully tested, for the universities and the Nazi student organizations were suddenly rocked by the ramifications of the *"Röhm Putsch"* of June 30, 1934, and the work of the Nazi women student leaders was brusquely interrupted. Nazi student boss Stäbel was forced to resign on account of his former close association with the SA, which lost its influence at the universities. The DSt and the NSDStB thus acquired new leaders as well as new patrons. Jurisdiction over the former, a body of public law, was entrusted to Reich Education Minister Rust, who appointed Andreas Feickert as its head. The NSDStB, on the other hand, an office of the Nazi party, was more closely integrated into the NSDAP "Political Organization" (*Politische Organisation*—PO) of Robert Ley (see figure 6). Albert Derichsweiler became the new *Reichsführer* of the NSDStB in the middle of August, and in order to preserve the semblance of unity between the Nazi NSDStB and the Nazified DSt, he and Feickert appointed each other as their deputies. It was a purely symbolic and futile gesture, for the months that followed were to witness the development of

Figure 6.
The National Socialist Student Organizations after Their Reorganization in July 1934

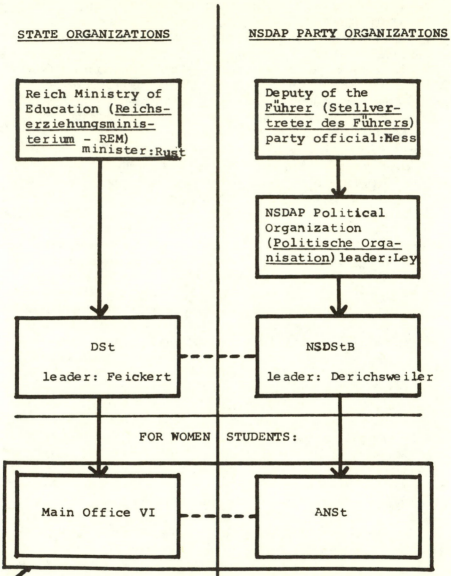

STATE ORGANIZATIONS

NSDAP PARTY ORGANIZATIONS

Reich Ministry of
Education (Reichs-
erziehungsminis-
terium - REM)
minister:Rust

Deputy of the
Führer (Stellver-
treter des Führers)
party official:Hess

NSDAP Political
Organization
(Politische Orga-
nisation)leader:Ley

DSt

leader: Feickert

NSDStB

leader: Derichsweiler

FOR WOMEN STUDENTS:

Main Office VI

ANSt

Held in personal union by Gisela Brettschneider until
October 1, 1934, by Liselotte Machwirth after December
1, 1934

an increasingly bitter rivalry between the two leaders and their respective organizations and patrons.[33]

All this naturally affected the status of the Nazi organizations for women students as well. The ANSt, the presumably elitist party organization, remained within the NSDStB and was subjected to yet another membership purge. This time, only those who had joined prior to January 30, 1933, were to taste the privileges and responsibilities of membership, although small numbers of selected students could be accepted as "probationary members" (*Anwärterinnen*). All studying female members of the NSDAP, on the other hand, were reminded of their duty to report for service in the ANSt.[34] These decisions aimed not only at reaffirming the role of the ANSt as an elitist National Socialist "leadership organization" vis-à-vis the apathetic majority of studying women assembled within the DSt's Main Office VI for purposes of Nazification, but also at strengthening the ANSt in the face of the encroachments of another Nazi organization, the League of German Girls (*Bund Deutscher Mädel*—BDM). For nearly one year, this department for girls within the Hitler Youth (*Hitlerjugend*—HJ) had been scheming to keep within its own ranks members who took up university studies, rather than turn them over to the ANSt, and this was mainly because they were sorely needed by the BDM as leaders. In April 1933 the League of German Girls had been given jurisdiction over girls and young women up to age twenty-one,[35] and as most young women started their academic studies at age eighteen or nineteen,[36] the BDM actually held a legitimate title to control over a considerable share, if not the majority, of all German women students. The ANSt, however, likewise suffering from an acute and chronic shortage of leaders, had proved unwilling to release BDM members from its service.[37] Frustrated, the League of German Girls saw no alternative but to try and eliminate the ANSt altogether and to replace it as the organization for National Socialist women students. In the spring of 1934, its leaders raised an "absolute claim" (*Totalitätsanspruch*) of jurisdiction over German female youth of all classes and occupations, and for a while the air was full of rumors of a pending incorporation of the ANSt into the BDM.[38]

It may seem odd that these two zealously competing antagonists, the ANSt and the BDM, were then still part of one single department within the NSDAP, the Reich Youth Leadership (*Reichsjugendführung*—RJF) of Baldur von Schirach. But this paradox is easily explained in terms of the recently developed theory of "institutional Darwinism" (*Ämter-Darwinismus*) in the Third Reich. We may assume that von Schirach was simply emulating within his own jurisdiction what Hitler was doing in the Nazi party and state as a whole, namely, allowing his subordinates to compete in a complex, social-Darwinian struggle from which, it was expected, the stronger would emerge victorious. Bollmus' apt description of Hitler's views in this respect also applies to Schirach: "Probably unconsciously, he practiced an 'institutional Darwinism' of sorts. As he saw it, 'the best' and 'the strongest' office would automatically prevail in the general struggle of life."[39]

There can be no doubt that in the struggle between the ANSt and the BDM, the former was by far the weaker and therefore predestined to fall prey to its stronger rival. The ANSt escaped this fate only because, together with the NSDStB itself, it was removed from the jurisdiction of the RJF in July 1934 and placed instead under the Political Organization of Robert Ley. Moreover, in the person of Albert Derichsweiler the NSDStB found an ambitious new leader who regarded Schirach as a dangerous rival. Consequently, he was not prepared to sacrifice the ANSt for the benefit of the Reich Youth Leader's BDM. Instead, he did his utmost to help shore up the weak Nazi coeds' association and to check the BDM's aspirations at the universities.

The NSDStB Reich Leader was likewise committed to preserve the ascendancy of the ANSt over Main Office VI of Feickert's DSt. He hoped to achieve this first by securing Rust's and Feickert's consent to his suggestion that "the political and ideological" education of Germany's women students would be the exclusive responsibility of the ANSt, the party elite, whereas less important tasks such as physical training would be in the hands of Main Office VI of the DSt.[40] The chronic shortage of reliable Nazi women students, coupled with the desire to avoid "overorganization," made it necessary to preserve the arrangement that had existed since the summer of 1933, whereby the same personnel had held the corresponding offices in both the ANSt and Main Office VI, even though there was no longer a personal union between the highest positions within the NSDStB and the DSt since the departure of Stäbel.[41] Derichsweiler aptly took advantage of this situation to force Gisela Brettschneider out of office, for he suspected that she was leaning towards Feickert, and to replace her at the head of both the ANSt and Main Office VI with Liselotte Machwirth, a dynamic individual and fanatic National Socialist who could be relied on to do his bidding under all circumstances.[42]

Being manipulated as mere pawns in the rivalry between the male-dominated NSDStB and DSt and their respective patrons was not likely to enhance the prestige and authority of the ANSt and Main Office VI in the eyes of Germany's female university students. And the reorganization of the Nazi student organizations took up most of the summer and fall of 1934. Consequently, nothing had been done to marshall the masses of women students and to organize a program of extracurricular activities for the winter semester 1934/35. Some local ANSt sections did display modest signs of life, and organized "cells" of approximately ten girls each for the purpose of political education in the National Socialist sense. But participation was voluntary and, in keeping with the ANSt's elitist aspirations, limited to the now again restricted numbers of the Nazi coeds' association alone.[43] Meanwhile, the majority of women students remained aloof and inactive. Efforts to involve them in these ventures were virtually doomed in advance because of the attitude of the male Nazi leaders. Derichsweiler himself was interested in the ANSt and Main Office VI only insofar as these organizations might be useful to him in his rivalry with Feickert, but he was not prepared to underwrite their ambitious plans and schemes, for which he probably had nothing but contempt. Like Stäbel before him, the new NSDStB leader at one time toyed with the idea of dissolving the obnoxious ANSt altogether, or of relegating it to the status of a mere "department" (*Referat*) within the NSDStB.[44] Friction and mutual antipathy thus continued to characterize the relationship between the ANSt and the unabatedly male exclusionist NSDStB in the fall and winter of 1934.[45] The greatest problem, perhaps, was posed by the fact that the male leaders who controlled the NSDStB's budget severely restricted the ANSt's freedom of movement by allocating woefully inadequate sums of money for its activities.[46] The same was true for the DSt, within which Main Office VI received only a very small fraction of the DSt contributions paid by female students.[47]

A way to escape this financial impasse was offered to the Nazi coeds' leaders in the late fall of 1934 by Frau Gertrud Scholtz-Klink, head of the Nazi women's organizations, who had just received the imposing title of Reich Women's Leader with jurisdiction, in theory at least, over all German women from age twenty-one on.[48] Since many female university students obviously fell into this category, and since Frau Scholtz-Klink herself was keenly interested in women students, if only because her own sprawling organizations suffered from a chronic shortage of qualified leaders, she sought to establish her patronage over the ANSt and Main Office VI. At a joint meeting of the top leaders of the *Nationalsozialistische Frauenschaft* (National Socialist Women's League—NSF) and the ANSt on December 12, 1934, manifestly convened at the initiative of the Reich Women's Leader, Scholtz-Klink enthusiastically described the benefits that would flow from an incorporation of the ANSt into the NSF. Not only would women students be freed from the male supremacist oppression they had suffered within the NSDStB and the DSt, they would also gain access to the cornucopian treasury of the Reich Women's Leadership and, by riding her coattails, would profit from her allegedly strong and influential position within the Nazi party. Machwirth and her associates, however, failed to be swayed by Scholtz-Klink's eloquence and were clearly offended by a casual reference of the Reich Women's Leader to the inefficiency and chaos that characterized the operations of Main Office VI. In the end, the meeting was adjourned without any agreements having been reached.[49] In any event, it is unlikely that the higher authorities of the NSDAP would ever have consented to a proposed transfer of the ANSt from the NSDStB to the already hulking private empire of Scholtz-Klink. The Reich Women's Leader's aspirations were in fact checked, at least for the time being, in February 1935, when she formally had to acknowledge that the ANSt was the party's sole organization for women students and that ANSt members, even when twenty-one years of age or older, would have to join the NSF only after their graduation. A few months later, on May 21, 1935, a similar agreement was concluded between the ANSt and the BDM.[50]

These agreements may have preserved the special status of the ANSt at the university as well as its autonomy from both the Reich Women's Leader and the Nazi League of German Girls, but they also ratified its fate as the penniless and powerless maidservant of the male exclusionist NSDStB. Nearly two years had passed since the ANSt had embarked on its ambitious schemes with great enthusiasm and determination, but the much-vaunted "new type" of National Socialist woman student had yet to make her grand appearance on the academic stage of the Third Reich. The majority of the women who attended Germany's institutions of higher learning were not appreciably different from those of the Weimar era. Most of them were primarily concerned with their studies and future career; they joined the traditional denominational coeds' associations and displayed little or no interest in the few extracurricular activities that Main Office VI managed to organize. Only a small minority were at home in the ANSt, now that opportunists were no longer welcome there and membership had little to offer in the way of authority or prestige anyway. In fact, events of the next few semesters were to demonstrate once again how little authority the Nazi coeds' organization enjoyed and how little fascination National Socialism itself generated among Germany's women students. And yet, wiser because of its previous disappointments, Main Office VI had lowered its sights and drastically reduced the number of compulsory extracurricular activities when it sent out its instructions for the summer semester in March 1935.[51] It was rationalized that most first-year women students had already received certain types of training, such as first aid or folk dancing, in the BDM or the "labor service," and were already better versed in the theory and practice of National Socialism, so that there was no longer an urgent need to subject them to many extracurricular activities at the university. Greater emphasis was therefore placed on voluntary actions during the holidays, such as the "agricultural service" (*Landdienst*), which involved the mobilization of Germany's students for the benefit of the peasantry of the Reich, particularly in late summer when the harvest generated a great need for additional agricultural labor.[52] The *Landdienst* scheme reflected the importance the Nazis attached to their agrarian ideology of "blood and soil" (*Blut und Boden*) and, with its romantic connotations of a "return to the land," it seemed ideally suited to arouse the enthusiasm of young women students. Small-scale experiments in 1933 and 1934 had been encouraging,[53] and it was decided early in 1935 to organize a massive, nationwide *Landdienst* in the spring of that year in cooperation with the male students. In spite of a massive propaganda campaign, however, the German universities failed to yield the expected masses of volunteers, and even a last-minute extension of the deadline for registration could not prevent a complete fiasco. The entire venture was unceremoniously cancelled, officially because of the "unforeseen" shortness of the Easter holiday.[54] A second attempt, improvised in the summer, was hardly more successful, as barely 2 percent of all German university students volunteered to help bring in the harvest.[55]

The Nazi student leaders were dismayed and embittered. Reflecting on the lack of success of the "agricultural service," one of them wrote dejectedly that they had "learned to take into account that the majority of the students are absolutely useless for such great tasks."[56] Widespread lethargy crippled not only large-scale schemes such as the *Landdienst* but also the more modest projects of Main Office VI. In the winter semester of 1935/36 and the spring semester of 1936, very few extracurricular activities were organized, but virtually no women students reported for duty, aside from a handful of zealous ANSt stalwarts and a number of opportunists who admittedly participated merely in order to obtain yet another certificate for possible future use (*"Testatjägerei"*).[57] Both the NSF and the BDM manipulated this malaise to encroach further on the position of the ANSt, and they did so in flagrant disregard of earlier promises and agreements. The Nazi League of German Girls encouraged its studying members not to serve in the ANSt, as agreed in May 1935, but instead to set up special female Hitler Youth working communities (*Arbeitsgemeinschaften*).[58] Scholtz-Klink's NSF freely raided the ANSt ranks in an effort to recruit new members, particularly among those rare birds who displayed leadership talents and who were therefore badly needed by the ANSt itself.[59] Meanwhile, Nazi student leader Derichsweiler, sublimely uninterested in the fate of his coeds' department, virtually sanctioned such practices by his order of April 18, 1936, which stipulated that ANSt members had to serve simultaneously in the ranks of another Nazi women's organization.[60] The Reich Women's Leader, in particular, was in a position to take advantage of this opportunity, for she could entice ambitious young women students with the lure of future career opportunities in her gargantuan Nazi women's organizations.[61] It is obvious that the ANSt was not likely to grow in prestige and authority under those conditions. Consequently, its leaders may well have welcomed yet another change in the structure of the Nazi student organizations, a change that occurred in the fall of 1936 and opened up prospects for a possible improvement in the fortunes of the ANSt.

The continuing rivalry between the DSt and the NSDStB and the apparent inability (or unwillingness) of their respective leaders, Feickert and Derichsweiler, to reach a compromise eventually exhausted the patience of their patrons in the Ministry of Education and the NSDAP leadership. Both Rust and Hess finally agreed that nothing short of a total merger of the DSt and the NSDStB could provide a definitive solution for the lingering friction between the two organizations. And since there was obviously no place in such a compromise for the two irreconcilable existing leaders, they both had to go. Derichsweiler and Waldemar Müller, who had become Feickert's successor as head of the DSt only shortly before, were dismissed on November 5, 1936, and on the very same day the DSt and the NSDStB were merged into one single organization, the Reich Student Leadership (*Reichsstudentenführung*—RSF). Gustav Adolf Scheel, a Nazi student leader from Heidelberg and high-ranking SS-officer, was simultaneously appointed head of the new organization, Reich Student Leader (*Reichsstudentenführer*).[62] A few months later, on April 19, 1937, the RSF was to be incorporated into Robert Ley's Political Organization of the NSDAP as a main office responsible for the political training of all German students. Oddly enough, however, both the DSt and the NSDStB somehow continued to exist within the RSF, the former as a sponsored organization (*betreute Organisation*) of the NSDAP, the latter as a genuine party formation (*Parteigliederung*). But since there was henceforth a complete personal union between the two at all levels, the distinction ceased to be consequential.[63] The ANSt and Main Office VI, too, were merged into one single office within the RSF, the Office for Women Students (*Amt für Studentinnen*) (see figure 7). The ANSt continued to exist separately within this office as an elite organization for National Socialist women students, but Main Office VI was never heard from again. Women students who were not members of the ANSt were henceforth simply said to belong to "the DSt," and all activities that had been organized by Main Office VI were now handled by the RSF Office for Women Students.[64]

One innovation, introduced by Scheel, was the system of NSDStB and ANSt "teams" (*Kameradschaften*) or "cells" (*Zellen*), to which students of the first three semesters were attracted. Membership was voluntary, at least in theory, and the teams' program included not only the standard Nazi fare of political education and sports but also more interesting activities such as visits to concerts and theatre performances. Scheel hoped that this might serve as an incentive for politically indifferent students to join the NSDStB teams.[65] In order to facilitate the recruitment of new members and to safeguard the continuity of the training within the teams, he issued an order that forbade students to change universities during their first three semesters. During that period of time they had to remain at the institution where they had first registered, their *Stammhochschule*.[66] Only on completion of their third semester could deserving team members be accepted as full-fledged NSDStB or ANSt members.[67]

The overhaul of the Nazi student organizations and the introduction of the system of teams, however, failed to arouse much National Socialist enthusiasm among the young men and women who studied at Germany's universities. Considerable pressure had to be brought to bear on freshmen to join the teams in the first place, so that membership, although voluntary in theory, was compulsory in practice.[68] The ANSt, in particular, found it extremely difficult to replenish its ranks in the face of widespread apathy among women students and the continuing encroachments of the BDM and the NSF. Its weakness and impotence was reflected in a new formal agreement with the Nazi League of German Girls, concluded on February 25, 1937. The BDM's promise to turn its student members over to the ANSt teams during their first three semesters secured a steady flow of recruits for the Nazi coeds' association, particularly since by 1937 virtually all high school graduates belonged to the Hitler Youth. But the actual value to the ANSt of these newcomers was highly questionable. They did not join the teams of their own volition, but merely on account of a bureaucratic stroke of the pen, so that the majority undoubtedly turned out to be indifferent, if not reluctant, recruits. Previous membership in the BDM hardly constituted a guarantee of National Socialist fervor or integrity, as membership in the Hitler Youth itself was not usually a question of free choice.[69] Even during the short period of time they served in the ANSt teams, BDM girls actually remained members of the Hitler Youth. The ANSt, therefore, could never really hope to command the full loyalty of these young women. On completion of their service in the teams, not only BDM members but all graduates of the teams, even those few

Figure 7.
The National Socialist Student Organizations after Creation of the RSF on
November 5, 1936

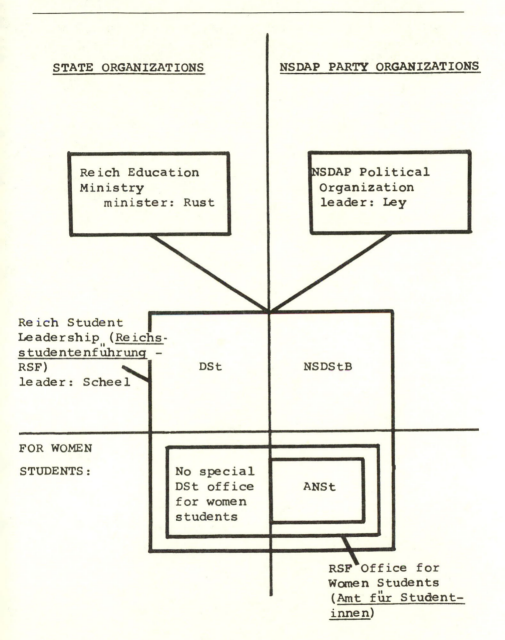

individuals who had not previously belonged to the BDM, had to be made available to the Nazi League of German Girls. The ANSt was allowed to retain only the minimum number of women it required for the training in the teams.[70] With this new agreement, the history of the ANSt had reached its nadir. Only a few years earlier, it had been the Nazi party's sole organization for women students; now it was merely a purgatory of sorts, where academic BDM members unenthusiastically served some time before they could return to the ranks of the League of German Girls. Not surprisingly, then, the achievements of women students within the ANSt in the late 1930s were far from impressive.

7

The National Socialist Performance of Women University Students

The "political education" (*politische Erziehung*) of women students of the first three semesters constituted the primary objective of the training within the ANSt cells. In theory at least, this might have been a feature of some interest to young women with academic and professional aspirations, for the name "political education" seemed to hold the promise of their future involvement in the political life of the German nation. But nothing could have been further from the truth. In fact, National Socialist tenets held that women simply did not belong in politics. Consequently, the "political education" of women students merely purported to teach them to "think politically," a euphemism for the uncritical acceptance of Nazi dogma and the glorification of Nazi rule.[1] The sessions in political education thus amounted to little more than dull lectures on *Mein Kampf* or NSDAP party history. And since most women had already had more than their fill of this kind of fare in the Hitler Youth, they were not likely to be impressed. Many consistently shirked the sessions, often on the pretext of duties within the BDM or the NSF. In an effort to stimulate interest, the curriculum was spiced with discussions of topics of particular relevance to young women, such as the issue of women's role in the professions or women's labor.[2] Emphasis was also gradually shifted from the obviously unpopular field of Nazi party ideology and politics to "cultural work" (*Kulturarbeit*).[3] The program of "political education" launched in order to imbue Germany's women students with the "racial-political" teachings of National Socialism, was thus soon watered down and later virtually abandoned in order to forestall the possible collapse of the ANSt teams in the face of widespread indifference and absenteeism.

The "cultural work" of the ANSt cells never developed into a going concern either. Women students received instructions to cultivate poetry, music, theatre, folk songs, folk dances, and the like and were repeatedly told that it was of the greatest importance to master such forms of "creativity" (*Lebensgestaltung*) because later, as homemakers and mothers, they would be responsible for the cultural life and customs (*Brauchtum*) of their families.[4] ANSt leaders also felt that consistent involvement in genuine German culture, particularly folk culture, might serve as the ideal antidote to the female student's long hours of studying and desk work, to the "scholarly hangover" (*Wissenschaftskater*).[5] The cultural work of the ANSt presumably focused on the "women's evening" (*Frauenabend*), a performance that included songs, ballads, poems, lullabies, and speaking choruses. Instructions for the organization of such festive evenings were frequently sent out by the ANSt leadership, but little evidence is available to indicate that the "women's evening" was a regular feature in German women students' social schedule in the late 1930s.[6] In order to help uphold their claims about the significance of the "cultural work" of women students, therefore, the ANSt leaders had to rely increasingly on individuals. Artistically gifted women students were encouraged to develop their talents and were given the opportunity to demonstrate their work to the general public. For example, much was made of the prizes won by women at the exhibition of student art held in Munich from February 9 to 12, 1939. But the kudos accorded the work of a mere handful of individuals only served to underscore the failure of a program that had purported to testify to the cultural achievements of *all* women students.[7]

Much the same can be said about the scheme of compulsory physical education for women students. In the pages of *Mein Kampf*, Hitler himself had ordained that physical training was to be emphasized above all else in the education of girls and young women, its sole goal being cultivation of "the future mother."[8] In keeping with this precept, the ANSt and Main Office VI had launched an ambitious scheme of compulsory extracurricular sports (*Pflichtsport*) as early as the fall of 1933.[9] It emphasized light athletic exercises as well as hiking, a pastime credited (among other things) with dissolving "bourgeois mentalities" and promoting "earth empathy" (*Erdverbundenheit*), whatever that may be.[10] Competitive sports were barred, however, since the extracurricular sports program purported to aim at "a general training of the body," at "healthy girls, women, mothers," and not at specialization and athletic records. Biological and eugenic objectives loomed uppermost in the minds of *Pflichtsport* protagonists; individual performances were of marginal importance at best. It was believed that undue stress on individual achievements of young women might lead to personality cults and "sports conceit" (*Sporteitelkeit*) and could thus breed "asocial individuals" (*unsoziale Einzelmenschen*) for whom the National Socialist state claimed to have no use. Furthermore, the extracurricular physical training of female university students was expected to compensate for the "overintellectualization" (*Intellektualisierung*) that presumably threatened all academic women (but apparently, for some unexplained reason, not men). These exercises were needed to bring about a harmonious "union of spiritual and physical development" in the higher education of Germany's women. In addition, sports were said to promote genuine femininity and natural grace and to exorcize the threat of "masculinization" (*Vermännlichung*).[11] Finally, *Pflichts-port* was to be put in the service of Nazi racial ideology; as one of the ANSt leaders had it, sports served to stimulate "racial purity" (*Rassereinheit*) and to promote "understanding of the racial-hygienical measures [of the National Socialist regime]."[12]

However, the poor performance of Germany's female students in this program of compulsory physical education soon deflated the high aspirations of the ANSt leadership in this field too. Lack of ministerial recognition and therefore of effective sanctions led to a wholesale boycott of the *Pflichtsport* scheme. The majority of female university students obviously did not share the ideologically motivated enthusiasm of their Nazi leaders for the compulsory exercises and hiking excursions, particularly since the latter were scheduled on Sundays, the only full day of leisure for women students.[13] Already in the spring of 1934 the *Pflichtsport* requirements had to be considerably relaxed, and in order to stimulate interest in the program an incentive was added in the form of a "university sport badge" (*Hochschulabzeichen*), to be awarded to women who completed a full training course.[14] But organizational difficulties and poor attendance continued to plague the scheme. Furthermore, its reputation was hardly enhanced by scandals such as the one at Erlangen University, where the physical exercises and hiking trips of women students allegedly degenerated into a "nudity cult" (*Nacktkultur*) of sorts in the summer of 1934.[15] Finally, in some cases, as in Leipzig in November of the same year, it was the impecuniosity of Main Office VI, undoubtedly combined with insufficient interest, which forced the sudden cancellation of the entire program of extracurricular physical education.[16]

Their sports illusions shattered, the ANSt leaders virtually abandoned the *Pflichtsport* scheme. A new "university sport decree," promulgated in February 1935, merely provided for a few hours of "basic training" (*Grundausbildung*) per week for women students in the first three semesters. Hiking, to which so much importance had been attached, was no longer even mentioned.[17] The ambitious *Pflichtsport* scheme of 1933 was no more than a distant memory, but in an effort to rationalize its failure, ANSt leaders pointed to the success of German women athletes at the 1936 Olympic Games, which was construed as more than sufficient evidence of the excellent physical condition of German women in general. Consequently, it was no longer necessary for women students to demonstrate their own collective athletic achievements, which were naturally much more modest in comparison and therefore unlikely to arouse much admiration.[18] In the years following the Olympic Games, individual top performances remained a useful alibi whenever the need arose to cover up the absence at the universities of the kind of eugenically and biologically meaningful training program for women which Hitler had called for in *Mein Kampf*. ANSt leaders increasingly emphasized the athletic performances of a handful of individuals in an awkward effort to demonstrate the physical fitness of all women students. This led them to abandon entirely the principles on which *Pflichtsport* had been based at the time of its inception and to place more weight on competitive sports.

At the annual student championships, separate competitions were now held for women students, and the winners were duly celebrated in solemn "victor proclamations" (*Siegerkundgebungen*).[19] Meanwhile, for the great majority of Germany's women students, sport remained a matter of marginal importance, as it had been before 1933.

Particularly in the months following the Nazi *Machtergreifung*, zealous ANSt leaders had been fond of denigrating the intellectual achievements of female university students in the Weimar era. The "bluestocking" or "old type" of woman student, it was claimed, had merely been capable of "assimilating lifeless subject matter" or had fallen into the trap of "an exaggerated and one-sided intellectualism."[20] Women students of the new Reich, however, had allegedly turned their backs on this lifeless "scholarship for the sake of scholarship." Inspired and spurred on by National Socialism, they embraced a new, *völkisch* ("racial," literally, "folkish") type of erudition, which was bombastically described as "a struggle for ultimate perception, a commitment to scrutinize the primeval racial values of our people in order to make them available to the entire racial community."[21] In addition, the new generation of women students were pledged to put much greater effort into their intellectual pursuits than their predecessors did. Characteristically, their Nazi leaders vowed nothing less than that they would henceforth "approach their studies with the same seriousness and sense of responsibility that is required from male students."[22] But in order to lend a measure of credibility to these extravagant claims, women university students of the Third Reich obviously had to accomplish more than attending the conventional lectures and passing the customary examinations. Consequently, the ANSt had launched a program that purported to provide a demonstration of the new, National Socialist kind of erudition as well as proof of the unprecedented academic diligence of the new generation of women students.

The first experiment, hailed as the cornerstone in the "reorganization of scholarship" and the formulation of truly National Socialist concepts of science, was the so-called "faculty work" (*Fachschaftsarbeit*). It was carried out by students of each individual faculty or discipline such as law or medicine, organized in "working communities" (*Arbeitsgemeinschaften*) within their respective "faculty groups" (*Fachschaften*, *Fachgruppen*, or *Fakultätsgruppen*), and was intended to provide these students with a more practical and ideologically relevant preparation for their future profession than the training they received in the traditional lectures, seminars, and laboratories. The working communities usually consisted of both male and female members, since there were only a few faculties with enough women students to justify all-female communities.[23] This created problems from the start, particularly since in 1933 and early 1934 both NSDStB and DSt leaders were still very much intoxicated by the ultramisogynic SA spirit. Somehow they consistently sabotaged the participation of women in the "faculty work." At Leipzig University, for instance, women students of all faculties were unceremoniously lumped together into one single working community, thus defeating the very purpose of the "faculty work," and in Berlin one working community was set up for all women students, with a single theme: cooking. At Königsberg University the "faculty work" was carried out in the SA student homes (SA-*Kameradschaftshaüser*), which were off limits to women.[24] It comes as no surprise that under these conditions women students simply opted out of the "faculty work," particularly since participation was strictly voluntary.[25]

The situation failed to improve even after SA-style male exclusionism went out of fashion at the universities in the wake of the Röhm affair. Women students were now encouraged to set up their own working communities,[26] but there were henceforth far too few girls in most disciplines to make that solution a feasible proposition. Between the winter semester 1933/34 and the summer semester 1935 alone, the total number of women students at all German universities had dropped by nearly one-third, from approximately 15,000 to 10,000.[27] At the Technical University of Dresden, for instance, each faculty group counted only a handful of women in the spring of 1935, thus ruling out the possibility of all-female working communities.[28] Medicine provided the sole exception to this general rule. Even in 1935, nearly 4,000 women continued to study in all medical faculties combined, averaging approximately 150 per university. Great efforts on the part of the ANSt resulted in the organization of female medical faculty groups in a number of places, but even some big universities, such as Munich, experienced difficulties or failed altogether in their attempts to launch medical "faculty work" for women students. In most cases, participation was virtually limited to the same dedicated ANSt members whose efforts also sustained the other tottering initiatives of the Nazi women student leaders.[29] The majority of female students of medicine evidently felt that they had better things to do in their free time than attend extracurricular lectures on such esoteric topics as "the professional duties of the female physician in the Third Reich, especially with regard to woman's duties as guardian of the race and blood," which was the official theme of the medical "faculty work" in those days. To be sure, a certain degree of success was achieved at certain universities, but characteristically only when the "faculty work" involved more useful and interesting activities than ideologically tinted discourses. Such was the case in Königsberg, where female students of medicine could perform their "faculty work" as trainees in a hospital during one semester and actually received credit from the university for this.[30] And at Freiburg in the spring of 1936 a faculty group team of twenty-six women students of medicine was probably inspired more by purely humanitarian impulses than by National Socialist zeal when these women worked voluntarily in a hospital during their holidays.[31]

After the ANSt-BDM agreement of February 1937, medical "faculty work" soon became the object of BDM encroachments. The female Hitler Youth badly needed medically trained personnel qualified to teach its members health care and hygiene and capable of serving as orderlies in its camps and providing assistance in the medical examinations of the millions of women within its ranks. Senior female medical students were extremely well suited for these tasks, and a better pool of inexpensive labor could hardly be imagined.[32] The submissive ANSt duly made its students of medicine available to serve in the BDM during their holidays, but there is some reason to suspect that the women themselves were not unhappy with this arrangement. To work as a BDM "camp physician" (*Lagerärztin*), whose travel expenses as well as room and board for the duration of the holiday were taken care of, was certainly interesting, useful, and even prestigious, at least in comparison with anything the ANSt had been able to organize in the "faculty work."[33] We should not forget that this kind of practical experience in the Nazi League of German Girls hardly prejudiced the future career opportunities of women medical students, particularly since the BDM itself engaged growing numbers of full-time women physicians. It is also clear that the "faculty work" of women students never amounted to much more than a perhaps somewhat unorthodox but certainly not very original extracurricular professional training. The program never even came close to achieving the lofty National Socialist objectives its proponents had in mind at the time of its inception. The experiences of the "faculty work" scheme proved that Germany's women students could be interested in certain extracurricular forms of practical training, particularly if these also served concrete humanitarian purposes as in the hospital service or enhanced future career opportunities as in the work for the BDM. They were utterly uninterested, however, when it came to exploring ways to fashion the new, National Socialist type of scholarship that, in the minds of the Nazi student leaders at least, was to conquer the German universities.

It comes as no surprise, therefore, that women students likewise fumbled a second opportunity offered them in this field, namely, the Reich Vocational Contest (*Reichsberufswettkampf*—RBWK) of university students, a competition launched for the first time in the fall of 1935.[34] Participation in this venture was entirely voluntary, as was the case in the "faculty work," and the contestants were expected to demonstrate their intellectual and scholarly skills as well as their social concern, patriotism, political reliability, and ideological purity by producing an essay on such subjects as "the Jew in community and art" or "the architectural creations of Adolf Hitler."[35] These projects were carried out not individually but collectively, by small groups of students, similar to the *Arbeitsgemeinschaften* of the "faculty work." As in the *Fachschaftsarbeit*, women did not normally organize their own groups, but were attached to predominantly male teams of their respective faculties.[36]

More than a year had gone by since Nazi student male exclusionism had been dealt a devastating blow as a result of the *Röhm Putsch* and its repercussions at the German universities. The ANSt leadership therefore looked forward to a harmonious and fruitful cooperation of female and male students within the teams and, implicitly, to a solid performance on the part of the female volunteers. Not without some hyperbole, the prevalence of mixed teams within the RBWK was hailed as the fruit of "the desire for intellectual collaboration between men and women at the universities."[37] But female students were undoubtedly turned off by a last-minute initiative of the Nazi student leadership, which appeared to prove that not all remnants of traditional misogyny had been cleared up within the national leadership of the DSt and the NSDStB, even though the scheme itself may have been well intended and perhaps even concocted by overzealous ANSt personnel. Participating women students were ordered to pass a supplementary "test in sport and home economics" (*sportliche und hauswirtschaftliche Prüfung*) intended to inject a dose of specifically feminine content into what was otherwise a purely scholarly contest and thus to prevent them from losing sight of women's main tasks in Nazi society, those of housewife and mother.[38] Particularly since no mention was made of a comparable requirement for male participants, this surprise engendered little enthusiasm among prospective female contestants and discouraged many from participating. The contest catered mainly to students of the higher semesters, from whom a high-caliber scholarly performance might more reasonably be expected. But these women were also "not exactly the youngest and most athletic," as one of them explained, and were therefore reluctant to undergo what looked like a strenuous physical-fitness test. Many senior women students, moreover, were already preoccupied with preparations for their final examinations and may have welcomed this supplementary test as a convenient excuse for dropping out of a contest in which they might otherwise have participated without much enthusiasm.[39] There can be no doubt that women students were also deterred from taking part in the RBWK on account of the rather humiliating aspects of the test. The "home economics" part, for instance, included a demonstration of each woman's talents in the cleaning of pans, pails, and other kitchen utensils; points were scored on the basis of "correct choice of cleaning product, cleaning skill, endurance, and thoroughness."[40]

It is not surprising, then, that the official figures on the students' first Reich Vocational Contest, which claimed a total of over twelve thousand participants,[41] do not make any mention of the performance of women students. We may speculate that the truth might have been somewhat embarrassing to the ANSt. We know that Erlangen University, an institution with approximately one hundred female students, produced only seven women contestants.[42] If this proportion had been characteristic for the entire Reich, the figures would come to a total of 685 women,[43] representing 5.7 percent of the total number of participants, a poor achievement at a time when women accounted for over 16 percent of the student population in Germany.[44]

In any event, the Nazi student leadership was obviously not pleased with the results, for it introduced important organizational changes in the fall of 1936, prior to the start of the second student RBWK. These innovations clearly purported to stimulate the enthusiasm of women students for the upcoming competition, to streamline the recruitment of female contestants, and to achieve a more effective administration and supervision of the women's effort.[45] A separate "contest division" (*Kampfsparte*) was now created to accommodate all-female contest teams[46] and was assigned what were believed to be specifically feminine topics, such as "health care in the female labor service." As in the first contest, each theme was to be tackled by a group of women from one faculty.[47] Whether these efforts were rewarded with success or failure we cannot know with certainty, since only fragmentary information is available on the contribution of female students to the Reich Vocational Contest of 1936–1937. Reports hinted at a "strong participation"[48] by women students, but such statements are so vague that they have no significance. Furthermore, they are belied by the fact that only thirteen assignments were handed in within the women's division.[49] But that did not prevent the Nazi student leadership, always eager to advertise its real or imagined accomplishments, from loudly bestowing honorable mention on the work of a number of teams and proclaiming seven female law students of Berlin University as "Reich victor" within their contest division for their paper on "the female industrial worker in German law."[50] The laureates were duly celebrated and honored with interviews by the NSDAP press agency, articles in various newspapers, and official receptions by Reich Women's Leader Scholtz-Klink and Reich Law Leader Frank in Berlin.[51]

The third Reich Vocational Contest for university students, scheduled for 1937–1938, was presented to female students as an unusually important undertaking, particularly relevant in view of the needs created by the Four-Year Plan. "To participate in the RBWK," the women were told, "is to heed the call of the nation, which demands the mobilization of each and every able woman."[52] Participating women students were reminded that their essays had to be relevant for "today's issues of our German life," and each team had to obtain the RSF's approval of the topic it proposed to deal with.[53] These instructions purported to help guarantee that the accomplishments of the contestants would constitute a genuine contribution towards the realization of the objectives of the Four-Year Plan, autarchy and rearmament, and on more than one occasion Nazi officials indeed stressed "the tight functional interrelationship between [their] economic planning and the Reich Contest."[54] But whereas teams of male students were duly mobilized to perform research in important fields such as the development of new synthetic products,[55] the RSF evidently did not have much confidence in the ability of women students to achieve anything worthwhile in this direction. Otherwise its leaders would not have recommended to them such totally irrelevant themes as "the changing ideal of women through the ages" and "the bridal crown as Germanic, and the bridal veil as foreign symbolism."[56] We do not know how many female students hurried to tackle such esoteric assignments, for the official (and probably strongly exaggerated) figures again failed to state how many women were included in the final tally of 14,593 participants.[57] In any event, the title of "Reich victor" went to the team of four medical students from Würzburg for a rather down-to-earth report on their "medical examinations of infants in the Rhön area."[58] It remained entirely unexplained, of course, in what mysterious way this admittedly worthwhile project might benefit the cause of the Four-Year Plan.

The fourth Reich Vocational Contest for university students lasted from May 1938 to April 1939 and was later reported to have involved 14,200 participants. Although both male and female students from Austria were taking part for the first time, overall participation was lower than the previous year.[59] The qualitative performance of women students was again far from impressive. In the important *Gau* ("region," or NSDAP party district) of Munich/Upper Bavaria, which accounted for a total of over one thousand students, there were only two female contest groups. At Halle University, only 5 women of a total of 58 took part, and in Würzburg the ratio was 8 out of 132, a decidedly poor achievement for the university that had produced the "Reich victor" the year before.[60] Within the female division, the highest honors were accorded Heidelberg University for an essay on "motherhood and women's labor in the tobacco industry."[61] Thorough research, the team reported, had led to the conclusion that the constant exposure to nicotine was not the direct cause of the lower-than-average fertility of women workers in Heidelberg's tobacco industry, although hygienic conditions in the factories might be improved.[62] Such findings, no matter how preposterous, sounded like music to the ears of the Nazi authorities. The labor shortage of the second half of the 1930s dictated full mobilization of Germany's female labor potential, and this objective was pursued in spite of the eugenic misgivings the Nazis themselves had voiced so loudly against women's work only a few years earlier. Whatever qualms they may have had about executing this about-face were now dispelled by the suggestion that female employment outside the home, even under obviously unhealthy circumstances, did not have to detract from women's biological functions, providing some basic hygienic precautions were observed. The Nazis' economic interests of the moment were thus reconciled with their supposedly timeless ideological concerns, and their ruthless exploitation of female labor was given the seal of approval by women themselves. It was undoubtedly on account of these merits that the Heidelberg women earned the "Reich victor" prize.

The Reich Vocational Contest, like the "faculty work," had been glorified by the Nazis as an experiment that would help create a new type of education and erudition that would no longer be "individualistic," "irrelevant," and "purely theoretical" but practical, politically and socially committed, and therefore relevant and beneficial for the entire nation.[63] It was supposedly "the form of scholarly work that [was]...most characteristic for the present development of German intellectual life."[64] But as had been the case in the "faculty work," women students displayed little or no enthusiasm for these experiments in National Socialist erudition. At a time when career opportunities were mushrooming in all professional fields from medicine to law, and Nazi authorities were virtually begging young women to help meet the requirements of the professional labor market, women students quite sensibly chose to concentrate their intellectual efforts on examinations, dissertations, and other conventional, unspectacular, but effective avenues to future careers.

The indifference of Germany's female university students was likewise mirrored in their lackadaisical response to undertakings of the ANSt in the sphere of Nazi social ideology and policies. In order to reconcile the masses of the lower middle class and the working class with social conditions in the Third Reich, the Nazi rulers shrewdly manipulated the slogan of the homogeneous community of all Germans, the *Volksgemeinschaft*, which served to obfuscate class differences and create the illusion of social equity.[65] The success achieved by this National Socialist "community ideology" (*Gemeinschaftsideologie*), to borrow a term coined by Reinhard Kühnl, can be fully understood only if one realizes that in times of crisis and hardship the idea of a genuinely classless society held out to the masses a promise of security as well as an opportunity to identify with the power and success of the entire nation.[66] An equally important factor in the effectiveness of the *Volksgemeinschaft* slogan was that this ideal ostensibly proved itself in everyday life, in the "labor service," in the Hitler Youth, in the Nazi welfare organizations, and in countless similar demonstrations of social solidarity.[67] University students of both sexes, then, played a potentially crucial role in the propagation of this *Volksgemeinschaft* myth. Since they traditionally were and continued to be the representatives of the upper middle class,[68] their participation in manifestations of social solidarity could not fail to make a great impression and thus to enhance the credibility of the Nazi theory that class barriers had been swept away. The Nazi rulers themselves were keenly aware of this and did not hesitate to prod Germany's students into action.[69]

ANSt leaders responded to this challenge with remarkable gusto.[70] Not only did they welcome this chance to ingratiate the Nazi authorities, but they also sensed a unique opportunity to render an invaluable service to the cause of the beleaguered *Frauenstudium* in the Third Reich. As they saw it, "social readiness" (*soziale Bereitschaft*) was to become the hallmark of Germany's female students and would "safeguard women's place at the university" in the Nazi state, just as the alleged social indifference of the "bluestocking" had jeopardized women's right to an academic education prior to 1933.[71] Still, tactical considerations made it desirable to convey the impression that the social activism of women students was inspired solely by an altruistic impulse to practice the "socialism of the deed" (*Sozialismus der Tat*), which formed such an essential part of Nazi community ideology. And ANSt leaders feigned deep indignation whenever someone dared question the idealistic purity of their intentions. After a confrontation with cynical male students, one ANSt woman wrote without a trace of humor: "[Women students] place themselves in the service of the *Volksgemeinschaft*, [not] in order to avoid being chased from the universities, as some extremely tactless male students have suggested with regard to our social work, but in order to fulfill the hopes which our *Führer*, Adolf Hitler, has invested in German women."[72] But such disputes about the sincerity of the social concern of female students were purely academic and rather irrelevant. In fact, if their performance in what was called the "socialistic service" (*sozialistischer Einsatz*) is to be used as the measuring rod of their social concern, it would appear that women students of the Third Reich were every bit as nonchalant in social questions as their bluestocking predecessors of the Weimar years were said to have been.

Much publicity was generated, for instance, about the contributions made by female university students in the aid actions sponsored by the National Socialist People's Welfare organization (*NS-Volkswohlfahrt*—NSV), particularly the "winter aid" (*Winterhilfswerk*—WHW) campaigns and the work of the NSV department Mother and Child (*Mutter und Kind*—MuK). To read the ANSt reports, women students of the Third Reich were forever roaming the streets collecting money, food, or clothes for some Nazi charitable project or other, acting as baby-sitters in the NSV nursery homes, helping out in its "people's kitchens" (*Volksküchen*) or "sewing centers" (*Nähstuben*), performing office work or odd jobs in local NSV headquarters, and even taking over financial responsibility or "godparenthood" (*Patenschaft*), as it was called, for a poor family from the welfare bureau.[73] In reality, however, things were somewhat different. Since Nazi charity was supposed to be solidly anchored in eugenic, racial, and political principles, only "politically reliable" women students could participate in it.[74] This meant that small numbers of dedicated ANSt members were practically the only women students to achieve much, if anything, in the field of National Socialist eleemosynary endeavor. Most of Germany's female students, on the other hand, found it very easy to stay aloof. For one thing, the simple excuse that one was too preoccupied with studies or exams proved to be singularly effective in this respect.[75] Furthermore, many women students evidently preferred to practice charity of a more conventional type than the racially inspired welfare efforts of the NSV. Thus in June 1935 the ANSt leader for Silesia was perturbed by reports that coeds from the Catholic Teachers College in Beuthen had the audacity to work for a confessional charity organization that committed the mistake, as she saw it, of aiding the "co-religionist" (*Glaubensgenosse*) rather than the "co-racialist" (*Volksgenosse*).[76] It would appear that the ANSt itself was not all that interested in the Nazi welfare schemes. Campaigns such as the "winter aid" were gigantic undertakings that relied on the cooperation of many other Nazi organizations to mobilize virtually the entire German population, and many of the tasks were basically dull and unspectacular. Consequently, the accomplishments of a handful of women students were not likely to earn much acclaim for the ANSt and Main Office VI. Since local Nazi welfare offices also frequently turned away female students offering their services,[77] the ANSt preferred to try to demonstrate the "socialistic" fervor of women students in other, more unorthodox and spectacular ways, such as the "factory service" (*Fabrikdienst, Fabrikeinsatz*) and the "agricultural service" (*Landdienst*).

David Schoenbaum has pointed out that the glorification of work and of the worker was a crucial ingredient of National Socialist labor ideology. Apart from a variety of empty slogans, such as "work ennobles" (*Arbeit adelt*), this attitude towards labor found expression in a series of symbolic manifestations of the Third Reich's professed respect for the working class.[78] The "labor service" may rank as the most prominent of these institutionalized demonstrations,[79] but other actions, although organized on a much smaller scale, could also produce effective psychological results. The "factory service" of women students fell into this category, for it purported to reflect the mutual respect and solidarity of female "workers of brain and fist" in Hitler's Germany.[80] In order to achieve this lofty objective, female university students were exhorted to work without remuneration in a factory during their holidays, usually for a period of two to four weeks. They were to take the place of working mothers with many children and other selected female workers who could thus be treated to a supplementary holiday without loss of wages and, incidentally, at no expense to management or to the state. Hence the term "job exchange" (*Arbeitsplatzaustausch*), which was frequently used as a synonym for "factory service."

On paper at least, it was a fine scheme, bound to make a profound impression on Nazi authorities as well as on the German public at large. ANSt leaders never tired of trumpeting its merits. In fact, they produced a flood of articles, creating a veritable *Fabrikdienst* myth in the process. The problem with the "factory service," however, was precisely that. It was never more than a myth, an illusion, for the vast majority of Germany's women students in the 1930s never did get to know what the interior of a factory looked like. Publicizing the "factory service" idea may have been an easy task, but implementing it was a different matter.

The project was apparently concocted in 1934 within the "women's bureau" (*Frauenamt*) of the German Labor Front (*Deutsche Arbeitsfront*—DAF), the Nazi mammoth union, whose members naturally stood to gain the most from this sort of action. But leaders of the ANSt and the NSDStB responded with meager enthusiasm. They feared that the Labor Front would not only reap all the benefits but also claim all the credit if the scheme proved to be successful. In addition, they were probably reluctant to try to mobilize women students on behalf of another Nazi organization at a time when they themselves found it virtually impossible to motivate them for their own purposes. Without much, if any, support from the ANSt, the "factory service" remained limited to a number of small-scale local initiatives in such cities as Königsberg, Munich, and Heidelberg in 1934 and 1935.[81] Gradually, however, the Nazi coeds' leaders started to appreciate the propagandistic potential of the "factory service." They simply could not resist the temptation to release exaggerated and often blatantly conflicting statistical data in order to impress the German *Volksgemeinschaft* with the "socialistic" performance of female university students. In particular, they liked to boast about the astronomic numbers of leisure days presumably created for women factory workers as a direct result of the efforts of the "factory service" volunteers.[82] Intoxicated by the sweet smell of fictitious success, the ANSt thus prepared to launch a first nationwide "factory service" in the summer of 1936. Nazi women student leaders evidently expected that masses of volunteers would step forward, so they permitted themselves the luxury of restricting participation to ANSt members, in order "to guarantee the politico-ideological integrity" of the candidates.[83] But this decision appears to have backfired. The painful silence observed throughout the rest of 1936 in ANSt reports and articles on the subject of the results of the "factory service" stood in striking contrast to the triumphant huzzas of the previous year and amounted to a tacit admission of failure and disappointment. This is not to say that no women students at all took part in the action. Certain ANSt sections probably achieved local successes and may have done as well as they had done in 1934 and 1935. In view of the high expectations of the spring and the planned nationwide scope of the action, however, this was simply not good enough.

In the summer of 1936, small numbers of women students of natural sciences—probably no more than a hundred throughout the Reich, if that many—were recruited to work for two to four weeks in ammunition factories. This project resembled the regular "factory service" but was referred to as the "special service" (*Sondereinsatz*) or "armament service" (*Rüstungseinsatz*). It was shrouded in the greatest secrecy, and for good reasons. This scheme had nothing to do with the "job exchange" idea of the normal "factory service" (although participating women were led to believe that it did) but was related to the Nazi regime's preparations for war. A group of thirty-one female students of physics, chemistry, and the like who were put to work in the German Weapons and Ammunition Enterprise (*Deutscher Waffen- und Munitionsbetrieb*) thus found out to their surprise that they were not replacing women workers but that they would receive the regular wage for the kind of work they were asked to perform. This, incidentally, included "revision of small metal parts," chemical and mechanical laboratory research, and drawing-board work, as well as purely administrative occupations. Moreover, it was impressed on them that they were to preserve the utmost discretion about these activities, which were labelled "strictly confidential" (*streng vertraulich*).[84] The raison d'être of this mysterious project was candidly described by ANSt leader Inge Wolff:

[The "special service"] is a preparation for the eventuality of war. Precisely those vital enterprises in which women students work during their holidays have to continue to operate when it comes to the worst and in spite of the departure of the male labor force [to the front]. To guarantee the replacement of the latter, that is the task of the coeds' preparatory work during their holidays.[85]

As clouds of war gathered ominously on the horizon, the "special service" was deemed worthy of an encore in 1937, and again in 1938 and 1939. Women students continued to work in armament industries in such centers as Lübeck, Karlsruhe, and Berlin,[86] but they were henceforth assured that they did replace female workers who could thus be treated to a supplementary paid holiday.[87] At least one woman, however, expressed doubt that this was really the case.[88] Because of the importance ANSt leaders attached to this project, and the secrecy that surrounded it, participation in the "special service" naturally remained limited to a handful of women students. Only the most reliable ANSt members in the faculties of natural sciences, economics, and technical studies qualified. But all these disciplines combined never counted more than a few hundred women in the late 1930s. Under those conditions, the "special service" drew only a few volunteers at best from each university, and the total number of participants did not exceed forty-two in a year like 1938.[89] Meanwhile, the regular "factory service" remained available as a forum where *all* women students could give free rein to their "socialistic" impulses. But this action, too, never attracted more than negligible numbers of women students. In 1938, Münster University produced a total of six volunteers, Leipzig seventeen, and Erlangen three.[90] Only Hamburg yielded a respectable crop of "factory service" recruits, eighty-seven to be exact, but that admittedly established an absolute record for the entire Reich.[91] One year later, in 1939, the "job exchange" action again exposed the indifference of the majority of Germany's women students towards the "socialistic" ideas and schemes of National Socialism. Bonn University produced twenty-two volunteers, Cologne and Königsberg sixteen each, Breslau nine, and Würzburg one.[92]

In the minds of its organizers, the "factory service" proved the solidarity of Germany's female factory laborers and intellectuals and of women workers "of fist and brain." The project was celebrated time and again as a magnificent achievement of "socialism of the deed," as evidence that traditional class barriers were no longer relevant in the "new" Germany. Here, if anywhere, was supposed to be a convincing sample of the esteem working-class people, and women at that, allegedly enjoyed in the Third Reich, for women factory workers were aided and honored by women who, on account of their family background and future profession, undeniably ranked as their social superiors. Measured by the yardstick of these lofty aspirations and exaggerated claims, the actual performance of women students in the "factory service" proved dismal. With only handfuls of volunteers involved in most of the actions, it is obvious that the majority of Germany's women university students were and remained quite insensitive to the fancy slogans of Nazi "socialism of the deed." Much the same lesson could be learned from the experiences in the "agricultural service" of female university students.

We have already seen how the "agricultural service" (*Landdienst*) project had been launched in the spring of 1935 but had achieved little or no success and had left Nazi student leaders embittered and disillusioned. With the adoption of the Four-Year Plan and Germany's outright commitment to autarchy, including agricultural self-sufficiency, in the fall of 1936, however, the "agricultural service" regained a great deal of attraction and interest in their minds. Originally a rather romantic enterprise in the "blood and soil" tradition, the project suddenly loomed as a potentially vital contribution of the student body to the achievement of the Reich's important economic objectives. In addition, Scheel was clearly eager to mark the beginning of his tenure as Reich Student Leader with some dramatic rhetoric and accomplishments. He called on German students to help "secure the nourishment of the German people within the framework of the Four-Year Plan" and announced his intention to mobilize studying men and women in the summer of 1937 for a "massive effort" aimed at realizing this ambitious goal.[93] The action did take place, and the results were reportedly impressive. Approximately 1,800 women students, 20 percent of the total, were said to have participated in this "agricultural service."[94] Even though this figure was probably somewhat exaggerated, it would appear that the "agricultural service" of 1937 provided Scheel with the success he had sought, at least as far as women students were concerned. The Nazi student leaders must have been greatly gratified. The "agricultural service" not only incorporated some of the most cherished ideological themes of National Socialism, specifically that of "blood and soil," but also purported to serve important political, cultural, and economic functions.

Politically, the "agricultural service" served a dual purpose in that it aimed at strengthening Nazism domestically and at protecting Germany externally. Each volunteer was expected to act as an envoy of National Socialism wherever she went during her service, and her task, in Nazi parlance, was "to educate the population in racial German thinking."[95] This was considered an important mission because the "agricultural service" usually took place in rural areas where people were backward and uninterested in politics, or even opposed to Nazism, as in the strongly Catholic eastern region (*Ostmark*) of Bavaria. In order to fulfill their mission, the women were instructed to cooperate closely with local Nazi organizations such as the BDM or the NSF and help boost the prestige and authority of their leaders.[96] They were also expected to disseminate propaganda for the Nazi cause within the family to which they were assigned, and to do this by word as well as deed. But that proved to be a very delicate task that called for a tactful and subtle approach, and the volunteers' efforts in this field often yielded frustration rather than success; in many reports we can find unflattering references to the "thick skulls" of the conservative peasants and complaints about their apathy.[97] Initial enthusiasm thus frequently turned into despair on realization that some peasants were very adept at quoting the Bible but had never heard of such Nazi celebrities as Hess, Frick, or Goebbels.[98]

In the minds of its protagonists, the "agricultural service" also served as a device to strengthen Germany against its foreign enemies, particularly the Slavs. It was no coincidence, therefore, that it usually took place in border areas, preferably in the east. The German character of that region was presumably threatened by the proximity of the despised Slavs and, more particularly, by the traditional seasonal influx of Polish agricultural laborers, a phenomenon that might be eliminated if sufficient German labor could be made available. The "agricultural service" of women students was thus conceived as an effort to help stem the "Slavic tide" in the east and to defend the "ancient German settlers' land" against the encroachments of supposedly inferior but more numerous races.[99]

The "agricultural service" was also regarded as a great cultural mission. The peasantry was viewed by the Nazis as the source of all authentic German folk culture, and women students, presumably the products of an arid urban environment of "asphalt culture," were expected to quench their thirst for primeval

German cultural values at this fountainhead. At the same time, it was their duty to help protect this source from drying up or being poisoned by nefarious foreign or modern influences. Hence they were encouraged to learn the peasants' traditional folk songs and dances and to arrange special festive evenings in the villages (*"Dorfabende"*) in order to stimulate cultural creativity. On the other hand, the volunteers had to discourage the rural population from imitating "empty forms of urban culture." All foreign cultural influences, such as jazz music or modern dances, had to be totally eradicated.[100]

Perhaps the most important aspect of the "agricultural service" was its economic function. The scheme must be understood in part as an attempt to supplement the dwindling agricultural labor force, itself the result of a continuing massive exodus from the land (*Landflucht*). The drive for agricultural self-sufficiency within the framework of the Four-Year Plan demanded mobilization of all available personnel for this purpose.[101] Heinrich Himmler, himself a graduate in agricultural sciences, thus wrote to Nazi student leader Scheel: "It is necessary in view of the great shortage of labor which plagues our agriculture...to do everything possible in order to provide additional labor for the work on the land."[102] Since women traditionally accounted for nearly 50 percent of the rural labor force in Germany, and since they too had been fleeing the land in ever-increasing numbers, it must have seemed particularly important to involve young women in these efforts.[103] In this respect, the "agricultural service" of women students served as a sort of pilot project, a prelude to the planned return to the land of thousands of working German women.

Women students who participated in the "agricultural service" could be found working in the fields, particularly at harvesttime. More often, however, this heavy work was left to their male comrades, and the women concentrated instead on a special task, namely, to assist the overworked peasant's wife in the household and on the farm. Thus they helped out in the kitchen, milked the cows, tended the garden, or simply looked after the children.[104] Sometimes a group of female students would set up village day-care centers, either permanently (called *Dauerkindergarten*) or for the duration of the harvest only (called *Erntekindergarten*), and this was usually accomplished in cooperation with the local Nazi welfare organization.[105] To serve the peasant's wife, this "guardian of German folk values" as she was sometimes referred to, was considered a task of the greatest importance, and special instructions were issued to the volunteers in order to help them to carry it out with success. It was suggested, for instance, that the student should always be the first to wake up in the morning, always be available to render assistance wherever it was required, and always be intent on finding things to do rather than waiting to be given a job. The women were also told to avoid conspicuous dress, to be pleasant and courteous under all circumstances, and to be extremely tactful whenever conversations touched on such delicate matters as religion, especially in Catholic regions.[106] It goes without saying that this was not always easy, the more so since the work could be hard and conditions primitive. The volunteers often had to rise as early as 5:00 A.M.

and work until 7:00 or even 9:00 P.M. The homes frequently lacked such basic amenities as electricity, and remuneration was out of the question. Worst of all, there was hardly ever any indication that their efforts were being appreciated.[107] But it was expected that the students would work well in spite of these problems and that they would exert a positive influence on the people with whom they came in contact. Each woman was to create a "relationship of confidence" (*Vertrauensverhältnis*) between herself and the farmer's wife, her family, and all the inhabitants of the village. Once she had gained their confidence and respect, she would be in an ideal position to influence her new acquaintances, not only politically but also in such trivial matters as good taste in dress and home decoration.[108] This function, and not the labor itself, was declared to be the raison d'être of the "agricultural service" of female university students.[109]

The importance of the "agricultural service" of female (and male) students was reflected in the attitude of the Nazi student leaders. In hundreds of speeches and articles, the "agricultural service" was praised to the sky and described as a magnificent experiment, successful in all its lofty objectives.[110] But these were spurious boasts. In spite of its great political, cultural, and economic significance, the *Landdienst* project of women students ended in utter failure.

Despite an emotional appeal by Reich Student Leader Scheel, asking university students to volunteer en masse for what he termed the "service of honor" (*Ehrendienst*) on the land,[111] participation in the "agricultural service" in the summer of 1938 was far from impressive. Munich University, an institution with more than 600 female students, produced a mere 6 female volunteers. Of Münster University's 237 women students, only 8 responded to Scheel's appeal, and a total of 6 women was all Erlangen could yield.[112] The ANSt leader in Breslau reported dejectedly on the disappointing results of her propaganda campaign: "Practically nobody reported for the *Landdienst*, although the need for this type of action ought to be best understood precisely here [i.e., in 'borderland' Silesia]. . . . We probably overestimate the sense of duty of the individual."[113] Nowhere did the RSF publish any figures on the overall participation of Germany's female students in the 1938 "agricultural service"; the results were almost certainly not impressive enough.

In 1939 the number of volunteers was equally low. Königsberg and Breslau reported three and five women respectively, Bonn University had two, and Würzburg none at all.[114] Moreover, according to some reports, the preparations for the "agricultural service" had been sabotaged and ridiculed by the students, as for instance in Bonn, where ANSt posters for the *Landdienst* had been "defiled in the most vulgar manner, . . . besmeared, . . . or ripped off," meetings had been disturbed, and the project had been the subject of what was called "an evil whisper campaign." Some professors were said to have encouraged this type of conduct, which was deemed "inimical to party and state," so that the local student leader had asked the Gestapo to investigate the matter.[115] Insofar as the "agricultural service" scheme incorporated some of the most cherished ideological, political, cultural, and economic values of Nazism, the general apathy towards it as well as these acts of outright sabotage can only be interpreted as evidence of the failure of National Socialism to win the hearts and minds of Germany's university women.

In spite of all the rhetoric and propaganda, the "social readiness," the "socialistic commitment," of female university students in the Third Reich was merely a sham. The service in the National Socialist welfare organizations attracted only a minority of dedicated ANSt stalwarts, and the "factory service," celebrated time and again as the embodiment of the enthusiasm of women students for the "socialism of the deed" promoted by the Nazis, never drew more than a handful of volunteers. The lack of success of the "agricultural service" experiment revealed perhaps most glaringly the indifference of the majority of German women students to the "community ideology" (*Gemeinschaftsideologie*) of the Nazis and, indeed, to National Socialism itself.

Virtually the only extracurricular project of the ANSt ever to achieve a measure of success was the "women's service," or *Frauendienst*, a sort of paramilitary training of women students which was viewed as the counterpart of the military service male students performed first in the SA and then, from 1935 on, in the new *Wehrmacht*.[116] Although women were in principle excluded from military matters by Nazi dogma,[117] they were nevertheless believed to share a "military obligation" (*Wehrpflicht*) of some kind towards the fatherland.[118] The paramilitary training of young women was allegedly necessitated by the realities of modern warfare and justified by tradition and history. Nazi women student leaders argued that "the next war" would be a "war between populations" (*Bevölkerungskrieg*), which would be fought not on some faraway front but "in the skies" and in the homeland (*Heimat*) itself. It would be unthinkable that this new front could be defended without the active support of half the population, women.[119] Of course it remained primarily a man's duty to be "soldier, fighter for the fatherland," but history had supposedly shown that "Nordic woman had always been the loyal companion of man" whenever the tribe, fatherland, or "race" had found itself in danger.[120] Germanic women, it was claimed, had always lent a helping hand in the defense of the nation, considering it their "natural duty" to assist "where female help was appropriate and even indispensable." Such arguments led to the conclusion that "women too had the right, even the duty, to put their strength in the service of the beloved community in the hour of danger" and provided a rationale for the efforts to prepare and train women students for an active role in the defense of Germany in future wars.[121]

Instructions for the *Frauendienst* of women students were first issued in October 1933.[122] Three different types of eight-hour courses—"air protection" (*Luftschutz*), "first aid" (*Erste Hilfe*), and "communications" (*Nachrichtenwesen*)—were introduced and declared compulsory for women students in the first six semesters. "Air protection" covered instruction on the air forces of foreign powers, "chemical warfare and the use of gas masks," and "practical protective measures," including the use of air-raid shelters and evacuation of civilians. In the first aid basic training, women were taught to cope with burns, hemorrhages, bone fractures, and cases of asphyxiation. Talented women were encouraged to take an advanced course to be trained as full-fledged Red Cross aides. The communications course introduced women students to the secrets of Morse code and naval semaphore messages. Expert instructors for all these courses were provided by such organizations as Hermann Göring's Reich League for Air Protection (*Reichsluftschutzbund*—RLB), the *Technische Nothilfe* (Technical Emergency Aid Organization—TeNo), the Red Cross, the Nazi physicians' association, the *Wehrmacht*, the SS, and the ordinary police as well as the national postal service (*Reichspost*).[123]

In spite of some initial confusion and lack of cooperation on the part of some local representatives of these organizations,[124] the ''women's service'' project was fairly successful from the start.[125] The objective of involving all women from the first six semesters in the three basic courses during the winter semester 1933/34 appears to have been achieved, so that only the newcomers of each consecutive first semester had to be enrolled from the summer of 1934 on.[126] Moreover, increasing numbers of local *Frauendienst* section leaders were taking special courses for instructors, so the ANSt became gradually less dependent on the goodwill of other organizations in this respect.[127]

The year 1935 proved to be an important year for the ''women's service,'' if only because two new laws seemed to underscore the relevance of the project and grant it both official sanction and greater prestige. The Conscription Law (*Wehrgesetz*) of March 16 of that year, which introduced general military service in Germany, also reaffirmed the principle that every German, regardless of sex, was committed to help defend the fatherland. And although the law did not state how this principle ought to be implemented in the case of women, Nazi female student leaders interpreted it as an endorsement of the ''women's service'' scheme. One of them explained: ''Just as our comrades serve in the *Wehrmacht*, we women students serve in the *Frauendienst*.''[128] Of even greater significance was the Air Protection Law (*Luftschutzgesetz*) of June 26, 1935, which in principle required ''every German man and every German woman'' to make a contribution towards the protection of the fatherland against attack from the air. It established ''air protection duty'' (*Luftschutzpflicht*) as an ''obligation of honor'' (*Ehrenpflicht*) for each and every German, thus vindicating once again the *Frauendienst* project of women students.[129]

Backed by the moral authority of this legislation, the ANSt experienced no problems in recruiting first-year women students for the basic ''women's service'' courses in the late 1930s. And many women students appear to have reported for the advanced courses on a voluntary basis, thus earning certificates that enabled them to serve as aides in the Red Cross or the RLB.[130] Women medical students, in particular, found their way into the Red Cross as ''nurse's aides'' (*Schwesternhelferinnen*), a practice made compulsory by a decree of the Reich minister of education in October 1936.[131] Because of its success, the *Frauendienst* section of the ANSt survived the reorganization of the Nazi student associations in the fall of that same year, and in the late 1930s it remained one of the most active departments within the RSF Office for Women Students.[132] The outbreak of World War II, finally, was to provide the ultimate justification of the "women's service" scheme and give German women students the opportunity to put the knowledge and experience they had gained in these courses to the test. All too soon, women students from university cities such as Dresden, whose ANSt section had been one of the first to promote paramilitary training and air protection, would have to make good on the promise made by one of them in a poem some years earlier:

> Die Mägdlein zeigen mutig sich
> Mit Wasser und mit Sand,
> Die Maske fest auf dem Gesicht,
> Den Stahlhelm angeschnallt,
> So tun sie ruhig ihre Pflicht,
> Wenn's rings auch pufft und knallt. . . . [133]

Compared with all the other extracurricular projects of the ANSt and Main Office VI, the "women's service" courses were a successful undertaking, and a good number of women students took part in them. Nevertheless, it would be a mistake to interpret this as evidence that Germany's women students wholeheartedly embraced the concept of paramilitary training for the benefit of the Nazi state or, for that matter, that they endorsed Nazi militarism itself. We must not forget that participation in the basic training was compulsory for all women students. Furthermore, it must have been a relatively easy task to stimulate interest in courses such as first aid, which were interesting and quite useful. The advanced courses also led to the certificate of *Schwesternhelferin* (nurse's aid) or similar diplomas, which might open the door to part-time employment and enhance future career opportunities. Finally, the *Frauendienst* benefited from the moral authority of highly vaunted new laws and did not constitute a very demanding obligation, as each of the three courses involved merely a few hours a week for the duration of only one month. The relative success of the "women's service" scheme undoubtedly owed more to these factors than to some hypothetical enthusiasm of Germany's women students for their coming active involvement in the horrors of war.

The case of the "women's service" proved merely that not all ANSt projects were total fiascoes all the time, but most of the time they were, as we have seen. The history of the ANSt in the 1930s indeed amounts to a virtually uninterrupted string of failures and disappointments to be credited to the antipathy of Nazi male students, the encroachments of competing Nazi organizations like the NSF or the BDM, and, above all, to the indifference of the overwhelming majority of Germany's women students. Exactly why women students remained so remarkably immune to the National Socialist siren call of the ANSt we cannot say with certainty, but their social origins may give us a clue.

A disproportionately large (and growing) share of the Third Reich's female university students came from the upper middle class, or *Oberschicht*, of German society. At Munich University in the winter semester 1935/36, for example, this *Oberschicht* accounted for 47 percent of all female students, as compared to only 34 percent in the case of men.[134] And no less than 50.3 percent of all newly matriculated German women students belonged to upper-middle-class families in 1939.[135] The attitude of the majority of women students towards National Socialism appears to have reflected the social and political beliefs of their upper-crust parents. High-ranking members of the civil service, senior *Wehrmacht* officers, wealthy businessmen, bankers, and professionals were not at all unsympathetic to the National Socialist regime, which could indeed be relied on to defend the interests and fulfill the ambitions of the army, big business, and other powerful and privileged groups within German society.[136] And yet they never fully *identified* with National Socialism. In their eyes, Hitler was and remained a philistine little Austrian corporal and a despicable (though extraordinarily arrogant) upstart of socially suspect background. They looked down on the NSDAP as a plebeian party for the vulgar masses, had nothing but contempt for its irrational ideology, and mistrusted its egalitarian, "socialistic," and "revolutionary" slogans and programs.[137] Therefore, in spite of the advantages and privileges they continued to enjoy in the Third Reich, Germany's upper middle class chose to keep some distance between itself and the Nazis, even if some of its representatives found it opportune to "purchase," as one might call it, an NSDAP membership card. And formal loyalty to the ostensibly legitimate authority of the Nazi state did not prevent them from continuing to cherish the traditional conservative (and rather elitist) political, social, and philosophical ideas of their class. Consequently, their academic daughters never developed a taste for the Nazi "socialism" and crude egalitarianism cultivated by the NSDStB and echoed clumsily by the ANSt.[138] These young women expected to be able to pursue the prestigious academic studies and career of their choice in relative peace and quiet. When in need of sociability or guidance, they chose to turn, as before, to the familiar and philosophically congenial denominational coeds' associations. If they were willing to go through the movement of joining the ANSt, it was purely because *not* doing so might have jeopardized their place at the university or their future career, just as many of their fathers joined the NSDAP for the same reason. But the last thing they were looking for in the ivory tower of academe was indoctrination, regimentation, and the pedestrian National Socialist activism dispensed by the Nazi women students' association.

PART 3

Women University Students and the Second World War

8

War: Catalyst of an Unprecedented Academic Emancipation of German Women

In the second half of the 1930s, Nazi Germany's economic preparations for war and conquest had not only solved (or so it seemed) the crisis of unemployment but actually spawned a serious personnel shortage in the professions as well as in industry. Consequently the Nazis had quietly abandoned their original misgivings about women's academic and professional aspirations and switched almost imperceptibly from a policy of official disapproval to a strategy of systematic and energetic support for the *Frauenstudium*. In spite of this about-face, however, German women had contributed little to the realization of Nazi labor objectives in the field of the academic professions, for they had continued to lose ground at the universities, both in absolute numbers and in relation to the male student population, and this trend persisted virtually until the very moment of the outbreak of the Second World War.

War, of course, merely served to exacerbate the existing labor shortages, since huge numbers of men were drained off to the battlefields. And they failed to return, as had been hoped, after a brief and victorious *Blitzkrieg*, so that Germany's labor needs assumed increasingly critical proportions as the war progressed.[1] Because of this, Nazi rulers found themselves compelled to tap alternative sources of labor, such as prisoners of war (POWs), concentration camp inmates, foreign civilian workers, and German women.[2] The professions were also affected by this personnel crisis, and the threat of dwindling supplies of students was a cause of great concern to the authorities. Reich Education Minister Rust himself alluded to the seriousness of the situation as early as January 1940 and declared that the primary objective of the Reich's wartime educational policies would be "to secure a steady, sufficient, and capable supply [*Nachwuchs*] for the academic professions, which are of so much importance to the racial community."[3] But he could not prevent the draft into the army of ever-growing numbers of young men who under normal circumstances would have gone to university to be trained as lawyers, teachers, and engineers, even as the war itself was generating an increased demand for academically trained personnel.[4] Between the summers of 1939 and 1941, for instance, the number of male students at all German universities fell by nearly 50 percent, from 50,325 to 27,327. And towards the end of the war, in mid-1944, only 14,285 male university students remained in the entire Reich.[5] (See figure 8.) To make things worse, men, on the average, took much longer to graduate during the war, since they were often drafted into the *Wehrmacht* for longer or shorter terms of service.[6] As a result of all this, numbers of male graduates dwindled rapidly in disciplines of great importance to the war effort, such as physics, chemistry, and engineering.[7]

To compensate for this shortage of male university-trained professionals by means of the same alternative sources of labor that supplied industry and agriculture was out of the question. POWs, concentration camp inmates, or foreign civilians could be used as farmhands or factory workers, but hardly as lawyers, scientists, or teachers, except in extremely rare cases. The only feasible solution was to rely on German women in order to fill the widening academic and professional vacuum. Among Nazi planners and authorities, this caused little gnashing of teeth. Faced with the hard realities of day-to-day economic and social life, they had long learned to mix some water in their heady National Socialist ideological wine. Already in the mid-1930s they had thus abandoned their opposition to the *Frauenstudium*, and ever since then they had consistently encouraged women's aspirations in the academic and professional field. The conditions created on the academic labor market as a result of the war did not call for a revision of this attitude but provided added justification for it—sanctioned it, as it were. Consequently, after 1939 the Nazi regime continued with even fewer inhibitions to support the academic ambitions of German women.

Barely one month after the outbreak of the war, on October 1, 1939, a Reich Labor Exchange Agency for Women (*Reichsvermittlungsstelle für Frauenberufe*) was opened in Berlin to help counsel female university graduates with regard to employment opportunities in their profession.[8] But it was not sufficient to direct university-trained women to places where they were needed; it was even more important to make it possible for still greater numbers of young women to acquire a university education in the first place. University admission requirements for women were therefore considerably relaxed. On January 19, 1940, the Reich education minister decreed that women who had graduated from secondary schools for home economics (*Oberschulen hauswirtschaftlicher Art*) could henceforth register at any university for any discipline other than medicine without having passed the special test that had hitherto been required in their case. This meant that knowledge of Latin was dropped as a prerequisite for university studies, except in the faculty of medicine.[9] In February 1942, moreover, Rust decided that women with children as well as childless widows of military personnel killed in action could take up university studies without having performed the "labor service."[10] This was a significant concession, for the married woman student

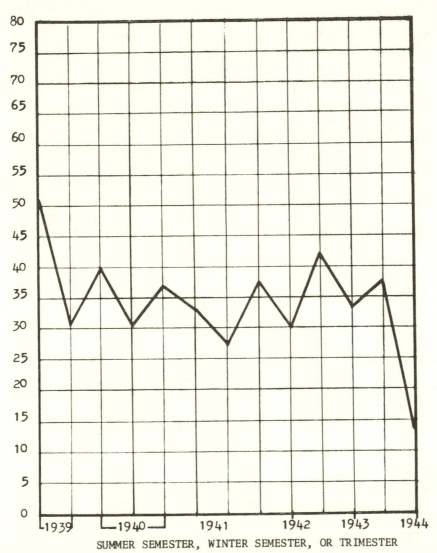

ENROLLMENTS
(IN THOUSANDS)

SUMMER SEMESTER, WINTER SEMESTER, OR TRIMESTER

was fast becoming a common phenomenon at Germany's institutions of higher learning during the war.[11]

Not only Rust's Reich Ministry of Education but also the RSF itself spared no effort to stimulate women's academic aspirations. In the spring of 1942, Scheel, in his capacity of Reich Student Leader and inspector of the Langemarck Foundation (*Langemarckstudium*),[12] established a special department within the latter, named Preuniversity Training for Women (*Vorstudienausbildung für Frauen*). Its purpose was to select gifted women between twenty and thirty-two years of age whose educational and financial background would normally make it impossible to study, and to train them for two years at the expense of the RSF in order to help them obtain the "certificate of university maturity" (*Hochschulreife*). Following that, these women would be free to take up university studies of their choice. The first candidates were selected by the RSF Office for Women Students in July 1942, and twenty young women started their first series of courses in the fall of that year. Another fifty were to follow suit a year later.[13] A second symptom of Scheel's wartime support for the *Frauenstudium* was the refounding, on November 23, 1942, of the University Community of German Women, the Nazi alumnae association.[14] And on May 10, 1944, a major obstacle on women's path to the university was removed. By special decree, Reich Education Minister Rust abolished the "labor service" as a precondition for academic studies. The six-month compulsory "war aid service" (*Kriegshilfsdienst*—KHD), which followed automatically on the "labor service" since July 29, 1941, was likewise dropped as a preuniversity requirement.[15]

During the war, female students also received a greater share of the scholarships of the Study Foundation (*Studienstiftung*). Whereas only 10.7 percent of all its beneficiaries had been women in the summer semester of 1938, their share increased to 18.8 percent in the first trimester of 1940 and to 25.5 percent in the winter trimester of 1941.[16] Since women's share of the entire student population in these two academic sessions stood at 15.7 and 28.3 percent respectively, one can say that women were receiving a fair share of all the scholarships of the Study Foundation. Even those many women who did not receive any grants did not necessarily have to rely solely on the financial support of their parents in order to finance their studies. The wartime labor shortage multiplied the opportunities for part-time employment for women students, and the female working student (a rare sight in Germany between 1933 and 1939) made her reappearance and became an increasingly common phenomenon during the war years.[17] Female representatives of the financially weaker classes were thus given a better chance to study, but the absence of statistical data on the social background of university students makes it impossible to investigate whether the social structure of the *Frauenstudium* changed significantly as a result of this factor, as one would suspect it would have done. In any event, the war years witnessed the fascinating spectacle of an intrinsically misogynic Nazi regime using all the incentives at its disposal in a shameless effort to bribe Germany's young women into taking up university studies.

To be sure, the Nazis had revised their attitude towards the *Frauenstudium* well before the outbreak of the world conflict, but the paternalistic benevolence they displayed vis-à-vis women's academic aspirations in the late 1930s, although quite spectacular in light of their earlier negative disposition, was almost insignificant compared with the energetic support the Nazis were to give the *Frauenstudium* throughout the war. For a number of reasons, Germany's young women had been unable to take advantage of the improved official climate in the late 1930s. Demographic and economic realities as well as social-psychological factors had combined to restrict access to the universities to all but a handful of predominantly well-off young women. In this field too, war was to act as a great catalyst, for it created conditions that motivated and enabled masses of young women to embark on academic studies and careers in order to fill the academic vacuum left by the departure of male students for the front.

Throughout the war, university studies constituted an ideal and popular alibi that permitted young women in general, but female representatives of the upper middle class in particular,[18] to avoid the threat of forcible mobilization for the war effort *and* the dishonorable appearance of inactivity in the fatherland's hour of danger. We know that the Nazi rulers never fully exploited the labor potential of Germany's women in spite of the acute personnel shortages generated by the war. Purely ideological misgivings are usually cited as the reason for this, but the availability of a seemingly inexhaustible alternative source of labor in the form of foreign workers also played an important part. In spite of their predilection for imported slave labor, however, the Nazis occasionally saw fit to mobilize (or threaten to mobilize) women for work in the armament industry, on the farms, or elsewhere. In March 1941, for instance, Hitler and Hess launched a campaign under the motto "Women contribute to victory" (*Frauen helfen siegen*). Its objective was to have women over sixteen years of age join the labor force. But disappointingly few of them stepped forward to place their names on the registration lists prepared by the NSF.[19] Nevertheless, the pressure was maintained,[20] so that many women found it opportune to look for an occupation that might exonerate them from the stigma of loafing.[21] Academic studies provided the ideal solution for those who could afford them, and it was probably no coincidence that new enrollments of women at Germany's institutions of higher learning increased dramatically during the next year, from 2,107 in early 1941 to 6,582 in the spring of 1942.[22] Later, after Fritz Sauckel, plenipotentiary for labor mobilization (*Generalbevollmächtigter für den Arbeitseinsatz*—GBA), decreed the compulsory draft of all women between the ages of seventeen and forty-five for a gigantic "labor mobilization" (*Arbeitseinsatz*) in January 1943,[23] the universities became veritable havens for thousands of young women who wanted to evade this labor dragnet. In the popular language of the day, this phenomenon was cynically referred to as "the flight to the university" (*Die Flucht ins Studium*).[24] Sauckel's decree turned out to be so ineffective that it earned the nickname "rubber decree" (*Gummiverordnung*).[25] One reason for this ineffectiveness was that no less than 8,917 women matriculated for the first time at the start of the next semester (the summer semester of 1943), causing an increase of 78 percent over the corresponding figure for the winter semester 1942/43.[26] Many young women had ostensibly become aware of their academic vocation just after Sauckel's proclamation of the "labor mobilization" for women.

Even so, there were many other reasons women wanted to study and earn academic degrees during the war. Fiancées and wives of military personnel, for instance, had to face the possibility that their partners might not return from the front, in which case they would have to look after themselves and their families. Academic studies were part of a contingency plan for this eventuality, a life insurance to be cashed in on the death of a partner.[27] The relatively generous state allowances paid to the wives of soldiers at the front facilitated such a strategy,[28] so that increasing numbers of married women, who would not normally have been interested in earning a degree, found their way to the universities during the war.[29] We may assume that this must have resulted in a rise of the average age of women students during the war, but no statistical data are available to confirm this.

The circumstances of war favored the *Frauenstudium* in yet another respect. In the depression-ridden 1930s, social-psychological factors operated in favor of the studies of a son and against the academic career of a daughter, since the latter appeared a far less promising investment. A family able to see one child through university would then most likely have chosen to send the son rather than the daughter. During the war, however, this situation was reversed, and social-psychological factors promoted the *Frauenstudium*. The studies of a son suddenly became a risky investment, since a young man could be drafted into the *Wehrmacht* at any time. His studies loomed as a long and expensive undertaking without guaranteed dividends, for death on the battlefield hung over his head like a sword of Damocles. But the same risks did not apply to a daughter's academic career, which consequently appeared as the more promising venture. Just as in the 1930s a family's savings were best invested in a son's studies, in the war conditions of the early 1940s it seemed more prudent to invest them in the studies of a daughter.

The wide range of facilities offered by the Nazi authorities, the desire on the part of young women to escape the threat of mobilization for the war effort in an honorable way, the need for fiancées and wives of soldiers to prepare themselves for a career in case of their partner's death, and the superior investment value of the academic studies of a daughter as compared to a son—all these factors formed a constellation capable of generating an unprecedented academic emancipation of German women during the war. But this potential could not have been realized had a large pool of young women not been available in Germany at the time. The demographic low tide that had ravaged the ranks of Germany's university students in the 1930s was turning during the war years. The last members of the World War I cohort were graduating, and now it was the turn of the much more numerous age-groups born in the 1920s to present themselves at the gates of the Reich's institutions of higher learning. In the years after the Treaty of Versailles, hundreds of thousands more births had been registered in Germany than during the Great War,[30] and some twenty years later, in the early 1940s, this produced a much larger supply of potential university students. This potential could not be realized in the case of men, primarily because of their military obligations, but the large young generation of women was free to take full advantage of the unique academic opportunity created by the circumstances of war.

During the Second World War, women indeed made spectacular gains at the German institutions of higher learning. The total number of women university students in the Reich[31] increased nearly sevenfold, from 6,342 in the summer of 1939 to 41,210 five years later. As early as 1942 all the losses incurred after 1933 had been wiped out, and by 1944 there were twice as many female students in the Reich as there had been in the first semester after the Nazi *Machtergreifung* (see figure 9). During the war, also, women's share of the total student population rose tremendously, from a mere 11.2 percent in the summer semester of 1939 to 49.3 percent in the summer semester of 1944. Whereas before the war there had been approximately one woman among every ten students, by the end of the war there was one coed for every male student.[32] The number of first-year women students increased fifteen times between 1939 and 1944, and women's share of all new registrations rose from 9.4 percent to 64.8 percent, although not without heavy fluctuations due mainly to the irregular wartime matriculations of men over the same period (see figure 10).[33]

During the war, moreover, women invaded those disciplines that had hitherto been nearly exclusively reserved for men. The number of women students of law thus increased from 151 in the summer of 1939 to 561 five years later. Their share of the total number of law students thereby rose from an insignificant 2.5 percent to a respectable 16.4 percent. Offices for vocational counselling actively encouraged women to study law and drew attention to the vast professional opportunities for women in this field.[34] While 310 women had accounted for 9.2 percent of all chemistry students in 1939, by the summer of 1944 their number had increased almost eightfold, to 2,395. With 63.3 percent of all students of chemistry, these women constituted a clear majority over the men, so much so that there was talk of a flooding of this discipline by women.[35] In the fall of 1939 there were 97 female students of biology; in the fall of 1944 there were nearly eighteen times as many, 1,728 to be precise, accounting for 89.3 percent of all biology students. In natural sciences, including chemistry and physics as well as mathematics and geology, women advanced from 10.8 percent to 63.5 percent of all students between 1939 and 1943. In technical sciences, too, their progress over the same period was truly remarkable: from 85 women and 0.7 percent, to 726 women and 11.7 percent. The most popular field here was architecture, which had attracted only 70 women in the summer semester of 1939, or 5.1 percent of all students, but had no less than 670 of them in the winter semester 1943/44, or 43.1 percent of all prospective architects. Even in such decidedly "unfeminine" fields as agricultural and forestry studies,

Figure 9.
Enrollments of Women Students at All German Institutions of Higher Learning during World War II, 1939–1944

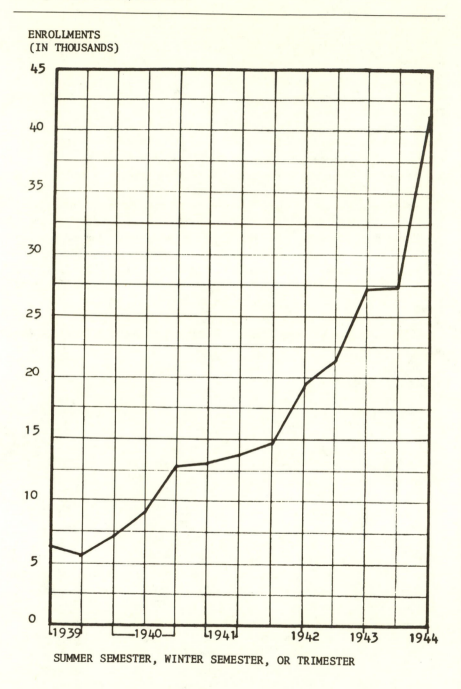

ENROLLMENTS
(IN THOUSANDS)

SUMMER SEMESTER, WINTER SEMESTER, OR TRIMESTER

Figure 10.
New Matriculations of Men and Women at the Institutions of Higher Learning of "Greater Germany," 1939-1944

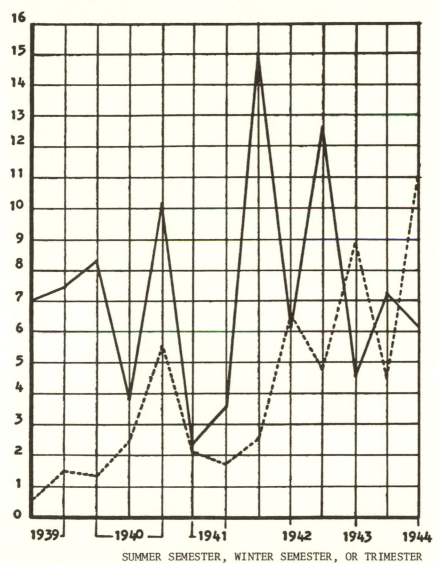

NEW MATRICULATIONS
(IN THOUSANDS)

SUMMER SEMESTER, WINTER SEMESTER, OR TRIMESTER

Men:_____   Women:_____

Figure 11.
Women Students at the Technical Universities of "Greater Germany," 1939-1943/44

PERCENTAGE

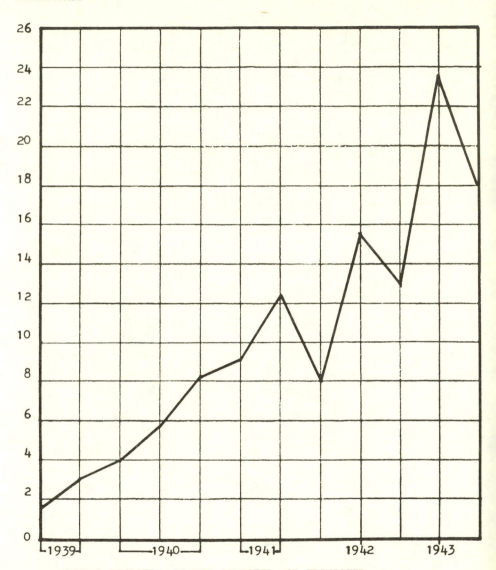

SUMMER SEMESTER, WINTER SEMESTER, OR TRIMESTER

women acquired a strong foothold. Between 1939 and 1943/44 the representation of women in those fields increased from 2.4 percent to 29.3 percent, representing 48 and 334 women respectively.[36] In the process, women conquered those universities from which they had hitherto been virtually excluded or in which they had been hopelessly underrepresented. At the technical universities, for instance, their share rose from 1.9 percent in the summer of 1939 to 23.5 percent a mere four years later (see figure 11). In absolute numbers, a sevenfold increase occurred, from 271 to 2,087.[37] At the commercial academies (*Handelshochschulen*), women advanced from 17.1 percent to 46.3 percent over the same period, representing 393 and 1,052 women respectively.[38]

In addition to their gains in these relatively new fields, women also continued to improve their position in those disciplines in which they had already been fairly strongly represented before the outbreak of the war. In general medicine their share more than doubled between 1939 and 1943, from 15.6 percent to 35.9 percent. The absolute number of women students of medicine quadrupled, from 3,352 to 14,078. Women's progress in the humanities during the same period was no less remarkable. The absolute number of females in that faculty rose from 2,160 to 9,245, and their share of all students of the humanities increased from 35.8 percent to 83.4 percent.[39]

9

German Women University Students, the ANSt, and the Fiasco of the "War Service" Scheme

The mood of the thousands of young women who found themselves crowded together at the German institutions of higher learning during the war was strictly businesslike. War in general, of course, was a serious matter that affected the lives of all Germans directly and inevitably colored the attitude of female students towards their academic career. Virtually all women students, moreover, owed their place at the university to a specific opportunity or need created by the circumstances of war. They were therefore determined to take full advantage of this opportunity, which might not present itself again, or to meet this need before it might be too late. The wartime generation of women students were concerned first and foremost with their studies, with earning a degree in the shortest possible period of time, and with their future professional careers. And this is precisely what the Nazi educational authorities expected from them. Since securing an adequate "supply"—to use Nazi jargon—for the academic professions was their main objective, the authorities welcomed the earnest attitude displayed by women students. But although the Nazi leaders had grounds to be pleased with the academic dedication of female students during the war, there was also a reverse side to this coin. Preoccupied with their studies, women university students showed little interest in National Socialism itself, and they clearly interpreted their mandate to graduate as soon as possible as a license to dispense with time-consuming and irrelevant displays of loyalty to the regime and enthusiasm for the Nazi cause. This was reflected, for one thing, in the poor fortunes of the ANSt, whose task it was to marshall the ever-increasing numbers of newcomers at the universities and to transform them into an elite of convinced National Socialist women.

The Nazi coeds' league had never been a very efficient organization, and this assignment proved to be far beyond its capabilities. Not that the recruitment of new members presented any problem: official reports invariably exaggerated the size of the ANSt's following,[1] but other—and more reliable—sources confirm that perhaps even the overwhelming majority of women students of the first three semesters joined the ANSt teams of their own free will. In the summer of 1940, confidential reports from Cologne and Halle indicated that "practically all" women of the first three semesters belonged to the teams, Berlin spoke of an "unprecedented influx of young women" into the ANSt, and the Frankfurt ANSt office informed the Reich leadership that it was nearly impossible to accommodate the masses of candidates for the teams.[2] But most women joined simply because it was expected from them as a matter of course and because *not* joining might prove to be a handicap, a curb on future opportunities for advancement and success. It is significant that at Halle University, to give but one example, the only women who did not belong to an ANSt team in 1940 were four students of theology and one girl of "mixed race" (*Mischling*);[3] on account of either choice of discipline or racial background, these young women were unlikely ever to be successful in Nazi society in any case, so that the added disadvantage of not being an ANSt member was hardly of much consequence to them. For the majority of female students, on the other hand, there were few pressing reasons for not joining a team. The ANSt was not the SS. Membership in a team did not stamp a person as a fanatical Nazi, so even anti-Nazis did not deem it worthwhile to remain aloof for that reason. Katharina Schüddekopf, a member of the White Rose student resistance group in Munich, thus belonged to the ANSt during her first three semesters at the university.[4] In addition, the duties that membership in the teams entailed were few and could easily be shirked.

Team members met once a week for an "educational evening" (*Schulungs-abend*) or "community evening" (*Gemeinschaftsabend*). These were supposed to be thorough sessions of political indoctrination, but more often than not they consisted solely of discussions on the significance of current developments at the front. The declaration of war on the United States, for instance, stimulated interest in the new theaters of war in the Orient and the Pacific, and this led to discussions on "the political importance of the Pacific Ocean," "rivalry between Japan and the United States," and "Indonesia and its mineral wealth between Japanese, British, and American interests."[5] The meetings were clearly not very demanding. Frequently they amounted to no more than an additional history seminar, as in 1940 in Cologne, where the discussion focused on the 1648 Treaty of Westphalia.[6]

The Nazi coeds' leaders liked to remind women students that "only a physically as well as spiritually fit people will be able to maintain its right to live in the long run," and they stressed the importance of extracurricular sports (*Pflicht-sport*), which was compulsory for members of the teams.[7] But that was only theory. No evidence whatsoever can be found that *Pflichtsport* regulations were ever enforced during the course of the war. In order to divert attention from this inactivity, the achievements of individual female student athletes continued to be loudly glorified, as on the occasion of the sports championships for women students, organized in Darmstadt from July 24 to 27, 1941. Not only was the alleged "world class" of some female participants praised to the sky, but "over a thousand" women were reported to have delivered proof that "a real physical education of women at the university is now guaranteed."[8]

Like sports, the "women's service" (*Frauendienst*) was compulsory for members of the ANSt teams, the more so since the war itself appeared to vindicate the principle on which these courses were based. But women who had already taken instruction in first aid, air protection, and gas protection in the BDM or the "labor service," as was the case with virtually every woman student, were exempted. Consequently, the "women's service" duties, like extracurricular sports, were merely a fictitious obligation during the war.[9]

If the burdens of ANSt members of the first three semesters were minimal, from the fourth semester onward they were virtually nonexistent. On completion of their service in the teams, ANSt women were promoted from "provisional members" to full-fledged members. Paradoxically, this ended their duties within the Nazi coeds' organization, except in the case of women students of medicine. Women of the fourth and higher semesters were supposed to engage in extra-curricular "scholarly work" (*Wissenschaftsarbeit*).[10] But since the scheme of an annual Reich Vocational Contest for university students had been discontinued shortly after the outbreak of the war, it was only the "faculty work" of the women medical students which displayed any signs of life. As had been the case prior to 1939, these women were usually committed to work for the BDM, but now they also found their way into Red Cross "squads" (*Bereitschaften*) as "nurse's aides." Only women students who faced examinations were exempted from service for either the BDM or the Red Cross.[11] Women students of faculties other than medicine, however, never bothered with any type of "faculty work" during the war; at least, no traces of such activities are to be found anywhere.

It is clear that membership in the ANSt, whether provisional or full, meant little more to the great majority of Germany's female university students during the war than possession of a membership card. There were very few obligations, and the Nazi coeds' leaders complained that even those were consistently neglected by the ANSt rank and file. Many women did not hesitate to display their indifference or even contempt for the activities of the RSF's Office for Women Students.[12] This widespread lethargy was likewise reflected in the difficulty the ANSt experienced in finding women who were willing and able to act as leaders and as instructors for the sessions in "political education." Throughout the war there was to be a great shortage of such personnel.[13] The indifference of women students was most glaringly revealed, however, by their disappointing performance in the "war service" (*Kriegsdienst*, also *Kriegseinsatz*).

Throughout the war, ANSt leaders argued convincingly that the privilege of being able to study in time of war called for a special "quid pro quo" (*Gegenleistung*) on the part of women university students. As early as January 1940, for instance, an ANSt brochure brought home this message: "Precisely because we are so privileged compared to many others, in that we are allowed to study in times like these, do we feel the strong obligation for a greater service...."[14] Furthermore, women students were warned that the Reich was still very much a man's world, and that the men at the front might resent seeing great numbers of women taking "their" places in the lecture halls. In order to forestall an antifeminist backlash, female students were advised to match the sacrifices of the soldiers at the front with an unselfish personal effort on behalf of the community and the fatherland. Gertrud Scholtz-Klink, for one, solemnly cautioned, "Our conduct and our service have to convince [the men] that the mark of distinction of the *Frauenstudium* during the war is not the petty ambition of the individual but selfless service."[15] Anna Kottenhoff, Reich Leader of the ANSt, was fond of appealing to the coeds' personal loyalty to the *Führer* himself. On April 20, 1942, at the occasion of Hitler's birthday, she took to the pages of the student paper *Die Bewegung* to pledge that women students would never cease "to deliver proof of the socialism of the German racial community." Even more than in peacetime, she promised, performance in the service of the *Volksgemeinschaft* was to be the mark of distinction of Germany's women students: "We acknowledge being part of the 'community of creativity and work' of all Germans.... We, German women students, will not lag behind anybody in the fulfillment of our duties."[16] This was fine National Socialist rhetoric, undoubtedly pure music to the ears of the Nazi bosses, but the masses of Germany's women students failed to be stirred into action by these catchwords. Throughout the war, they were to display an utter lack of enthusiasm for the very "war service" their Nazi leaders proclaimed as the sine qua non of the *Frauenstudium* in wartime. Insofar as the coeds' contribution to the Reich's war effort was expected to provide a resounding demonstration of their loyalty to the National Socialist state, their manifest lack of "enthusiasm for service" (*Einsatzfreudigkeit*) was proof of Nazism's failure to captivate Germany's female students and future professionals.

In order to provide for a speedy deployment of women university students for the "war service," Reich Education Minister Rust issued a decree on November 15, 1939, that allowed students of both sexes to interrupt their studies temporarily in order to make "a full-time contribution to the war effort" by joining the labor force. Such volunteers were officially considered "on leave" from the university. They retained their student status but were exempted from both DSt dues and from the "welfare contributions" levied on students during the war.[17] In spite of the ringing exhortations of their leaders, only a very few women students ever took leave from their academic pursuits in order to devote themselves full-time to the war effort of the Reich. In the winter trimester 1941, for instance, 694 female university students were officially on leave, representing an unimpressive 3.7 percent of all women students. Their number did rise gradually during the following semesters, to 1,342 in the summer of 1943, but their share of the entire female student body continued to hover around a low 3.5 percent. It was only in the winter semester 1943/44 that the situation improved somewhat.

During that academic session, a total of 2,334 women were on leave from their studies, and these volunteers accounted for 5.5 percent of all women students.[18] On the whole, it is clear that during the war German women students were more interested in pursuing their studies and future careers than in serving the National Socialist fatherland in its hour of danger.

It is true, on the other hand, that women who continued their studies did not escape the obligations of the "war service." Special "service communities" (*Dienstgemeinschaften*) of ten to twenty members each were created early in 1940 at all institutions of higher learning. Membership in these communities was compulsory for all students of both sexes and involved a minimum of five hours of service per week, at least in theory. This "service duty of the students" (*studentische Dienstpflicht*) was placed under the jurisdiction of the head of the RSF Office for Political Education, and an ANSt leader was in charge of the coeds' section within this office.[19]

We must wonder, however, whether much was ever accomplished by these "service communities," for little was ever heard from them. Germany, of course, was enjoying success after success during this early stage of the war, and with victory taken for granted, it is likely that virtually nobody seriously believed in the need for a "war service" of women university students. Still, some female students did take part in an action launched by Rust and Scheel, which displayed many characteristics of the prewar RBWK. It was a competition sometimes referred to as the "War Performance Contest" (*Kriegsleistungskampf*), although it was more commonly known as the "War Propaganda Service" (*Kriegspropagandadienst*). The objective of this scheme was to have university students of both sexes help "to unmask the true nature and aims of the plutocratic powers of destruction," in other words, to contribute to the defamation of Germany's western enemies, and to do this by means of pseudo-scholarly propaganda.[20] Initially this work was aimed at France as well as England. Early in 1940 a woman student at Berlin University was thus instructed to scan the combined works of Nietzsche for Francophobe quotations, which were to be published in the infamous Nazi periodical *Der Stürmer*.[21] But after France had been overrun by the German war machine, only England remained as a target for the participants in the War Propaganda Service. Women students were directed "to explore the history and culture of all nations, including the English people itself, for arguments against England."[22] Participating women were told to concentrate especially on the allegedly sad plight of women under the British "plutocratic" regime. A number of essays were produced on such topics as "plutocratic exploitation of women's and children's labor," and the conclusions were predictably devastating. England emerged from these writings as a bastion of misogyny, a women's hell.[23] The best essays were actually published, as was the case with an investigation of social conditions in England and with a treatment of hygienical conditions in the British colonies.[24]

It is undeniable that the scholarly talents of Germany's women university students were manipulated in this manner in order to produce grist for the Nazi propaganda mill. However, it seems unlikely that many women ever took part in the "War Propaganda Service" or, for that matter, that the results were consistently gratifying to the Nazi rulers. For instance, the Berlin woman who scrutinized Nietzsche's writings for anti-French quotations reported to her ANSt leader that she had found only two derogatory remarks about France, but "at least a dozen" about Germany.[25]

The War Propaganda Service may have been an important project, but it was clearly not there that Germany's female students were performing the kind of community service which, in the minds of their Nazi leaders, was to justify women's wartime academic activities. Much the same can be said about a number of other "war service" schemes that were organized throughout the academic year. There was a great deal of publicity about the "soldiers' service" (*Soldatendienst*; *Soldatenbetreuung*) of female university students. Thousands of parcels and letters were reportedly sent by women students to soldiers at the front and to members of the Todt Organization who were working on the western defense line (*Westwall*) in 1940.[26] A similar project was the "hospital service" (*Lazarettendienst*), which had female students visit wounded soldiers in military hospitals (*Lazaretten*) in order to bring them presents, entertain them with music and songs, and sometimes even to teach them minor chores such as woodcutting and painting.[27] In their free time, other women helped out in day nurseries of the Nazi welfare organizations; some were mobilized to assist refugees, repatriates, and wounded soldiers in railway stations, and individual women even worked as streetcar conductors.[28] But whether these actions did indeed involve massive numbers of women students, as official reports suggested, is an open question. In any event, the Nazi coeds' leadership must not have been entirely satisfied with the performance of their following during the academic year, for it was decided to mobilize all women students in the 1940 summer holiday for a large-scale action on the fields or in the factories.

Participation in an "agricultural service" was compulsory for all women in the first three semesters, with the exception of those from a number of faculties whose members were assigned to a "factory service." "War service passes" (*Kriegsdienstpässe*) were issued to all female students, who were sternly warned that no one would be allowed to register in the fall for the second, third, or fourth semester without either an entry proving the holder's participation in the "agricultural service" or a special "certificate of exemption" (*Beurlaubungsbescheinigung*).[29] Official reports later claimed that five thousand women had taken part.[30] This figure is impressive and may well reflect the truth, considering the sanctions involved. Still, mere statistics do not tell the entire story. In reality, the implementation of the "agricultural service" project in the summer of 1940 met with considerable difficulties. At Cologne and Aachen, for example, three to five hundred women students reported for the service, but were flatly turned down because the influx of prisoners of war after the successful campaign in the west had suddenly solved the labor shortage on the farms of the Rhineland. Approximately three hundred women ended up taking odd jobs in or around their hometowns; the rest were sent to war industry enterprises to perform a "factory service."[31] Of all the female students of Cologne University, only seventy-five managed to work the harvest as planned; all other volunteers worked in factories.[32] In the Frankfurt region, no women students at all ever reached the fields. This was said to be the result of slipshod organization on the part of the responsible official in the regional employment office. The students were simply told that the farmers of the area had an adequate labor force in the form of a large contingent of prisoners of war.[33] Organizational difficulties also arose in Berlin, where only thirty-five women were to serve in the "agricultural service"; others worked in factories, as in Cologne, but failed to accomplish anything worthwhile. Reports spoke of a general lack of enthusiasm and condemned the immature ("*Backfisch*") behavior of many participants.[34] Anecdotes such as these suggest that the "agricultural service" of the summer of 1940 was not at all the unmitigated success official reports later claimed it had been.

Available evidence indicates that the concomitant "factory service" did not fare any better. Participation in this action was compulsory for all women of the first three semesters in law, economics, natural and technical sciences, and architecture.[35] Each woman was committed to four weeks of work in a militarily important enterprise, and during this period she was to relieve a female worker.[36] It was later reported that 2,700 women students had taken part in this "factory service," performing a grand total of 650,000 work hours and creating no less than 64,800 leisure days for female factory workers.[37] One source even put the number of participants as high as 4,000.[38] But the available figures for individual universities, which are more reliable, are considerably more modest. Freiburg University, for instance, yielded only 11 volunteers, Cologne 76, and Frankfurt 48. The entire Berlin region produced no more than 300 candidates for the "factory service."[39] The suspicion that the official figures were greatly inflated is also confirmed by the case of Hamburg University. According to the students' yearbook for 1941, some 45 female students had taken part in the 1940 "factory service,"[40] yet a confidential report of the RSF in the Hamburg region put their number at a far less impressive 8.[41] The RSF in general, and its Office for Women Students in particular, undoubtedly tended to exaggerate the number of participants in these student aid actions in order to reap greater acclaim for the wartime performance of women university students and also to enhance the status of the RSF within party and state. Verification of the official figures, in the unlikely event that anybody would ever have raised any doubts about their accuracy, would certainly have been difficult, if not entirely impossible. One reason for this was that actions often overlapped, resulting in an extremely confused overall picture. Who was ever to know if, as may well have happened, the number of women who had reported for the "agricultural service" but had ended up performing a "factory service" were credited to the final tallies of both these actions?

The myth of a successful "factory service" is further undermined by reports of cases of friction and ill feelings between participants and factory management.

During the ''factory service'' of the Hamburg girls, complaints were voiced about the choice of the female factory workers who were to be relieved by the students. In particular, the selection of the sister-in-law of a shop steward of the Labor Front had annoyed the volunteers and infuriated other workers.[42]

The optimistic and sometimes almost triumphant tone struck in official reports only served to becloud the disappointment of the Nazi coeds' leadership with the major ''war service'' schemes of the summer of 1940. Some consolation could be derived, however, from the relative success of an entirely new sort of experiment, which involved women students in the implementation of Nazi settlement (*Siedlung*) schemes in conquered Poland. This was the so-called ''service in the east'' (*Osteinsatz*).

On October 7, 1939, Hitler appointed Heinrich Himmler as Reich Commissar for the Strengthening of German Folkdom (*Reichskommissar für die Festigung deutschen Volkstums*—RKF).[43] Himmler was thus given carte blanche to proceed as he saw fit with the ''resettlement'' of the population of Danzig, West Prussia, Posen, Upper Silesia, and parts of Congress Poland, conquered Polish territories that were incorporated into the Reich on the following day by virtue of a special *Führer* decree.[44] Since these relatively backward areas held little attraction for native Germans, the SS had to rely predominantly on ethnic German ''resettlers'' (*Umsiedler*; *Rücksiedler*), ''repatriated'' from the Baltic nations, the ''Government General'' of Poland,[45] and areas of the Soviet Union and Romania such as Galicia and Bessarabia.[46] In order to make room for them, hundreds of thousands of Poles and Jews were deported, and before the end of the war approximately 350,000 ethnic Germans had been ''resettled,'' the majority (245,000) in the so-called *Warthegau* (or *Wartheland*), the area around Posen and Lodz, a city rebaptized ''Litzmannstadt'' by the Nazis.[47] The Nazi rulers expected that these settlers would reconvert the ''ancient German land in the east'' into truly German territory,[48] but this was no easy task for people who were often illiterate, spoke German only badly and sometimes not at all, and had no knowledge of German history or National Socialist ideology. Consequently, educated native Germans were needed to help, and when this call for help reached the German universities in the first weeks of July 1940, women students responded favorably. Romantic visions of pioneering work in a strange yet fascinating frontier area proved a strong incentive. Departing for the east, one woman student wrote: ''Now I would have the opportunity to turn into deeds what I had sung in my songs about the eastern lands; I would help to Germanize the east liberated by the German sword, and carry hence our German culture.''[49]

The first *Osteinsatz* of women university students got under way on August 1, 1940, and was carried out in the eastern border districts of the *Warthegau*. As each woman was made to perform a type of work for which she was being trained academically, the *Osteinsatz* resembled the prewar ''faculty work'' and was referred to as a ''professional service'' (*Facheinsatz*).[50] Women from teachers' colleges thus lent a hand in the organization of elementary schools for the settlers' children. They usually accomplished this by simply occupying formerly

Polish schools and installing a Hitler photograph above the blackboard.[51] In addition, these women filled in as teachers, an achievement of some importance, since the war had caused a serious shortage of teachers even in Germany proper and since the children of the repatriates often had little or no previous schooling. One female student-teacher wrote in exasperation: "Even the older boys and girls have never heard of the Rhine, of Hermann Göring, of paratroopers....Many have no idea where Berlin is!"[52] On the other hand, the work could be gratifying. A woman student later recalled with nostalgia how she had instilled the children of the settlers with love for the *Führer*, who had brought their families "home" into the Reich: "I told them of Germany and its *Führer*, of our leader's love for children. The kids' eyes flashed up....I could make them happy with a mere photograph of the *Führer*. The adults, too, were happy as children with a picture of our beloved *Führer*."[53] The *Lehrerinneneinsatz*, as the work of the student-teachers was called, lasted from six weeks to three months, and each woman spent approximately seven hours daily teaching reading, writing, arithmetic, geography, and, for the older children, National Socialist *Weltanschauung*.[54] There was also a "professional service" in the east for students of medicine, referred to as *Medizinischer Facheinsatz Ost*. Its total of approximately one hundred participants included only eight females, however. The reason for this was that the work was generally considered too dangerous and demanding for young women. For instance, epidemic diseases such as typhus were widespread among the German repatriates in the east.[55] An activity for which women students were believed to be better qualified was the work in the nurseries set up by the NSV in the *Warthegau*.[56]

The most important type of student action in the east, however, was the "settlers' care" (*Siedlerbetreuung*). It was a complex and delicate assignment, combining material assistance to the settlers with political supervision and ideological indoctrination. Consequently, the "settlers' care" fell under the direct jurisdiction of the SS. Although the NSV financed the operation, it was the SS Settlement Staff (*SS-Ansiedlungsstab*) in "Litzmannstadt" which supervised the work of all organizations involved, namely, the BDM, the NSF, the Nazi eleemosynary organizations, and the ANSt.[57] Male organizations are missing from this list, for the "settlers' care" was virtually an exclusively feminine prerogative: it was the work of a "[female] sponsor" (*Betreuerin*), usually but not necessarily a student, who was attached to a settlers' family in order to help in the household and on the farm. This young woman also gave advice in matters of hygiene, diet, baby care, and child-rearing and was supposed to work herself into a position of family confidante who could instill Nazi political, ideological, and racial values into her hosts.[58] Here, then, was a mission for which feminine talent, tact, and skills were required, and to coeds and other young women alike this assignment constituted a privilege and an opportunity to assert their value within Nazi society.

Aside from her duties within the settlers' family, each "sponsor" also had to supervise her village and the entire "settlement cell" (*Siedlungszelle*), the cluster of settlements in the area.[59] She organized afternoons for the children (*Kinder-nachmittage*), social evenings (*Heimabende*), and a host of other social activities.[60] Moreover, she had to set up local cells of the NSF, the BDM, and other party organizations and select and train leaders for them, other symptoms of the highly political character of her mission.[61] During her visits to the homes of the settlers, the "sponsor" had to inspect hygienic conditions, but she was also to inquire about each family's relationship with the Polish population. Here again the women were performing a political service for the Nazi regime, for it was their duty to instill "master race" (*Herrenvolk*) notions into the settlers. Friendship with Polish neighbors was sternly frowned on. The "sponsors" were instructed that Polish servants had to sleep in the stables, never in the settler's home, that Polish pictures and decorations (belongings of the former occupants of the farm) had to be destroyed, and most of all, that the children of the settlers were not allowed to play with Polish children.[62] Daily reports had to be entered into a special diary (*Arbeitstagebuch*). The most important part of this diary was the "village mirror" (*Dorfspiegel*), a collection of detailed notes on the "racial-political and private-human behavior of the settlers," which was to serve as the basis for a future "frontier card-index" (*Grenzkartei*). The women were told to pay special attention to the ideological and political reliability of the repatriates whenever they made an entry in this "village mirror."[63] Since this material eventually found its way to SS headquarters in Lodz, the "sponsors" in effect acted as spies for Himmler and his henchmen, the new overlords of the eastern territories, who were evidently determined to supervise their ethnic German subjects very closely. The women must have lived up to the expectations of these sinister patrons of the "settlers' care," for in April 1941 the SS commander in "Litzmannstadt" described their performance in highly laudatory terms.[64]

There can be hardly any doubt that the *Osteinsatz* of female university students was of considerable value to the Nazi rulers of the occupied eastern territories. But whether the "service in the east" may therefore be viewed as evidence of the "performance impulses" (*Leistungsdrang*) and the enthusiasm for the National Socialist cause of the majority of Germany's female students is a different question. For one thing, it must be kept in mind that only a relative handful of women ever made the long journey to the *Warthegau*. The student-teacher work involved exactly 100 women, the medical faculty work, merely 8, and the related work in day-nurseries (*Kindergarteneinsatz*), 64; with 203 participants, the "settlers' care" was also numerically the most important activity.[65] The *Osteinsatz* of 1940 thus attracted a grand total of precisely 375 women students, a fair number in itself, but merely 2.9 percent of the 12,797 females who populated the Reich's institutions of higher learning in the summer semester of that year.[66] The *Osteinsatz* was conceived as an elitist undertaking, a privilege granted a few deserving individuals. One precondition for participation was prior experience in the "agricultural service" in eastern Germany.[67] Under such conditions Cologne University, to give but one example, yielded only six candidates.[68] It is clear that the organizers of the *Osteinsatz* intended to attract only convinced

National Socialist women, a sensible decision in view of the highly political nature of the women's duties in the east. On the other hand, great efforts were made to draw the largest possible number of women who met the Nazis' criteria. Emphasis was deliberately placed on the elitist character of the project in order to lure more volunteers, and more concrete incentives included the granting of credit for student-teacher service in lieu of the otherwise compulsory teacher training (*Landschulpraktikum*) as well as free travel to the *Wartheland*.[69] Since more than 95 percent of Germany's women students either failed to qualify for participation or, if they did qualify, did not bother to heed their leaders' pressing appeals even in spite of the benefits they held out, it can be argued that the 375 participants in the 1940 *Osteinsatz* represented the larger part of the Reich's truly convinced National Socialist women students. Viewed in this light, the *Osteinsatz* was not such a gratifying experiment to the Nazi coeds' leaders after all.

The balance sheet of the performance of women students within the ANSt and in the "war service" during the early years of the war was far from impressive. Women students clearly refused to submit to the National Socialist indoctrination their leaders hoped to dispense to them in the ANSt, and failed to respond to the RSF's passionate appeals for an energetic performance in the "war service" actions. In addition, many women students demonstrated their indifference to or even contempt for National Socialist political, ideological, and racial tenets in a different manner. By Nazi standards of morality, for instance, the lifestyle of many women students was hopelessly decadent, so that confidential reports spoke of a wholesale "degeneracy" of the female student population. And it was not just that women university students participated in clandestine dance parties and indulged in other relatively innocuous frivolities forbidden by the authorities for the duration of the war;[70] they also permitted themselves far-reaching sexual liberties for which Hitler's professedly "chaste Reich" (*saubere Reich*), as Hans-Peter Bleuel cynically calls it, claimed to have no use. To make things worse, women students did not restrict their favors to the racial comrades; on the contrary, they often displayed a predilection for "southern, foreign types of non-Aryan outlook." In October 1941 a case was cited of a woman student of music and an East Indian, whose affair allegedly caused "unpleasant sensation" in the staid Prussian city of Königsberg. But in the more cosmopolitan atmosphere of Munich University, the situation was far worse, as "virtually every foreign student had a German girlfriend." Turks and Bulgarians were reportedly the most ardent suitors of German female charms there, but even they had to recognize their master in a Peruvian who left three "half-breed" (*Mischling*) descendants behind when he departed from the Bavarian capital. The women who became involved in these affairs—and there evidently were many of them—displayed not only a total indifference to the racial purity the Nazis were promoting so diligently, but also an utter lack of patriotism as the Nazis understood it. This is illustrated by the case of one woman who refused to stand at attention when the national anthem was played. Reproached by the student leader, she flatly declared "to have married a Bulgarian national and therefore no longer to feel German in any way." Similar incidents occurred in Berlin, Leipzig, Dresden, Hamburg, and Darmstadt.[71] When a love affair led to an unwanted pregnancy, women students reportedly did not hesitate to have an abortion,[72] although in the Nazi book this constituted a cardinal sin, an act of sabotage against Germany's racial future, at least if the father was of "Aryan" background. The lack of National Socialist conviction and loyalty, reflected in these cases, was also revealed in other fields. Reports circulated that women students monitored enemy radio stations, a particularly grave offense, that they violated war-economy regulations, and that they were not even above criticizing the regime and its conduct of the war.[73] Finally, dissatisfaction with National Socialism often went hand in hand with a renewed interest in traditional values. Evidence indicates that a religious revival of sorts may have occurred during the war, particularly among Protestant women students, who were reported to be organizing "communities" (Gemeinschaften) and electing "leaders" (Obleute). The matter was considered serious enough by the RSF to warrant a request for a Gestapo investigation of these underground activities.[74]

10

The Supply Crisis in the Academic Professions and the Nazi Attitude Towards Women's Academic Aspirations During the War

Incidents such as those just described did not amount to genuine acts of resistance, but they did reflect a widespread indifference to, if not outright repudiation of, National Socialism on the part of many female university students. Below a thin veneer of professed loyalty there lay a mass of apathy, skepticism, disenchantment, or hostility, an iceberg of which these acts were but the tip above the surface. And nobody was more keenly aware of this than the Nazi authorities themselves, including the SD (*Sicherheitsdienst*—Security Service) and Gestapo, the RSF, and naturally Reich Education Minister Rust. Yet somehow the wrath of the National Socialist potentates failed to descend on the heads of the recalcitrant women students. This surprising leniency had nothing to do with noble magnanimity on the part of the Nazis but was dictated by necessity. The prime concern of Germany's rulers was to secure an adequate flow of university-trained professionals to meet the demands created by the war on the academic labor market, and they realized only too well that women alone could supply this demand. To take sharp measures against women students, such as expulsion from the university, would therefore have been counterproductive. The words Hitler himself once used in one of his famous monologues perfectly illustrate the Nazis' dilemma, although he was in this case referring to intellectuals in general: "When I look at the intellectual classes among us, well, unfortunately we need them, you know; otherwise we might some day...exterminate them or something. But unfortunately we need them."[1]

Within the complex hierarchy of Nazi party and state, it was Rust, the Reich minister of education, who championed and virtually personified the policy of leniency under all circumstances vis-à-vis women students. His ministry, after all, was responsible for turning out the masses of academics and experts Germany needed, so the personnel "supply crisis" (*Nachwuchsfrage*) in the academic professions remained his top priority for the duration of the war. Hitler himself, and most Nazi planners with him, appreciated and respected Rust's objectives. But a number of Nazi leaders, while admitting the importance of allowing women to supplement the dwindling numbers of professionals, were nevertheless more concerned with the need to solve the thousand and one problems the war created each day. In particular, acute labor shortages in industry made them cast covetous eyes on the thousands of female students at Germany's universities, who constituted an ideal pool of labor from which, as they saw it, they ought to be permitted to draw from time to time, whenever the exigencies of war required it. Fritz Todt, the Reich minister of armament, proposed in March 1941 to mobilize young women students for a large-scale compulsory "war service" in the armament industry during the summer holiday. He took his cue from a suggestion made by Hitler in a speech a few days earlier, to the effect that a greater contribution to the war effort would be demanded from German women.[2] Todt must have been aware, moreover, that the coming attack on the Soviet Union would entail the mobilization of huge numbers of men, so that the labor market would be subjected to increased pressure, which might be relieved somewhat by putting women students to work in the factories during their holidays. Rust, however, strongly opposed any initiative that threatened to send even the slightest ripple through the relatively privileged academic world where Germany's new crops of professionals were being trained. This episode was to set the stage for a tug-of-war over women students which was to last until the end of the war. Other than Todt, Rust's antagonists in this struggle would include the plenipotentiary for labor mobilization, Fritz Sauckel; "labor service" leader Konstantin Hierl; the chief of the high command of the armed forces, Wilhelm Keitel; and eventually Todt's successor as Reich minister of armament and ammunition, Albert Speer.

In spite of Rust's opposition, Todt prevailed, and on March 17, 1941, the *Führer*'s deputy, Hess, formally ordered the mobilization of women students for a compulsory action in the armament industry during the summer.[3] But Rust managed to limit the damage by proclaiming that this "armament service" (*Rüstungseinsatz*) was to be the only obligatory "war service" action involving women students in 1941.[4] In addition, he restricted the duration of the project to ten weeks of the summer recess. It was to start on July 28 and end on October 4.[5] Women students thus salvaged at least the early part of their holiday, but their "armament service" was still two weeks longer than a similar action involving male students. In almost apologetic terms the deputy leader of the RSF, one Gmelin, explained that this was justified by "the fact that female students may continue their studies during the war without interruption, while male students may be and are in effect drafted for military service." He added that such an action was necessary because 1941 was to be "the year of decision," implying that it was to be a one-time sacrifice that would not have to be repeated in the future since the war would soon be over.[6]

At first the instructions for the "armament service" looked draconic. All women students, regardless of semester or faculty, were to be called up by the local representatives of the RSF. Then between July 7 and 12 they were to report to the labor office (*Arbeitsamt*) of their hometown, which would assign them to a factory. The women were sternly warned that any attempts to dodge the service were not to be treated lightly but would make the perpetrator subject to criminal prosecution.[7] In reality, however, exemptions from the service could be obtained for a plethora of reasons. Women could be excused from participation if they could present a certificate of poor health or physical disability signed by a physician of the Student Aid Foundation (*Studentenwerk*), or if they could demonstrate that they had final examinations in the winter semester 1941/42. The same was true for female working students who could convince authorities that they relied on a summer job to finance their studies, and for women from peasant families who could prove that they were needed to help on the parental farm. Women from large families likewise qualified for an exemption, and so did women students who had been accepted for the *Osteinsatz* or the "war propaganda service."[8] Female students who felt they were entitled to an exemption for a reason other than those listed above were given ample opportunity to plead their case. For one thing, they were granted a personal interview with the local ANSt leader in order to discuss the merits of their case, and the official instructions clearly specified that the ANSt leader had full authority to grant such requests.[9] There is little doubt that those who decided to apply to be freed from the service stood a good chance of succeeding. Available statistics bear this out. At Frankfurt University, 136 out of a total of 343 women students—nearly 40 percent—were in effect freed from participation in the "armament service."[10] In the Brandenburg region, the flood of applications for exemptions was so high that, in an effort to stem it, the RSF leader resorted to financial sanctions. On June 21 he decreed that all exempted students had to pay a special "exemption fee" (*Beurlaubungsgebühr*) of two Reichsmarks.[11] It was a futile effort, for the "armament service" was so unpopular that the payment of a few marks was considered a small price to pay to escape its obligations. Confidential reports of the SD, the Security Service of Himmler's SS, leave no doubt that the attitude of the university students of both sexes towards the "armament service" left much to be desired. Informants noticed very little enthusiasm for the service but found widespread lethargy and even open criticism.[12] Students who had not been able to obtain an official exemption used a thousand and one tricks to dodge the service. Some changed their addresses without telling the authorities, so that they never received the official summons to report to the labor office. Another subterfuge, brilliant in its simplicity, was widely used: students would officially ex-matriculate at the end of the summer semester of 1941 in order to escape the jurisdiction of the RSF and the obligations of the "armament action," which affected only students; at the start of the new semester they simply rematriculated. Practices such as these were so widespread that the RSF found it necessary to send out a special circular to warn its regional and local leaders to be on guard against them.[13] But it is hardly likely that these instructions produced substantial results, since the enforcement of the "armament service" obligations was impeded not only by the resourcefulness of the dodgers but also by an obvious reluctance on the part of Reich Education Minister Rust to take strong action against them. Rust was simply not willing to impose sanctions that might jeopardize anyone's studies. After all, he remained infinitely more concerned about the issue of the personnel supply for the academic professions, which was the responsibility of his ministry, than about the "armament service," a scheme that had been forced on him by the minister of armament and the labor minister because it served *their* purposes. The attitude of Rust in this respect is best illustrated by his curt refusal of a proposal to make registration or re-registration at the university conditional on written proof of participation in the "armament service." He used the excuse that such a sanction would be very difficult to implement, but that was pure hypocrisy. In reality, he was only too happy to be able to obstruct the enforcement of "armament service" regulations.[14] "Departmental jealousy" (*Ressortegoismus*), an aspect of the "institutional chaos" (*Ämterchaos*) that characterized the Third Reich,[15] thus played into the hands of students who wanted to shirk their "war service" duties. Rust's recalcitrance vis-à-vis his ministerial colleagues gave those students who had not already received an official exemption from the "armament service" carte blanche to dodge it.

The RSF, concerned more with its own reputation than with the truth, was not about to admit that the performance of women students in the "armament service" had been less than impressive. Instead, its leaders chose to cover up the failure with specious rhetoric and spurious figures. It was claimed, for instance, that over nineteen thousand students of both sexes had taken part in the "armament service" of 1941[16] and that women students had performed excellently in such vitally important enterprises as the Heinkel and Junker aviation industries, Krupp's artillery factory, the electro-technical Siemens works, and the chemical enterprise IG-Farben.[17] Furthermore, the "armament service" of the female students was described as "a great social experiment," "a patriotic service,"[18] and even "a contribution to the victory in our struggle against world plutocracy, Bolshevism, and Jewry."[19] The coverup was successful indeed: on October 6, 1941, the *Führer* himself sent a telegram to Reich Student Leader Scheel to congratulate him on the presumably outstanding performance of Germany's young men and women students in the "armament service."[20]

If the achievement of women students was far from impressive in the "armament service," which was compulsory, it cannot have been much better in the other, voluntary "war service" actions. This suspicion is borne out by the evidence contained in the relatively few reports that survived the war. Female students behaved very poorly in the *Westeinsatz* ("service in the west"), a scheme modelled on the *Osteinsatz* but carried out in the territories Germany had acquired as a result of the victorious western campaign of the spring of 1940, mainly Alsace-Lorraine. Here too the Nazis' plans called for the expulsion of the local population and the settlement of ethnic Germans. Like the *Osteinsatz*, the *Westeinsatz* was intended as an elitist undertaking restricted to students whose National Socialist integrity was firmly established. Only 260 university students of both sexes were thus found worthy of participation in the "service in the west" in 1941.[21] In view of the presumably high caliber of the volunteers, however, the performance of the women was disappointing. To give but one example, a group of ANSt members from Hamburg were dissatisfied with the quality of their lodgings and protested loudly. Their general conduct was so bad that their leader was arrested in Paris by the SD. Other groups did "not better at all," according to confidential reports, and nowhere was the service taken seriously, although the *Westeinsatz* was supposed to be an elitist action of great responsibility and importance. Some women, together with a number of *Wehrmacht* officers, painted the town red; others left prematurely on leaves or returned too late from leaves. Incidents such as these were not at all isolated cases, but were said to occur "practically everywhere."[22] The debacle of the German coeds' "war service" of 1941 was thus every bit as much the work of the relatively few convinced Nazi women students as of the mass of those women who were either indifferent or opposed to National Socialism. Meanwhile, in numerous articles and reports the ANSt leadership sought to create the image of a German female student who devoted every minute of her leisure time to the war effort, be it in the "armament service," in the Red Cross, as railway conductor or as postal clerk, as "communications aide" (*Nachrichtenhelferin*) for the *Wehrmacht*, as laborer on her parents' farm, or in some other capacity.[23]

As the *Blitzkrieg* phase of the war drew to a close towards the end of 1941, the Nazi leadership awoke to the realization that Germany could no longer escape the economic implications of a long, drawn-out war. This had important consequences with regard to the labor policies of the regime. Since the failure to decide the war against the Soviet Union in a brief and victorious campaign made it impossible to replenish the German labor force with the hundreds of thousands of men at the front, the Hitler government had to face the fact that the Reich's economy would have to rely on alternative sources of labor for a long time to come. It is against this background that Sauckel's appointment as plenipotentiary for labor mobilization in March 1942 must be viewed. As the Nazi leadership invested great confidence in the potential of forced foreign labor, Sauckel was to devote his efforts mostly to the compulsory mobilization of foreign civilians for work in Germany. Consequently, the number of foreign workers (*Fremdarbeiter*) increased spectacularly, from 2.6 million in May 1942 to 4.6 million a year later.[24] Sauckel was in effect putting all his money on this one horse, for comparatively little was done to mobilize the labor potential of Germany's women, an alternative championed by Speer.[25] As a matter of fact, the number of female workers was allowed to decline in 1942, from 2.58 million in May to 2.49 million in November.[26] All this had relatively little to do with ideological objections to the use of women's labor. Of greater importance was the pragmatic calculation that there was no need to draft women, at least for the time being. Having the German collapse of 1918 in mind,[27] Hitler undoubtedly feared that drafting women might do a great deal of damage to the morale of the home front. If ideological considerations had taken precedence over practical calculations, he would certainly have done something to check the influx of women into the labor force in the years before the war, when practical objections to ideological considerations had been much less urgent than they were to be during the war. Even then, however, he had not lifted a finger.

On occasion, Sauckel faced localized and short-term labor shortages that required small numbers of highly mobile and relatively skilled personnel and that often presupposed a certain amount of National Socialist and patriotic loyalty, preconditions that precluded the utilization of foreign workers. In such cases Sauckel liked to resort to the compulsory mobilization of university students of both sexes, not only during the holidays but also during the academic year. Women students were thus forced to interrupt their studies in order to serve temporarily in the Red Cross or to help out in such operations as the *Kinderlandverschickung*, the evacuation of children from two to six years of age from cities threatened by air attacks to the countryside.[28] This greatly alarmed Reich Education Minister Rust, who felt that students ought to be able to pursue their academic activities without interference. On May 19, 1942, he sent a strongly worded protest to Sauckel, asserting the priority of the students' study over their involvement in these aid actions. The Reich education minister curtly informed his colleague that he would no longer permit the organization of any type of aid action during the academic year, and reminded him that the Reich could ill afford a disruption of the training of the vitally needed academic professionals. In addition, he denied the local offices of Sauckel's organization the right to interfere in the preparation of the students' "war service" actions during the holidays. In order to guarantee its effectiveness, Rust claimed, the "war service" of the young academics had to be organized on a nationwide scale by the RSF alone. In concluding, Rust reemphasized his standpoint that even during the holidays students should have plenty of time to devote to their studies.[29].

As a result of Rust's exertions, Germany's women students were free to concentrate on their academic work and future professional career during virtually all of 1942. They certainly did not have to worry much about "war service" obligations, for the only major "war service" action turned out to be a second large-scale "armament service" organized during the summer recess. In an effort to prevent this venture from finishing as ingloriously as the "armament service" of the previous year, the planners of the RSF took certain precautions this time. They set up a special department, the "Aid Action Leadership" (*RSF-Einsatzleitung*), to supervise the operation and installed its headquarters in the prestigious Adlerhof Hotel in Berlin.[30] It was hoped that the students would thus be made aware that the eyes of the nation would be on them, so that they would feel obliged to deliver a particularly impressive performance in the "war service." On the other hand, the new "armament service" was to be shorter than the first one. Instead of ten weeks, the women only had to serve eight weeks, and they were offered a choice between the period from July 6 to August 29 and the time between August 3 and September 26. Participants in the "armament service" were thus not forced to sacrifice their entire holiday. In addition, they were promised financial remuneration for their work, based on the prevailing wages for working students.[31] But in spite of these incentives, the second "armament service" was no more successful than the first. Many students, both male and female, again neglected the "war service" obligations or served only reluctantly.[32] Official reports abounded with references to cases of loafers who dodged the service in spite of threats that "the sharpest punishment" would be meted out to them.[33] In view of the experiences of the previous year, however, almost everybody was aware that these were empty threats and that the authorities were reluctant to take drastic measures against dodgers. Although twenty thousand students of both sexes had been expected to take part,[34] only slightly more than twelve thousand actually fulfilled their "war service" duty, and even that figure may have been inflated.[35] But such unpleasant technicalities did not deter Scheel from publicly claiming that the second "armament service" of the university students had been an overwhelming success.[36]

Since the catastrophe at Stalingrad forced the Nazi leadership to replenish the Reich's armed forces by withdrawing 1.5 million men from its labor force,[37] the German labor market was subjected to increased pressures from 1943 onward. Moreover, as the potential of forced labor from the occupied territories had been virtually exhausted by that time, the Nazis were left with no alternative but finally to turn to Germany's women in order to resupply the labor force.[38] As early as January 1943, Sauckel thus decreed the compulsory mobilization of all women between seventeen and forty-five years of age into a gigantic "labor draft" (*Arbeitseinsatz*), a decision endorsed by Goebbels in his famous speech on "total war" of February 18, 1943.[39] But although it was specified that exemptions to this draft were to be granted only in exceptional cases—on account of pregnancy, for instance—Sauckel's decree was practically left unenforced and soon earned the popular epithet of "rubber decree."[40]. Still, hundreds of thousands of "Sauckel women" (*Sauckelfrauen*) joined the German labor force as a result of it.[41]

In the weeks following the proclamation of Sauckel's decree, Reich Education Minister Rust was greatly concerned that the labor draft regulations might herald the end of the *Frauenstudium*, as all young women over seventeen years of age were liable for the draft. Since women accounted for 33.9 percent of all university students in the winter semester 1942/43,[42] the personnel supply for the academic professions would conceivably have been in jeopardy. Rust therefore appealed directly to Hitler, and with success. He secured a blanket exemption from the labor draft for female university students, and on March 16 or 22 the *Führer* even issued a statement in which he declared academic studies to be "important for the war effort" (*kriegswichtig*).[43] Rust himself reciprocated with a promise intended to impress Hitler, to pacify those within the Nazi leadership and the German public at large who may have questioned the wisdom and fairness of the exemption, and to warn women (and men) students that he was running out of patience with their lackadaisical attitude towards National Socialism in general and the war effort in particular. He publicly pledged nothing less than to remove all "lazy, unqualified, or unreliable" students from Germany's institutions of higher learning. A special committee was set up at all universities, consisting of the rector, one professor, and the local Nazi student leader; it was called the "Committee of Three" (*Dreierausschuss*) and was supposed to investigate complaints about individual students and to punish them if necessary. In principle, furthermore, each student was to be thoroughly checked after his or her second semester on "performance, conduct, and 'war service'." This investigation was referred to as the "scrutiny" (*Überprüfung*), and it purported to eliminate all those who failed to meet the rigid criteria that were henceforth to apply to Germany's academic youth.[44]

In the case of women students, who were notorious for their nonchalance, this *Überprüfung* was to be carried out "with special vigor and thoroughness."[45] Nazi coeds' leaders extolled the virtues of the new institution with great enthusiasm. It would pave the way, they claimed, for the admittedly belated emergence of "the new type of woman student who is the synthesis of study and 'war service,' the lively, intelligent young woman who thinks and acts according to National Socialist principles." On the other hand, it would guarantee the ruthless elimination of "women students who fail to meet those standards in their conduct and performance, and who fail to be models of duty towards the outside world, as every German woman student should be,...or those who are buried behind their books, stay-at-homes who do not take an active part in the history of our time."[46] ANSt leaders received orders to report such women, particularly those who neglected their studies in favor of "personal enjoyment" and those whose conduct revealed a lack of "human and psychological maturity or intellectual, moral, and ideological integrity."[47]

But Rust's vocal firmness, duly echoed by the chorus of Nazi women student leaders, was to yield no more impressive results than his leniency had produced in previous years. First, unprecedented numbers of young women who would not normally have considered an academic career "fled to the universities" in order to escape the obligations of Sauckel's labor draft.[48] No less than 8,917 young women thus matriculated for the first time at the start of the summer semester of 1943, an increase of nearly 80 percent over the 4,985 who had done so in the winter semester 1942/43.[49] Exasperated, Sauckel watched these women slip through the net of his draft, but he had no choice except to comply with Hitler's directive, which had created this loophole. Nevertheless, with the support of Wilhelm Keitel, Hans Lammers, and Martin Bormann, Sauckel managed to persuade Rust that women students ought to make some contribution to the war effort in the form of another large-scale "armament service" during the summer holiday.[50] But the familiar pattern of a disappointing "war service" performance of women students remained unbroken in 1943. In contrast to previous years, the RSF did not even try to claim any credit for their efforts this time. And in private at least, Nazi student leaders vented their frustration at what one of them termed "the exceptional underperformance" (*die ausserordentliche Unterleistung*) of female students in the "war service."[51] In spite of this, the "Committees of Three" remained remarkably inactive. The RSF freely admitted that "only in the most extreme cases" were women ever expelled from the university, although this was supposed to be the standard punishment for neglect of "war service" duties.[52] In all of 1943, a grand total of 250 students fell victim to the *Überprüfung*,[53] not quite 0.5 percent of the approximately 60,000 men *and* women who were studying in the Reich at the time. Among those very few, moreover, there were at least some women who appealed the verdict and actually managed to obtain permission from the Reich ministry of education to return to their studies.[54] All this revealed only too clearly that Rust's tough rhetoric had been intended for the gallery, that his promises and measures had been tactical maneuvers aimed at softening the impact of the proclamation of Sauckel's labor draft, and that in reality Rust was not prepared to do anything that might have jeopardized his efforts to keep the Reich supplied with sufficient numbers of university-trained professionals.

In fact, it took acts of outright resistance to exhaust Rust's patience and force him to resort to sharp punitive measures. To our knowledge, this happened only once—in the case of the White Rose (*Weisse Rose*) student resistance group in Munich and Hamburg. The Munich episode is well known and need not be recounted here.[55] But it is interesting that, aside from Sophie Scholl herself, various other women students were involved in the circle around Professor Kurt Huber, including Traute Lafrenz, Gisela Schertling, and Katharina Schüddekopf.[56] After their arrest, these women were formally expelled from the university by the Munich "Committee of Three" and on the following day, February 22, 1943, Sophie Scholl and her brother Hans were executed as "former students."[57] The other female members of the White Rose group were sentenced to one year imprisonment.[58]

Of particular interest within the frame of reference of this study are the circumstances that led to the intensification of the pamphlet campaign of the White Rose, which had already started in the summer of 1942, and thus to the arrest of its members in early 1943. In a speech to the students of Munich University on January 13, 1943, regional Nazi leader Paul Giesler alluded to the phenomenon of "the flight to the universities" (*Die Flucht ins Studium*). His remark that "universities should not be safe havens for little rich girls who want to shirk the obligations of the labor draft" offended his female listeners especially. Moreover, when he suggested that women would do better "to donate a child to the *Führer*" than "to waste their time at the university," and added that his crafty assistants would be available for that purpose,[59] a number of female students walked out. Some male students are reported to have left with them in a show of solidarity.[60]

This incident reflected the defiant attitude of many women students who were aware that, in view of official personnel objectives in the academic professions, the Nazis could ill afford to remove them from the universities. Merely the fact that they could stage this walkout with impunity proved how correct they were. It also demonstrated that the totalitarian Nazi state was willing to tolerate a surprisingly high degree of defiance. Yet at the same time this event marked the limit of both the students' recalcitrance and the Nazis' patience. White Rose members totally misread the situation when they interpreted this incident as evidence that the university was ripe for a showdown with the regime. They viewed the walkout as merely a prelude to even greater acts of opposition on the part of men and women students. With an intensified pamphlet campaign they hoped to sustain the momentum and fan the flame of student resistance. Characteristically, Sophie Scholl would respond to her condemnation to death with the almost triumphant remark, made to a cellmate, ''Now it is certain that the students will revolt!''[61] In reality, however, the defiant reaction to Giesler's speech had marked the high tide of student opposition, and the frantic activities of the White Rose in the following weeks failed to touch off the hoped-for rebellion. But now the Nazis' patience was exhausted, and when the conspirators were arrested, partly because of their own recklessness in handing out pamphlets in broad daylight, no mercy was shown. The sudden draconian measures of the authorities were more than sufficient to bring into line those male and female students who had previously permitted themselves the luxury of nonconformity because the Nazis had appeared reluctant to take sanctions. A DSt rally, organized one week after the execution of the Scholls in order to condemn the actions of the White Rose, drew masses of students undoubtedly including some of those who had walked out on Giesler only a month earlier.

The White Rose affair was an uncharacteristic but not entirely isolated episode of resistance at the German universities. In late 1942 or early 1943, a student resistance cell had also been founded at Hamburg University. Here too a number of women students were involved, including one Greta Rothe. Traute Lafrenz, mentioned earlier in connection with the Munich White Rose, also studied at Hamburg for a while and brought the Scholls' pamphlets there in the fall of 1942. The Hamburg group was not directly affected by the events in the Bavarian capital in February 1943 and was able to continue its activities. These activities included discussion sessions on such topics as Marxism, art, literature, and resistance at the universities, as well as the distribution of pamphlets, both those of the Munich group and their own. Greta Rothe, for instance, wrote a tract, ''Against Hitler and the War'' (*Gegen Hitler und Krieg*), with Heinz Kucharski. Contact was also established with other anti-Nazi groups, and financial support was organized for the widow of Professor Huber. Between November 1943 and March 1944, however, one member after another of the Hamburg group were arrested, including Greta Rothe. Some committed suicide; some perished in concentration camps; some fortunate ones were freed in the spring of 1945 by the Allies.[62] Even in Munich, finally, all forms of student resistance did not disappear with the liquidation of the White Rose. A few months after the execution of the Scholls, in April 1943, a so-called ''action Scholl'' (*Aktion Scholl*) opposition cell started to spread pamphlets that demanded "the liberation of Germany from Hitler and his co-criminals" and advocated somewhat unrealistically "the method of enlightenment and passive resistance" to achieve this end. The authors of the pamphlet cited the Scholls as "example[s] for the entire German opposition" and urged readers to spread their message to all their acquaintances. This appeal did not fall on deaf ears, for the tract spread as far as Frankfurt, where copies were confiscated by the SD in November 1943.[63]

In the fall of 1943, Rust's continuing efforts to secure an adequate supply of university-trained professionals for Germany were again threatened by Sauckel. This time Sauckel was scheming to call up all women from the last years of the secondary schools for the "labor draft." Had he succeeded, these women would have been prevented from completing their secondary school education and thus from ever moving on to the university. To make things even worse for Rust, Sauckel had found an accomplice in the person of "labor service" boss Hierl, who simultaneously prepared to call up ten thousand female high school graduates as "communication aides" for the air force and who was also putting pressure on female high school graduates to remain in the "labor service" organization as leaders on completion of their "labor service" duties rather than take up academic studies.[64] Rust responded to this twin challenge by seeking help from Lammers, chief of the Reich chancellery, and Göring.[65] Their joint efforts were crowned with success, for Sauckel's plans were rejected by Hitler, who realized—as Rust gleefully reminded Sauckel in a letter on November 2, 1943— that "these women are the last reserves for the academic professions."[66] A few months later, the Reich education minister likewise had his revenge against Hierl. On April 24, 1944, Rust was allowed to abrogate the "labor service" duty for female candidates for university studies, thus putting an end to Hierl's machinations with regard to the female high school graduates.[67]

For a short time, Rust could enjoy his triumph. Unprecedented numbers of women were allowed to register at the universities and pursue the studies of their choice without having to worry about the "labor service," "war service" actions, or other delays and interruptions. Occasional displays of loyalty to National Socialism, perhaps in the form of minor contributions to the work of the anemic ANSt, absolutely delighted the Nazi authorities, particularly since such gestures were no longer expected from women students. At the start of the summer semester 1944, no less than 11,387 young women matriculated for the first time at Germany's institutions of higher learning, compared to 4,515 in the previous semester.[68] Over forty thousand women accounted for 49.3 percent of all university students in the Reich during that spring,[69] and women could be found firmly entrenched even in faculties that ten years earlier had loomed as the impregnable bastions of academic male exclusionism. But this happy state of things changed quickly in the summer. The Allied armies landed in Normandy, and their rapid advances soon threatened the Reich itself. In the face of this

130   Women, Nazis, and Universities

danger, the Nazis proceeded to mobilize the nation's remaining energies for a desperate, ultimate effort.

On July 25, 1944, Hitler officially proclaimed the "total mobilization" (*totale Mobilmachung*; *totaler Einsatz*) of the German population and appointed Joseph Goebbels as Reich Plenipotentiary for Total Mobilization (*Reichsbevollmächtigter für den totalen Kriegseinsatz*).[70] Long-range considerations were hardly relevant at a moment when survival itself was the order of the day. Consequently, Rust's objective of securing an adequate supply of professionals for the future was subordinated to the efforts of men like Sauckel, Speer, Keitel, and Goebbels, whose immediate objective was nothing less (and little more) than survival.[71] Rust suddenly discovered that his Reich Education Ministry was a beleaguered fortress. Hitler himself had suggested in his decree of July 25 that all university students be mobilized without any further ado for a labor draft in the armament industry, and in the following weeks the Reich education minister was subjected to pressure from all sides to proceed immediately with the implementation of the *Führer*'s wishes. In early August, Rust was still struggling to forestall the inevitable, procrastinating and trying desperately to convince his colleagues and Hitler himself of the seriousness of the supply crisis in the academic professions.[72] But shortly thereafter he had to give in. Rust openly acknowledged defeat by accepting the fact that "the immediate day-to-day needs of the army and the armament industry [had] become so urgent that the securing of an adequate supply of academic professionals [had] to retreat before these needs."[73] In an undated letter to Goebbels, he declared his readiness to do whatever was necessary in order to make his contribution to "the present series of measures [which] represent a brief but intensive effort to bring about, by means of a mass levy on the front and in the country, and in a relatively short time, a decision in Germany's favor." He therefore consented "to place into the background his own concerns with regard to the training of academic professionals, which had hitherto determined his standpoint."[74] Although Rust clearly clung to the illusion that all this was to be only a temporary measure, he had thus nevertheless taken the step from which he had shrunk so long.

On September 1, 1944, Reich Education Minister Rust issued his first instructions for the implementation of the promises he had made to Goebbels. He introduced a total restriction on new matriculations from which only wounded soldiers and war widows were to be exempted. All graduates of secondary schools, who were thus prevented from taking up academic studies, were made available for work in the armament industry, and so were all students who had been in their first, second, or third semester in the summer of 1944, with the sole exception of the students of a number of important disciplines, such as mathematics, physics, and ballistics. Also drafted were all students of higher semesters in the faculties of law and political sciences, humanities and social sciences, foreign studies, agricultural sciences, architecture, and theology. Finally, medical students of the fourth to seventh semester were likewise called up.[75] These thousands of male and female students were to report immediately to the regional labor offices (*Gauarbeitsämter*) of Sauckel's organization, where they were to receive specific instructions with regard to their labor assignment.[76] As a result of these measures, seventy-seven faculties and five higher technical institutes (*Fachhochschulen*) closed their doors entirely, and in fifty-eight other faculties only the fifth and higher semesters continued their activities. Many faculties were merged in an effort to consolidate both human and material resources. The law faculties of Freiburg, Heidelberg, and Strassburg thus all moved to Tübingen; those of Munich and Würzburg moved to Erlangen; and those of Frankfurt, Giessen, and Cologne moved to Marburg.[77] But the mobilization of so many students at such short notice constituted a gargantuan task, encumbered further by frequent Allied air raids.[78] In addition, the local offices of Sauckel's organization often proved unable to accommodate all draftees and had to turn them back because no employment could be found for them. The students themselves displayed no more enthusiasm for the "war service" than in previous years and again proved their ingenuity in finding ways to shirk their obligations. Sauckel was infuriated, for example, by reports that many healthy young academics somehow managed to obtain certificates declaring them unfit for service. Finally, as late as the end of October great numbers of students, including 4,400 female students of medicine, had not yet been called up. It was therefore decided to allow them to register for the winter semester after all, on the understanding that they might be drafted at any time.[79] By the end of 1944, some 26,403 (or 64.1 percent) of all 42,210 women who had studied at German universities in the preceding summer semester had been drafted for the "total mobilization."[80] But even as National Socialist Germany struggled through its death throes, over ten thousand women were permitted to continue their studies by the same Nazi rulers who, it had been expected in 1933, would not rest before they had driven the last woman from the German universities.

In his recent impressive study of education in modern Europe, Fritz Ringer suggests two criteria for gauging the socially "progressive" character of a system of higher education, that is, the degree to which an increasing proportion of representatives of the lower and lower middle classes get to share in the benefits of a university education traditionally reserved for the socially privileged. One method consists in the calculation of absolute and comparative "[university] access percentages," the percentage of children within various social groups which eventually reach a university level of education. This permits an assessment of the comparative "university access chances" of young members of the working class, the middle class, and so on. Second, by dividing its share of the entire university student population by its share of the occupational census, one may arrive at the "educational opportunity ratio" of a given class, whereby a ratio of 1 amounts to the statistically perfect level of social progressiveness.[81] In a similar way, one can also monitor the level of emancipation of women within systems of higher education. Just as social progressiveness is measured by the "university access chances" and "educational opportunity ratios" of the representatives of the lower strata of the social pyramid, the degree of academic emancipation of women depends on their "university access percentage" and "educational opportunity ratio." Judging by these criteria, it cannot be denied that an unprecedented academic emancipation of German women took place during the war, even though its fruits were unevenly and unfairly distributed among social classes: the "university access chances" of women soared as the absolute number of women students rose from just over six thousand to more than forty thousand in a mere five years, between 1939 and 1944; and in 1944, when women (representing approximately 50 percent of all Germans) also accounted for half the German *student* population, their "educational opportunity ratio" virtually reached 1, the statistically perfect reflection of academic emancipation achieved.[82]

But the intrinsically misogynic Nazi regime deserves no credit for the impressive advances of German women in the field of higher education during the Second World War. The academic emancipation of women had never been among the objectives listed in the NSDAP party program. If increasing numbers of women were in fact allowed to study, it was merely because they alone were available to satisfy the professional personnel needs of the Nazi state at war. Women students were cynically manipulated as an "academic reserve regiment,"[83] which would undoubtedly have been disbanded as soon as a victorious end to the war had created the precondition for a return of men to the lecture halls. Moreover, we must question whether better educational opportunities for women were complemented by corresponding improved chances on the professional job market and by increased job satisfaction, remuneration, and prestige, in other words, by a proportionate amount of social mobility, but that is beyond the scope of this study.[84] In any case, Dörte Winkler suggests that female physicians, to name but one group of women professionals, remained excluded from better-paid positions and did not fully share in the prestige associated with the medical profession.[85]

There can be little doubt that even during the war the Nazis remained uninterested in the principle and opposed to the realization of a genuine academic (and professional) emancipation of German women. Moreover, the incentives they used to induce more women to study (solely because that suited their purposes) were hardly more effective than the measures they had introduced ten years earlier in an attempt to deflate female academic ambitions. Women's enrollments at the German institutions of higher learning had not declined in the 1930s on account of Nazi policy; in the 1940s they increased not (or only marginally) in response to initiatives of the Nazi regime but mainly on account of specific needs and opportunities created by the war, combined with favorable demographic realities, as we have seen.

A genuine academic emancipation of German women was not among the objectives of Nazi educational policy during the war, nor was it the accidental by-product of a number of Nazi initiatives in the sphere of university recruitment. Even though other causes were clearly at work, it is remarkable that an unprecedented academic emancipation of German women did take place at a time when the Reich was being ruled by a clique of rabid and avowed misogynists. We may question, moreover, whether better educational opportunities would have accrued to German women had another, presumably Weimar- or Bonn-style government been in power during the war. Uninhibited by awkward ideological objections to the use of women's labor, such a regime would probably not have balked, as the Nazis did, at ordering a full-scale mobilization of young women for work in the nation's vital industries, thus necessarily restricting their access to the universities. In any event, a government committed to a modicum of social fair play in the implementation of labor mobilization schemes would not have permitted masses of young (and not so young) well-to-do women to escape the hardships of the factory workshop in favor of the relative comforts of the university lecture halls, as happened in Germany during the war.

The fact that an unprecedented academic emancipation of German women was achieved under the auspices of a reactionary and misogynic rather than a democratic and progressive regime is not necessarily a historical anomaly. The distinguished political scientist Maurice Duverger has pointed out that women's *political* emancipation, too, as epitomized by their acquisition of the suffrage, was usually effected not by feminist efforts but by the exertions of men (and not necessarily sympathetic men) motivated by their own specific interests and objectives. This tended to be the case during periods of national emergencies in particular, such as revolutions and wars.[86] Germany during the Second World War, then, represented merely one such case, in which *antifeminist* men tolerated and even encouraged an academic emancipation of women because they hoped to use its fruits for their own purpose, namely, winning the war. In the bottom of their misogynic hearts, the Nazis were undoubtedly far from enthusiastic about the unexpected educational opportunities and benefits German women were thus allowed to enjoy. But the circumstances of war left them with no choice. Modern war proved to be an irresistible catalyst of change not only in the field of social stratification, as Arthur Marwick has demonstrated in the case of Great Britain,[87] but also with regard to women's role in society, at least in the case of Germany. It is one of the more subtle ironies of history that it fell to Mars, the eminently masculine god of war, thus to provoke the metamorphosis that transformed the misogynic masters of the Third Reich into reluctant emancipators of German women. But if the Nazis were forced to accept and even promote changes in the educational status of women which, to apply a remark made by Leila Rupp in a more general context, they would "normally [have] considered undesirable on a permanent basis,"[88] it is also true that German women would soon have been deprived again of their academic gains had Hitler's regime survived the war. As it turned out, they were unable to sustain the momentum of their academic emancipation and preserve its fruits, even though Nazi rule was obliterated and replaced in the two new German states by social and political systems that both purported to be democratic, progressive, and unprejudiced with regard to women. For precisely this is the most remarkable feature of the net gains made by German women in the field of higher education during the Second World War: that they have not (or just barely have) been equalled in West or East Germany to this very day.[89]

Conclusion

Throughout the 1920s and in the first half of the 1930s, the Nazis were unequivocally opposed to female academic aspirations. The National Socialist movement had originated as a sort of "male league" whose members liked to cultivate a tough brand of masculinity and sought to dissociate themselves from women and everything feminine. Male supremacist attitudes and misogynic prejudices had thus permeated the entire NSDAP from Hitler, the charismatic "male hero" at the top, down to macho paladins such as Alfred Rosenberg and to the lowliest storm trooper. Virtually without exception, these Nazis believed that women were intellectually unfit for university studies, that they were not (and could not be) genuinely interested in academic matters but attended university mainly in hopes of meeting a future husband, that women had no need for a higher education in any case, and finally, that a university was (or ought to be) a *Männerhaus*, a sanctuary reserved for men alone, like the army.

But Hitler and his followers opposed the *Frauenstudium* not merely on account of admittedly sterling male exclusionist principles. Concern about the decline of German fertility, which appeared to jeopardize the *Führer*'s dreams of conquest, provided a supplementary and more practical rationale. The Nazis were convinced that intellectual ambitions could only detract from what they considered to be women's "natural" vocation in society, namely, marriage and motherhood. Important eugenic benefits were therefore expected to flow from the proposed removal from the universities of young women in their childbearing prime. As the Nazis saw it, the academic disenfranchisement of women, like that of Jews, would also greatly relieve the twin evils of overcrowding at the universities and unemployment in the academic professions.

After Hitler's accession to power in January 1933, the Nazis were free to implement their misogynic views in the field of higher education, and they did.

But the campaign waged against women's academic aspirations consisted of intrinsically ineffective or irrelevant (although ostensibly energetic) measures. A *numerus clausus* on new matriculations of women was thus never enforced, and the restrictions on scholarships for female students affected a mere fraction—less than 2 percent—of all women students. "Tactics of exhortation and counsel" in guidance offices for female high school graduates proved futile, as no coercion was involved, and the formal exclusion of women from the allegedly unfeminine professions of judge and attorney merely closed careers that had never really been open to women anyway. An outburst of male supremacist chauvinism among both professors and male students certainly served to make life at the German universities unpleasant for female students in those years, but it failed to touch off a wholesale exodus of women from academe. Even the introduction of a compulsory pre-university "labor service" for female high school graduates did not restrict their access to the academic world in a significant way, as its protagonists had hoped.

There is no doubt that the Nazis could have taken much more drastic measures to curb the academic aspirations of German women, but perhaps they had hoped it would not be necessary to go that far, that young women would realize that they now lived in a men's world and stay away from the academic male bastions of their own volition. By 1935 at the latest, it was clear that this was not the case. It no longer mattered, however, for in the mid-1930s the Nazi attitude towards the *Frauenstudium* was changing dramatically.

From 1934 onward, the German birthrate was on the rise again, so that the eugenic argument against female academic ambitions gradually lost most of its urgency. In addition, the crisis of "academic unemployment" was solved as a result of the Hitler government's inflationary policies and the elimination from the liberal professions of innumerable "non-Aryans" and other enemies of National Socialism. The demands of the Four-Year Plan, moreover, soon created a very real shortage of university-trained specialists in all fields. But inadequate numbers of young men were available to replenish their ranks; impressed by the Nazis' own antiintellectual and militaristic propaganda, more and more ambitious male adolescents opted for the more exciting and prestigious careers unfolding in the new *Wehrmacht* and the SS. Furthermore, new enrollments of men at the German institutions of higher learning suffered badly as a result of the introduction of general military service in March 1935. The Reich could ill afford to be without sufficient numbers of engineers, chemists, and all other types of university-trained specialists at the very moment that it was pursuing self-sufficiency and preparing for war. And women alone could supplement the dwindling supply of these professionals. Germany's Nazi rulers thus reluctantly swallowed their male supremacist pride and muffled their antifeminist slogans. Without much fanfare, the admittedly ineffective restrictions they had earlier imposed on the *Frauenstudium* were removed. To give but one example, the *numerus clausus* was dropped as early as February 1935. All faculties and all institutions of higher learning henceforth welcomed with open arms young women equipped with the necessary intellectual qualifications.

The concomitant purge of the most fanatic misogynists within the NSDAP contributed greatly to the smooth execution of this about-face in the Nazi attitude towards female academic aspirations. On June 30, 1934, Röhm and many other high-ranking SA leaders, the proponents par excellence of National Socialist *Männerbund* mystique, were ruthlessly eliminated. Homosexuality, male supremacism, and misogyny were discredited in the process. Nazi male students, for instance, formerly always eager to establish bona fide male exclusionist credentials at the expense of their female colleagues, now openly declared their readiness to accept women as their academic "comrades" (*Kameradinnen*) at the university.

Although the campaign the Nazis waged against the *Frauenstudium* in 1933–1934 had been a lackluster affair, women's enrollments at the Reich's institutions of higher learning declined dramatically, not only in those years but until the end of the decade. But this decline had little or nothing to do with Nazi misogyny. It was a development that had started well before the *Machtergreifung*, affected male students as well, and persisted in the second half of the 1930s in spite of Nazi efforts to recruit more women for academic studies and careers. The inordinately small size of the age-groups born during the First World War, which were to come of university age from 1931 on, constituted the real cause of the decline in the number of both male and female students in the Reich in the 1930s. The impact of the Great Depression on the budgetary considerations of lower-middle-class families, and to a certain extent Nazi antiintellectualism, also played a role. The discrepancy between the dwindling enrollments of men and women reflected a marked tendency on the part of the students' lower-middle-class parents to favor studying sons over daughters, particularly in those years when the Great Depression dictated financial retrenchment and austerity. Although Nazi policy with regard to women students had a marginal effect at best on their matriculations, it did contribute to a shift in the social structure of the *Frauenstudium* after 1933 in favor of women of upper-middle-class background and at the expense of female representatives of lower-middle-class and working-class families.

When the Nazis came to power in 1933, German women had good reason to believe that the academic franchise they had won only a few decades earlier was in serious danger. Judging by its rhetoric, the Hitler regime was clearly determined to curb female "intellectual pretensions" once and for all and to send women into academic exile. In order to prevent the worst, Germany's women had to react. They never dreamed of challenging National Socialism itself but hoped to appease it and to awaken it to the *Frauenstudium*'s potential usefulness. Women described as "Nazi feminists" thus attempted cautiously to refute the eugenic and economic objections that had been raised against female academic ambitions and to demonstrate that it was not at all unbecoming for women to engage in intellectual activities, as the male supremacists contended. Logical arguments, however, never had much effect on the Nazis. They were more likely to be impressed (if not convinced) by the servile and flattering approach of Nazi women student leaders who promised, ostensibly on behalf of all the Reich's female university students, to make the social-Darwinian principle of "performance" the keystone of the *Frauenstudium* in the Third Reich. The "bluestocking" of the Weimar years, they pledged, was to make way for a new type of woman student, characterized by scholarly devotion, social activism, unconditional political commitment to the cause of National Socialism, and a guarantee of future eugenic performance.

Women did not lose the academic franchise in the Third Reich, mainly because its Nazi masters realized in due course that the *Frauenstudium* was a small yet indispensable cog in the gigantic economic machine they were gearing up for war. Therefore it did not matter much that the new, revolutionary, National Socialist type of woman student promised by the Nazi coeds' leaders never did make her appearance on the academic stage of the Third Reich. The reason for this was a patent lack of interest on the part of the majority of Germany's young female academics. Indeed, the history of the ANSt and Main Office VI reveals all too clearly the failure of Nazi women student leaders to implement the "performance principle" by means of an impressive series of extracurricular projects. Insufficient sanctions, lack of cooperation on the part of male student leaders, and chronic organizational difficulties made it virtually impossible to coerce women students into participation. And the vast majority of Germany's female student population displayed a total lack of interest in projects that were organized on a voluntary basis.

The service in the National Socialist welfare organizations thus attracted virtually only dedicated ANSt members, and the "factory service" drew disappointingly small numbers of volunteers in spite of massive recruitment propaganda. The lack of success of the "agricultural service" scheme, except perhaps in one summer, in 1937, was all the more conspicuous in view of the great economic, social, cultural, and ideological importance attached to it. If anything, the manifestations of the "socialistic" performance of women students revealed their immunity to the Nazi slogans of *Volksgemeinschaft* and "socialism of the deed." Other demonstrations of the "performance" of women students were even less convincing. Extracurricular sessions in "political education" purported to bear witness to the desire of all coeds to assimilate the "racial-political" teachings of National Socialism but were restricted to members of the ANSt only. Women students were strongly encouraged to demonstrate their intellectual prowess in experiments hailed as the harbingers of a new, genuinely German, and truly National Socialist scholarship. But the "faculty work" was hampered by the small number of women in each discipline, and practically only the medical "faculty work" turned out to be a viable undertaking. Furthermore, in the Reich Vocational Contest female university students generally did not perform impressively, although participating teams of zealous individuals went to great lengths to tell the Nazi organizers precisely what they wanted to hear and thus earned some imposing prizes, including the title of "Reich victor." The paramilitary "women's service" training was the only extracurricular activity of women students to achieve a measure of success, but this was at least partly due to the useful practical experience to be gained in courses such as those in first aid. In contrast, "cultural work" was largely a fiasco, and the Nazi women student leaders ended up trying to becloud the failure of their attempt to raise the cultural level of the female student population by emphasizing the artistic accomplishments of a few individuals. Much the same was true for the physical performance of female university students. A grandiose program of compulsory extracurricular sports, intended to improve the physical condition of all women students, failed miserably, but the ANSt leaders found consolation in the accomplishments of German women athletes in the 1936 Olympics and in the individual athletic performances of women students at the occasion of the annual student sport championships.

With the exception perhaps of a few difficult years in the wake of the *Machtergreifung*, women of the Third Reich were quite free to register at a university, pursue the studies of their choice, and graduate, if they possessed the necessary intellectual qualifications and could afford the rising cost of academic studies. Outward displays of conformity and loyalty to the regime were required, but that was accomplished easily enough by the acquisition of an ANSt membership card or by occasional token participation in the activities of Main Office VI. Because the overwhelming majority of women students were primarily (if not solely) concerned with their studies and future career, they readily complied with these conditions, but beyond that they would not go. Their general mood was one of apathy and indifference to the slogans of National Socialism. In this respect they resembled their upper-middle-class fathers, who did not mind going through the formality of joining the NSDAP but loathed its pedestrian activism and "socialistic" appeal. Membership in the Nazi coeds' organizations meant little more to the rank and file than possession of a membership card. Many women preferred to vent their energies in the familiar, denominational organizations for women students, which continued to exist until 1938, or even in the BDM or the NSF, not because of Nazi sympathies but because these party formations offered plentiful prospects for future career opportunities. But the widespread lethargy was most glaringly reflected in the failure of women students to display any enthusiasm for the extracurricular activities. If they ever did participate voluntarily at all, it was hardly as a result of sympathy for the Nazi cause. More likely they calculated that they occasionally had to remit this small token in order to safeguard their place in the academic sun or to protect future professional opportunities in what was after all a Nazi state. Furthermore, participation sometimes yielded a certificate that might benefit their studies and career. As a general rule, however, female students other than a small nucleus of fanatic ANSt members could not be counted on to fulfill their "duty of honor" vis-à-vis the regime and the entire *Volksgemeinschaft*. And they never even came close to implementing the "performance principle," which in the minds of their Nazi leaders was to have been the sine qua non of the *Frauenstudium* in the Third Reich.

The considerations that prompted the about-face in the Nazi attitude towards female academic ambitions in the mid-1930s argued even more strongly in favor of the *Frauenstudium* during the war. Since growing numbers of young men were needed to serve as fodder for Hitler's insatiable war machine, the Reich suffered from an increasingly severe shortage of university-trained professionals. Unlike the labor shortages in agriculture and industry, this presented a problem that could not be alleviated by the forcible mobilization of prisoners of war, concentration camp inmates, or foreign slave labor. Instead, the Nazis were forced to capitalize more and more on the same "female intellectual pretensions" they had so frivolously despised and condemned a few years earlier. Conse-quently, the war years were to witness the interesting spectacle of an intrinsically misogynic regime virtually humiliating itself in an effort to induce young women to take up university studies. An impressive although not very effective series of incentives and facilities thus combined with other, more important factors to touch off an unprecedented rise in female university enrollments. Foremost among these factors we must rank the desire of many young upper-middle-class women to escape the obligations of the "labor draft." Whereas young working-class women were forced to take up poorly paid, unpleasant, and often dangerous jobs in the war industry, academic studies were available to women of the financially stronger classes as a medium that permitted them to absolve—or at least *appear* to absolve—their patriotic duty in a pleasant, privileged, and ul-timately profitable way. No wonder, then, that innumerable well-to-do women of all ages, regardless of marital status, became aware of an academic vocation at some time during the war, particularly when Nazi leaders like Sauckel or Hitler himself rattled the "war service" saber.

The circumstances of war also served to crack the thin veneer of outward loyalty that had covered up the apathy of the great majority of German women students in the 1930s, and revealed the indifference or even outright hostility to National Socialism which lay beneath the surface. More than ever before, joining the ANSt was a meaningless formality, and reports of Nazi coeds' leaders in-dicated that the few membership obligations were consistently neglected by the rank and file. But women students not only declined to swallow the tasteless Nazi medicine their leaders would have liked to administer to them in the ANSt dispensary; their "exceptional underperformance" in a multitude of "war serv-ice" projects also exposed their lack of National Socialist loyalty and patriotic dedication as the Nazis understood it. And even as social discipline was breaking down everywhere in the Reich under the pressures of war, women students earned particular notoriety on account of spectacular violations of conventional and National Socialist precepts of morality. Finally, relatively small numbers of women students, exemplified by the courageous female members of the White

Rose group, engaged in full-fledged acts of resistance and eventually paid for their opposition to the Hitler regime with their freedom or even their lives.

The White Rose episode, however, was atypical not only with regard to the attitude of women (and men) students, but also with regard to the reaction of the Nazi authorities. Throughout the war the Nazis displayed a surprising degree of leniency in response to the well-known recalcitrance of female university students. The reason for this was that they could not afford to take effective punitive measures such as expulsion from the university, since that would have jeopardized the vital personnel supply for the academic professions. Reich Education Minister Rust, in particular, who was responsible for this supply, thus became an indulgent protector of Germany's women students. Not only did he look the other way whenever they permitted themselves disloyal liberties or flagrantly neglected their "war service" duties, he virtually encouraged his vassals in the RSF and the ANSt to orchestrate cynical coverup actions that permitted female students to bask publicly in the glory of fictitious patriotic exploits. This enabled him to enlist Hitler's decisive support in his struggle to prevent Speer, Sauckel, Goebbels, and other Nazi bosses from dislodging women students from the ivory tower of academe in order to mobilize them for the war effort. It was not until the fall of 1944, when the war was already lost, that Rust had to give in. But even though he had promised to close the universities and make all students available for service in the war industries, the Reich education minister kept scheming until the very end to allow large numbers of women to continue their studies.

The incongruous result of twelve years of misogynic Nazi rule, then, was that—for an admittedly all-too-short moment in the history of higher education in Germany—women achieved academic parity with men at the universities of the Reich.

Appendix: Statistical Data

Table 1. Crude Birthrate, Absolute Number of Live Births, and Absolute Number of Marriages in Germany, 1871–1943

Year	Birthrate	Live Births	Marriages
1871/75	38.8	—	—
1901	35.7	—	—
1910	29.8	1,924,778	496,396
1913	27.5	1,838,750	513,283
1914	26.8	1,818,596	460,608
1915	20.4	1,382,546	278,208
1916	15.2	1,029,484	279,076
1917	13.9	912,109	308,446
1918	14.3	926,813	352,543
1919	20.0	1,260,500	844,339
1920	25.9	1,599,287	894,978
1921	25.3	1,581,130	740,330
1922	23.0	1,424,804	690,947
1923	21.2	1,318,489	588,069
1926	19.6	—	—
1930	17.6	1,144,151	570,241
1931	16.0	1,047,775	522,881
1932	15.1	993,126	516,793
1933	14.7	971,174	638,573
1934	18.0	1,198,350	740,165
1935	18.9	1,263,976	651,435
1936	19.0	1,278,853	609,770
1937	18.8	1,277,046	620,265
1938	19.6	1,348,534	645,062
1939	20.4	1,413,230	774,163
1940	20.0	1,402,040	612,946
1941	18.6	1,308,367	504,543
1942	14.9	—	—
1943	16.0	—	—

Sources: *Statistisches Jahrbuch*, 1917, p. 5; 1921/22, pp. 34–36; 1930, p. 32; 1935, p. 36; 1941/42, pp. 66, 72; Knodel, p. 5; Loewenberg, p. 1475.

Table 2. Scholarships for Women Students, 1932–1934

| Semester | Number of Scholarships | | Women's Percentage of: | |
	Total	Women	All Scholarships	Student Body
SS 1932	4,212	471	11.18	15.4
WS 32/33	4,472	489	10.93	15.8
SS 1933	4,107	354	11.05	15.5
WS 33/34	4,280	389	9.09	14.5
SS 1934	3,925	274	6.93	11.4

Source: "Förderung von Studentinnen," in *Reichsstudentenwerk...1935* [not paginated].

Table 3. Women's Share in the German Labor Force, 1933–1940

Year	Total Employed (in thousands)	Employed Women (in thousands)	Women's Percentage of All Employed
1933	13,433	4,751	35.36
1934	15,470	5,052	32.65
1935	16,424	5,246	31.94
1936	17,592	5,507	31.30
1937	18,885	5,894	31.20
1938	20,114	6,306	31.35
1939	20,813	6,822	32.77
1940	19,604	7,115	36.29

Source: *Statistisches Jahrbuch*, 1941/42, p. 410.
Note: Percentages computed. The figures cover all *Arbeiter* and *Angestellten*.

Table 4. Decline in the Number of Women Students at All German Universities, 1933–1939

Semester	Total Students	Female Students	%	SS 1933 = 100
SS 1933	113,247	17,685	15.6	100
WS 33/34	104,409	15,176	14.5	85.8
SS 1934	91,224	12,630	13.8	71.4
WS 34/35	84,704	11,717	13.8	66.2
SS 1935	71,624	10,190	14.2	57.6
WS 35/36	75,205	10,286	13.6	58.1
SS 1936	66,548	8,849	13.3	50.0
WS 36/37	62,810	8,313	13.2	47.0
SS 1937	57,001	7,296	12.8	41.2
WS 37/38	56,395	6,721	11.9	38.0
SS 1938	54,873	6,337	11.5	35.8
WS 38/39	55,944	6,587	11.7	37.2
SS 1939	56,557	6,372	11.2	35.8

Source: Lorenz, I, pp.148–51.
Note: The figures are for all *Hochschulen*. At the *Universitäten*, the number of women students declined from 16,210 in SS 1933 to 5,777 in SS 1939, their share of the student population from 18.2% to 14.2%, according to data in Lorenz, I, p. 104.

Table 5. New Registrations of Women at All German Universities, 1932–1939

Semester	Absolute Number of All Female New Registrations	Women's % of All New Registrations	1932/33 = 100
1932/33	4,618	18.46	100
1933/34	3,544	17.27	76.74
1934/35	1,595	13.25	34.54
1935/36	2,046	15.70	44.30
1936/37	1,642	17.57	35.56
1937/38	1,511	12.37	32.72
1938/39	1,898	13.99	41.10

Source: Lorenz, I, p. 52. Kotschnig, p. 207, has slightly different figures.

Table 6. The Decline of the German Student Population, 1931–1939

Year	A. All Students Absolute Numbers	SS 1931 = 100	Rate of Decline
SS 1931	130,886	100	
WS 31/32	—	—	
SS 1932	126,381	96.5	−3.5
SS 32/33	119,702	91.4	−5.1
SS 1933	113,247	86.5	−4.9
WS 33/34	104,409	79.7	−6.8
SS 1934	91,224	75.4	−4.3
WS 34/35	84,704	64.7	−10.7
SS 1935	71,624	54.7	−10.0
WS 35/36	75,205	57.4	−2.7
SS 1936	66,548	50.8	−6.6
WS 36/37	62,810	47.9	−2.9
SS 1937	57,001	43.5	−4.4
WS 37/38	56,395	43.0	−0.5
SS 1938	54,873	41.9	−1.1
WS 38/39	55,944	42.7	−0.8
SS 1939	56,667	43.2	−0.5

Year	B. Male Students Absolute Numbers	SS 1931 = 100	Rate of Decline
SS 1931	109,812	100	
WS 31/32	—	—	
SS 1932	106,384	97.8	−3.2
WS 32/33	100,889	91.8	−5.0
SS 1933	95,562	87.0	−4.8
WS 33/34	89,233	81.2	−5.8
SS 1934	78,544	71.5	−9.7
WS 34/35	72,987	66.4	−5.1
SS 1935	61,434	55.9	−10.5
WS 35/36	64,919	59.1	−3.2
SS 1936	57,699	52.5	−6.6
WS 36/37	54,497	49.6	−2.9
SS 1937	49,705	45.2	−4.4
WS 37/38	49,674	45.2	—
SS 1938	48,536	44.1	−1.1
WS 38/39	49,358	44.9	−0.8
SS 1939	50,325	45.8	−0.9

Year	C. Female Students Absolute Numbers	SS 1931 = 100	Rate of Decline
SS 1931	21,974	100	
WS 31/32	—	—	
SS 1932	19,997	94.8	−5.2

Table 6—Continued

	C. Female Students		
Year	Absolute Numbers	SS 1931 = 100	Rate of Decline
WS 32/33	18,813	89.2	−5.6
SS 1933	17,685	83.9	−5.3
WS 33/34	15,176	72.0	−11.9
SS 1934	12,630	59.9	−12.1
WS 34/35	11,717	55.5	−4.4
SS 1935	10,190	48.3	−7.2
WS 35/36	10,286	48.8	−0.5
SS 1936	8,849	41.9	−6.9
WS 36/37	8,313	39.4	−2.5
SS 1937	7,296	34.6	−4.8
WS 37/38	6,721	31.8	−2.8
SS 1938	6,337	30.0	−1.8
WS 38/39	6,586	31.2	−1.2
SS 1939	6,342	30.0	−1.2

Sources: Lorenz, I, pp. 30, 148-51; *Statistisches Handbuch*, p. 622.
Note: The figures are for all *Hochschulen*.

Table 7. Women's Share of the Student Population at German Institutions of Higher Learning, 1931–1939

Year	All *Hochschulen*	Universities Proper
SS 1931	16.1%	18.6%
WS 31/32	—	—
SS 1932	15.8	18.5
WS 32/33	15.7	18.5
SS 1933	15.6	18.2
WS 33/34	14.5	17.1
SS 1934	13.9	16.5
WS 34/35	13.8	16.1
SS 1935	14.2	16.9
WS 35/36	13.6	16.3
SS 1936	13.3	15.9
WS 36/37	13.2	16.0
SS 1937	12.8	15.6
WS 37/38	11.9	14.5
SS 1938	11.5	14.4
WS 38/39	11.7	14.6
SS 1939	11.2	14.2

Sources: Lorenz, I, pp. 30, 148-51; *Statistisches Handbuch*, p. 622; Kater, "Krisis," p. 208.

Table 8. Women University Students in Individual Faculties, 1928–1939

Semester	SS 28	SS 32	WS 32/33	SS 33	WS 33/34	SS 34	WS 34/35	SS 35	WS 35/36	SS 36	WS 36/37	SS 37	WS 37/38	SS 38	WS 38/39	SS 39
General Medicine	14.9	24.5	26.1	28.9	30.4	34.8	34.8	37.9	37.1	39.0	41.0	44.7	43.7	44.4	40.8	41.3
Dentistry	3.4	7.1	7.5	7.5	7.6	7.7	7.6	7.4	7.2	6.5	6.0	4.7	4.9	4.8	4.5	4.0
Pharmacy	—	2.2	2.4	2.9	3.1	3.5	3.9	4.8	4.9	5.0	4.7	5.6	5.5	6.1	6.5	7.0
All Medical Studies	19.1	33.9	35.8	39.5	41.4	46.2	46.6	50.4	49.4	50.7	51.9	55.3	54.2	55.2	52.1	52.5
Law	6.0	5.6	5.2	4.2	3.3	2.9	2.6	2.0	1.7	1.3	1.0	0.9	0.8	0.6	0.7	0.9
All Legal and Political Studies	14.3	14.3	13.1	12.0	10.3	9.0	8.2	7.1	6.7	6.4	6.3	8.3	9.8	9.9	11.5	12.6
German Language and Literature	—	9.1	8.7	8.8	9.2	9.3	9.5	8.1	9.0	9.0	8.1	7.5	7.1	6.3	6.0	4.6
Physical Education	—	0.9	0.7	1.0	1.2	1.5	1.7	1.5	2.2	2.1	2.6	2.5	3.4	3.2	4.7	4.6
Humanities	43.2	33.9	33.0	31.9	32.3	30.2	30.7	29.6	30.7	30.4	30.2	25.9	25.8	25.0	25.6	24.9
Theology	1.1	1.7	1.7	1.8	1.8	1.8	1.7	1.5	1.3	1.1	0.9	0.8	0.5	0.6	0.5	0.5
Technical Sciences	0.5	0.7	0.8	0.7	0.7	0.6	0.7	0.8	1.0	0.8	0.8	0.7	0.8	0.8	1.0	1.1
Natural Sciences	20.9	15.0	14.1	13.6	13.0	11.7	11.5	10.1	10.2	10.0	9.2	8.4	8.1	7.6	8.6	7.7
Mathematics and Physics	—	5.9	5.6	5.5	4.8	3.7	3.7	3.1	2.9	3.0	2.4	1.9	1.4	1.2	1.5	1.2

Sources: Lorenz, I, pp. 148-51; Statistisches Handbuch, p. 623.

Table 9. Women in the Faculties of Medicine and Law at German Institutions of Higher Learning, 1932–1939

Semester	SS 1932	SS 1933	SS 1934	SS 1935	SS 1936	SS 1937	SS 1938	SS 1939
MEDICINE								
Total Students	24,808	25,264	23,028	19,974	19,470	18,158	16,980	17,476
Women	4,919	5,123	4,417	3,871	3,456	3,266	2,814	2,623
Women's Percentage	19.8	20.2	19.1	19.3	17.7	17.9	16.5	15.9
LAW								
Total Students	18,364	15,115	11,255	7,400	6,583	4,694	4,275	4,555
Women	1,137	742	374	205	122	68	42	57
Women's Percentage	6.1	4.9	3.3	2.7	1.8	1.4	0.9	1.2

Sources: Lorenz, I, pp. 148-51; *Statistisches Handbuch*, p. 623.

Table 10. Percentages of All New Matriculations of Women Students According to Father's Occupation

Class	Father's Occupation	SS 1933	WS 1934/35	SS 1939
Upper *Middle* *Class*	-high-ranking civil servants	21.3	24.0	23.4
	-officers and high-ranking military personnel	2.6	1.9	2.2
	-academic professions	8.4	8.2	13.1
	-great landowners, owners of factories and banks, wholesale dealers	0.8	0.5	—
		4.9	4.5	7.3
	-high-ranking employees	7.4	7.7	4.3
Totals for Upper Middle Class		45.4	46.8	50.3
Lower *Middle* *Class*	-intermediate civil servants	27.7	25.9	21.8
	-other military personnel	—	0.1	—
	-non-academic free professions	1.5	1.9	4.3
	-intermediate and small farmers	1.4	2.7	—
	-independent craftsmen and small businessmen	14.4	10.8	9.8
	-other employees	5.8	7.8	8.6
Totals for Lower Middle Class		50.8	49.2	44.5
Working *Class*	-clerical workers	0.9	1.2	—
	-industrial workers	1.5	1.7	1.2
Totals for Working Class		2.4	2.9	1.2

Source: Lorenz, I, p. 372.

Note: Totals do not add up to 100 percent because "other occupations" and "no occupation or no occupation given" are not included here.

Table 11. Male Students at German Universities during World War II

Semester	Absolute Numbers	1939 = 100
SS 1939	50,325	100
Fall Semester 1939	31,031	61.6
1st TR 1940	39,913	79.3
2nd TR 1940	30,788	61.1
3rd TR 1940	36,905	73.3
Winter TR 1941	32,895	65.3
SS 1941	27,327	54.3
WS 1941/42	37,457	74.4
SS 1942	30,179	59.9
WS 1942/43	42,029	83.5
SS 1943	33,892	67.3
WS 1943/44	37,341	74.1
SS 1944	14,285	38.3

Sources: Statistisches Handbuch, p. 622; REM circular WA 1960, December 30, 1944, appendix: "Die Massnahmen zum totalen Kriegseinsatz...," p. 6, BA R21/29.
Note: Figures are for all *Hochschulen* in the *Altreich*.

Table 12. New Matriculations at All Institutions of Higher Learning of "Greater Germany," 1939–1944

Semester or Trimester	Total New Matricula- tions	Men	Women	Women's Percen- tage	New Matric- ulations of Women Based on SS 1939 = 100
SS 1939	7,738	7,004	734	9.4	100
TR 1939	9,095	7,532	1,563	17.1	212
1st TR 1940	9,667	8,299	1,368	14.1	186
2nd TR 1940	6,474	3,965	2,509	38.7	341
3rd TR 1940	15,711	10,147	5,564	35.4	758
TR 1941	4,583	2,476	2,107	45.9	287
SS 1941	5,604	3,768	1,836	32.7	250
WS 1941/42	17,792	15,026	2,766	15.5	376
SS 1942	12,770	6,188	6,582	51.5	896
WS 1942/43	17,631	12,646	4,985	28.2	679
SS 1943	13,578	4,661	8,917	65.6	1,214
WS 1943/44	11,725	7,210	4,515	38.5	615
SS 1944	17,570	6,183	11,387	64.8	1,551

Source: Lorenz, II, appendix: "Entwicklung," pp. 20–23.

Table 13. Women Students at All German Institutions of Higher Learning during World War II, 1939–1944

Semester or Trimester	Absolute Numbers	Percentage of Student Population	SS 1939 = 100	SS 1933 = 100
SS 1939	6,342	11.2	100	35
TR 1939	5,903	15.9	93	33
1st TR 1940	7,487	15.7	118	42
2nd TR 1940	8,615	21.8	135	48
3rd TR 1940	12,797	25.7	201	72
TR 1941	12,964	28.2	204	73
SS 1941	13,641	33.3	215	77
WS 1941/42	14,887	28.4	234	84
SS 1942	18,974	38.6	299	107
WS 1942/43	21,607	33.9	340	122
SS 1943	27,174	44.5	428	153
WS 1943/44	27,442	42.4	432	155
SS 1944	41,210	49.3	665	238

Sources: *Statistisches Handbuch*, p. 622; REM circular WA 1960, December 12, 1944, BA R21/29.

Note: Figures are for the *Altreich*.

Table 14. Women at the Technical Universities of "Greater Germany" during World War II, 1939–1944

Semester or Trimester	Women Students	Women's Percentage of All Students	Women's Percentage Based on SS 1939 = 100
SS 1939	271	1.9	100
TR 1939	251	3.2	92.6
1st TR 1940	406	4.0	149.8
2nd TR 1940	594	5.9	219.1
3rd TR 1940	922	8.1	340.2
TR 1941	907	9.3	334.6
SS 1941	897	12.3	330.9
WS 1941/42	984	8.0	363.0
SS 1942	1,458	15.6	538.0
WS 1942/43	1,731	13.1	638.7
SS 1943	2,087	23.5	770.1
WS 1943/44	2,088	18.0	770.4

Source: Lorenz, II, appendix: "Entwicklung," pp. 16–19.

Notes

INTRODUCTION

1. Stierlin, p. 11. Full references for this work and those that follow can be found in the bibliography at the end of this book. Abbreviations used here can be found in the list at the front of this book.
2. On the phenomenon of the "Hitler wave," see, e.g., Janssen, "Bleibt uns Hitler nicht erspart?"
3. Hörster-Phillips, p. 9.
4. See Bossmann's work on this topic.
5. We refer to the impressive series of Hitler biographies from Bullock to Fest and, most recently, the psycho-historical studies of Waite, Stierlin, and others.
6. See, e.g., the studies by Jacobsen, Weinberg, and Hillgruber.
7. Among the best treatments of the "final solution" are those of Hilberg and Schleunes; Höhne and Broszat have produced authoritative studies of the SS.
8. Leading in this respect are the studies of Mosse.
9. The English version of Bleuel's study is entitled *Strength Through Joy: Sex and Society in Nazi Germany*. Page references for this work are to the English edition.
10. See Stephenson, *Women in Nazi Society*, pp. 130–46; a more elaborate version of this study appeared earlier as an article in *JCH*, January 1975. Since these lines were written, one more contribution to the history of women students in the Third Reich has been published; however, Irmgard Weyrather's "Numerus Clausus für Frauen: Studentinnen im Nationalsozialismus" relies heavily on Stephenson's work and on my own 1976 dissertation.
11. Quotation from Renate Bridenthal's review of Stephenson's book in *AHR* 81 (December 1976).

CHAPTER 1

1. Huber, p. 122.
2. Friedrich, p. 20.

3. In "German Women and the Triumph of Hitler," Evans, e.g., calls the Nazi party "the ultimate in male chauvinism"; Merkl, p. 121, refers to the NSDAP as "the epitome of male chauvinism." See also Schoenbaum, pp. 187, 189–90; Fest, *Face*, p. 385; Thalmann, pp. 65ff.

4. Goebbels as quoted in Kirkpatrick, p. 107. See also Friedrich, p. 20.

5. Blüher, pp. 308ff.

6. Kirkpatrick, p. 95.

7. See, e.g., Heuss, pp. 133, 135; Mierendorff, p. 501.

8. Maschmann, p. 90; Gersdorff, p. 39 (quoting Gertrud Bäumer); Rupp, pp. 27–28.

9. Blüher, p. 28.

10. Tiger, p. 102.

11. See, e.g., Mosse, *Crisis*, p. 229; Fest, *Face*, p. 385; Glaser, *Eros*, p. 119; Evans, "German Women," p. 18; Langer, pp. 99, 178–79.

12. On Rosenberg, see his *Mythus*, pp. 494–95; Glaser, *Eros*, pp. 119–20; Viereck, pp. 263ff.; Kater, "Krisis," p. 248; Rupp, p. 16; Thalmann, pp. 66ff. On the SA, see Mosse, *Crisis*, p. 229; Höhne, pp. 66ff.; Glaser, *Eros*, pp. 119–20; Fest, *Face*, pp. 385–86.

13. Kater, "Ansätze," pp. 817ff.

14. Waite, pp. 283–84; Stierlin, p. 121.

15. Blüher, pp. 26–28.

16. Steakley, pp. 110, 119.

17. See, e.g., Langer, pp. 176–78.

18. Waite, p. 461.

19. Ibid.

20. Stierlin, p. 32; Waite, pp. 56, 59–60; Payne, pp. 71, 73, 118, 346.

21. See, e.g., Friedrich, pp. 39ff.; Kutzleb, pp. 41ff.; Glaser, *Eros*, pp. 118–19.

22. Hitler in a speech on September 8, 1934, as quoted in Domarus, I, part 1, pp. 449–51.

23. Rosenberg, *Mythus*, p. 495. See also Thalmann, pp. 68ff.

24. Lange, "Die weibliche Begabung und die neue Schule," as quoted in Köberle, p. 177; Rompel, pp. 4, 17.

25. Tritt, p. 1; Salomon, p. 419.

26. "Verstand bei Mann und Frau," *VB*, October 2, 1926. On Wieth-Knudsen, see Kater, "Krisis," p. 221.

27. Budde, p. 132.

28. Bumm, pp. 6ff. On the prejudices against the *Frauenstudium* in Germany prior to World War I, see Ruge, pp. 30ff.; under the Weimar Republic, see Kater, "Krisis," pp. 219ff.

29. B. Täfe's undated manuscript entitled "Die Leute haben Sorgen," ARNW II *532. (The asterisk [*] is a part of the ARNW reference system.)

30. Hitler on April 10, 1942, as quoted in Picker, p. 269. Similar statements are quoted in Picker, p. 194.

31. Friedrich, p. 18. Similar views in Paatero, p. 2, and Rompel, p. 9.

32. Rompel, pp. 7–8.

33. Bleuel, p. 96.

34. Glaser, *Spiesser-Ideologie*, p. 185.

35. Grün, p. 153.

36. See, e.g., Beard, p. 445.

37. Nitsch, p. 444; Gerstein, p. 82; Pross, pp. 45ff.

38. Feickert, pp. 17, 23. Baeumler developed his ideas in a treatise entitled, appropriately, *Männerbund und Wissenschaft*.

39. See table 1.

40. Knodel, p. 39; Kuczynski, p. 16.

41. See, e.g., the studies of Korherr and Grotjahn.

42. McIntyre, p. 183; Koonz, "Mothers," p. 462. Ironically, Hitler justified his claims for "living space" by referring to Germany's alleged overpopulation; see *Mein Kampf*, pp. 137–40.

43. Rosten, p. 160. See also Beyer, p. 8.

44. Hartnacke, p. 75; see also McIntyre, p. 189. On motherhood as women's sole "natural" vocation, see Frobenius, pp. 29, 54; Siber, p. 6; Rosten, p. 162; Frick, p. 10. Hitler's views are in Domarus, I, part 1, pp. 449ff.

45. Grün, pp. 151–53.

46. Salomon, p. 419; Paatero, p. 2.

47. Grün, p. 152. On these mythical statistics, see also Kirkpatrick, p. 215.

48. Grün, pp. 151–53.

49. Friedrich, pp. 16–18.

50. In 1933, e.g., there was a surplus of 2 million women in the Reich. See Kirkpatrick, pp. 117, 124.

51. See, e.g., the ideas of Fritz Lenz, professor of "racial hygiene" in Berlin, as described in "Auslesewirkung," p. 189, and Köberle, p. 178.

52. Friedrich, pp. 16ff.; see also Kirkpatrick, p. 119.

53. See, e.g., Nemse's "Die Frauenfrage vom eugenischen Standpunkt aus betrachtet," *Deutsches Ärzteblatt*, 1933, no. 4, parts of which are quoted in "Zur Frage des Frauenstudiums," pp. 165–68. See also Rompel, pp. 35–36; Kirkpatrick, pp. 234–35.

54. Grün, p. 154.

55. Bridenthal, p. 158.

56. Bloch, p. 133.

57. Bridenthal, pp. 163–64; McIntyre, pp. 177–78; Gaebel, p. 25.

58. Steinberg, p. 83. On the problem of academic unemployment in the Weimar Republic, see Kater, *Studentenschaft*.

59. Kotschnig, pp. 118–19; Hartshorne, *German Universities*, p. 77; von Soden and Zipfel, p. 28. The literature on this subject is quite extensive; see, e.g., the studies of Schairer, Ruoff, Kotschnig, and Kater.

60. Puckett, pp. 199ff.; Stephenson, "Girls' Higher Education," pp. 42ff.; Bäumer, *Krisis*, p. 6; Winkler, pp. 23–25, 50.

61. See, e.g., the remarks in Bridenthal, pp. 163–64; also Bäumer, *Krisis*, p. 4.

62. Kater, "Krisis," p. 208 (table 1).

63. See, e.g., the undated pamphlet "Der weibliche akademische Nachwuchs," ARNW II *524; also Sikorski, pp. 5ff. The percentages for 1911 and 1913 are computed from figures in *Deutsche Hochschulstatistik*, 1928/29, p. xiv.

64. *Der Deutsche Hochschulführer*, 1933, p. 8; for a similar view, see Rompel, pp. 4ff.

65. Kater, *Studentenschaft*, pp. 145ff.; Kater, "Der NSD-Studentenbund," pp. 154–55.

CHAPTER 2

1. Kirkpatrick, p. 235; Hartshorne, *German Universities*, pp. 79–80; Kotschnig, pp. 201–2; Stephenson, "Girls' Higher Education," pp. 48–49; Hervé, p. 16; von Soden and Zipfel, p. 28.

2. *Deutsche Hochschulstatistik*, 1935, p. 5.

3. Kotschnig, p. 207; Stephenson, "Girls' Higher Education," p. 50.

4. Stephenson, "Girls' Higher Education," p. 48.

5. Lorenz, I, p. 53.

6. See, e.g., "Förderung von Studentinnen," *Umschau*. We refer to Schlömer for a history of the *Studienstiftung* in the Third Reich.

7. Minutes of the meeting of the committee of the *Studienstiftung* of October 9, 1933, ARNW I *6 f586.

8. "Merkblatt für Studienförderung," n.d., ARNW II *XV a498 (a400).

9. See, e.g., "Förderung von Studentinnen," *Umschau*.

10. See table 2.

11. "Die Hochschulförderung der Studentin," p. 16.

12. In the summer semester of 1933, 2.0 percent of all female students (354 out of 17,685) received an official scholarship; in the winter semester 1933/34 it was 2.5 percent (389 out of 15,176) and in the summer semester of 1934, 2.1 percent (274 out of 12,630) (computed from data in "Förderung von Studentinnen," *Umschau*).

13. For a fictionalized account of the hardships suffered by women students in the Third Reich, see Wirth-Stockhausen, "Barbara."

14. "Ausführungsbestimmungen über die Durchführung der Arbeitsdienstpflicht der Abiturienten und Abiturientinnen von Ostern 1934," February 23, 1934, ARNW II *500; Köhler, p. 260; Benz, p. 342.

15. See, e.g., Seipp, pp. 30–33; Böttcher; Mosse, *Nazi Culture*, pp. 145–46; "Arbeitsdienst und Studentin"; Dreissig, "Frauenarbeitsdienst."

16. See the descriptions of life in the "labor service" camps in Seggel, pp. 217–18; Winslow, p. 35; Kirkpatrick, pp. 88–89; Tormin, p. 1027; Maschmann, p. 38; Vinke, p. 81.

17. Wunderlich, pp. 320–21; Kirkpatrick, p. 85. The Catholic clergy were so concerned about these rumors that they published a pamphlet in which prospective "labor maids" were warned about the dangers awaiting them in the service; see Breit, *Das Jungmädel im Arbeitsdienst*.

18. Quoted from "Die Studentin von heute"; see also Dreissig, "Die Abiturientinnen," p. 11.

19. Tormin, p. 1031; Kleiber, p. 200.

20. Report "Referat Frauenarbeitsdienst," June 1936, ARNW I *84 g553.

21. DSt Office for Labor Service, circular 7, April 17, 1935, ARNW II *543; Tormin, p. 1031.

22. "Labor service" leader in Stuttgart to a Dr. Bendler in Offenbach, letter of April 27, 1935, ARNW II *504.

23. Dreissig, "Der Ausgleichsdienst"; report "Referat Frauenarbeitsdienst," June 1936, ARNW I *84 g553; letter of the leader of the DSt office for the "labor service" for women to the Nazi welfare office in Königsberg, September 7, 1935, ARNW II *XV a498 (a400).

24. Leader of the DSt office for the "labor service" for women to a Mr. Rosenberger

in Würzburg, October 11, 1935, ARNW I *85 g931; DSt Office for Labor Service, circular 37, March 30, 1935, ARNW II *543.

25. See Hervé, p. 17; von Soden and Zipfel, p. 29.

26. *Keesing's Contemporary Archives*, December 13, 1933, p. 1052A.

27. Kirkpatrick, pp. 226ff.; Newitt, pp. 58ff.; Winkler, p. 51.

28. Newitt, p. 58.

29. Bridenthal, pp. 163–64.

30. Newitt, pp. 57ff. The mouthpiece of this association was the journal *Die Ärztin*.

31. Eben-Servaes, p. 10; Newitt, p. 65; Kirkpatrick, p. 218.

32. Bridenthal, p. 164; McIntyre, p. 201; Gaebel, p. 25; Bäumer, *Krisis*, p. 27.

33. Bridenthal, p. 164; McIntyre, p. 203.

34. See, e.g., McIntyre, pp. 208–9; Noakes and Pridham, p. 367.

35. Lorenz, II, p. 69.

36. See, e.g., Kater, "Krisis," pp. 223–24, on the antifeminist attitude of professors in the Weimar Republic.

37. Alfred Baeumler, e.g., was transferred from the relative obscurity of Dresden University to the prestigious chair of political pedagogy at Berlin University. See Bollmus, p. 68; Franze, pp. 230–31. Another notorious antifeminist was Professor Dresel in Greifswald; see the report of ANSt leader G. Rothe in Greifswald, March 13, 1934, ARNW II *547.

38. Kater, "Krisis," pp. 224–25; Blüher, pp. 308ff.

39. Kater, *Studentenschaft*, pp. 193ff.; Berndt, p. 75; Franze, p. 218; Faust, II, p. 123.

40. Franze, p. 219.

41. Düning, p. 63; Franze, p. 216. On SA influence at the universities in 1933/34, see also Steinberg, pp. 772–74; Faust, II, p. 123; Giles, "National Socialist Students' Association", pp. 131ff.

42. See, e.g., Sevin, p. 974; report of ANSt leader I. Brandt in Frankfurt, October 30, 1933, ARNW II *499.

43. Woman student H. Köbel in Dresden to the local minister-president, January 11, 1934, ARNW II *542.

44. Schuster.

45. Quoted in a report by ANSt leader U. Schmidt in Leipzig, February 17, 1934, ARNW II *505.

46. A Würzburg woman student thus declared in May 1933 that she had feared that "should the [National Socialist] movement come to power her studies would be jeopardized" and that she had opposed the NSDAP "in order to safeguard the *Frauenstudium*" (declaration of E. Wiegand in the report "Disziplinarverfahren wegen Verdachtes kommunistischer Betätigung," May 22, 1933, ARNW IV x4).

CHAPTER 3

1. See table 1.

2. The Nazis themselves credited their own pronatalist policies; others have emphasized the importance of the overall improvement of the economy after the worst years of the Great Depression. But even Knodel, author of the most recent study of Germany's demographic development in those years, avoids a definite commitment to either one of these theories. See Knodel, pp. 51–52.

3. Burgdörfer, *Kinder*, p. 54.

4. In fact, statistics indicated that women were making an important contribution to the demographic revival; see, e.g., the figures on female nuptiality and fertility in *Statistisches Jahrbuch*, 1941/42, pp. 73, 77.

5. Garraty, p. 917. See also Heyl, pp. 83–96, esp. pp. 84, 92–93; Mason, "Labour," p. 126.

6. Milward, pp. 19–20; Garraty, p. 917; Petzina, pp. 53, 159.

7. Mason, "Labour," p. 126.

8. Däubler-Gmelin, p. 31.

9. "Studentinnen und Berufseinsatz."

10. Winkler, pp. 55ff.; Mason, "Labour," p. 139; Bajohr, p. 226.

11. See table 3.

12. Meissner, p. 127.

13. Lorenz, II, pp. 72–75.

14. Stephenson, "Girls' Higher Education," p. 53. As early as 1935, e.g., the demand for engineers rose dramatically; see Kotschnig, p. 121.

15. Ibid., p. 120.

16. Luetkens, pp. 208–9; Schoenbaum, pp. 249–50. On Nazi antiintellectualism, see, e.g., Fest, *Face*, pp. 365ff.; Kühnl, pp. 146–50.

17. Lorenz, I, p. 52.

18. Bäumer, *Krisis*, pp. 3–4.

19. Stephenson, "Girls' Higher Education," p. 50. See also Kirkpatrick, p. 216; Kotschnig, p. 207.

20. Meissner, p. 117.

21. Brünneck, pp. 9–10.

22. Bäumer, "30 Jahre"; Stephenson, "Girls' Higher Education," p. 53; Kottenhoff, "Wert und Bedeutung," p. 139.

23. See, e.g., *Frauenkultur*, November, 1937; *NSK*, March 29, 1938; Scholtz-Klink, "Studentinnen"; "Berufsmöglichkeiten"; "Frauenstudium aussichtreich."

24. Kottenhoff, "Zur Lage," pp. 689–90; Kottenhoff, "Aufgaben und Ziele," p. 86; Scholtz-Klink, *Die Frau*, pp. 368–69.

25. *Reichsstudentenwerk: Kurzbericht...1938*, p. 25; *Reichsstudentenwerk: Kurzbericht...1939*, p. 28.

26. *Reichsstudentenwerk: Kurzbericht...1937*, p. 39.

27. Shirer, p. 312; Bullock, p. 306; Steakley, p. 108.

28. Glaser, *Eros*, p. 120.

29. Coler and Pfannstiehl, p. 288.

30. Kater, "Zum gegenseitigen," p. 368.

31. NSDStB circular St.F. 5.34, September 28, 1934, ARNW II *551; Franze, p. 219; Kater, "Zum gegenseitigen," p. 366.

32. Gesa, pp. 5–6; Wolff, pp. 103–5. One of the first Nazi student leaders to refer to women students as "*Kameradinnen*" was von Leers, see his "Unsere Kameradinnen."

33. Kottenhoff, "Fragen."

CHAPTER 4

1. See table 4.

2. Computed from data in *Der Deutsche Hochschulführer*, 1933, pp. 27–47; 1934, pp. 34–47; 1935, pp. 31ff.; 1936, pp. 34–35; 1937, pp. 44–45.

3. Lorenz, I, pp. 148–50.

4. See table 5.

5. See table 4.

6. See table 5.

7. Kotschnig, p. 73.

8. Lorenz, I, p. 30.

9. Eilers, pp. 19–20.

10. Hervé, pp. 16–17.

11. Von Soden and Zipfel, p. 28.

12. Reuter and Poneleit, p. 55; Elling, p. 15.

13. Thalmann, pp. 92–93; see Ringer, *Education*, p. 64, and Winkler, pp. 52, 64, for similar views. The importance of the *numerus clausus* is likewise emphasized in Weyrather's recent essay on the *Frauenstudium*.

14. See table 6.

15. See, e.g., Lorenz, I, pp. 148–51; *Statistisches Handbuch*, p. 622.

16. See table 6. For the corresponding figures at universities proper, see Kater, "Krisis," p. 208.

17. Hartshorne, *German Universities*, p. 72.

18. Luetkens, p. 196. Within Germany, the importance of this demographic factor was mentioned by Burgdörfer, *Volk ohne Jugend*, pp. 172–74, and by Bäumer, "30 Jahre," p. 583. On the problems involved in relating enrollments to demographic trends, see Ringer, *Education*, pp. 24–25.

19. See table 1.

20. Eighteen to nineteen was the average age at first matriculation at universities in the Third Reich; see Lorenz, I, p. 53. The cohort concept is borrowed from Loewenberg, esp. pp. 1465–66.

21. According to Ringer, *Education*, pp. 62, 66 (tables 1.5 and 1.6), university enrollments thus dropped from 2.7 percent to 1.5 percent of all Germans in the 20-to-23-year age-group.

22. See table 6.

23. See tables 4 and 5.

24. Hartshorne, *German Universities*, p. 74; Luetkens, pp. 197ff.

25. See, e.g., Hitler's diatribes against intellectuals in *Mein Kampf*, pp. 224, 253, 262, 410; also Fest, *Face*, pp. 365ff.; Kühnl, pp. 146–50.

26. Luetkens, pp. 208–9; Schoenbaum, pp. 249–50.

27. See, e.g., Stephenson, "Girls' Higher Education," p. 50.

28. See table 7.

29. Focke and Reimer, p. 161; Winkler, pp. 52, 64. See also Hervé, p. 17, and von Soden and Zipfel, p. 29, for similar views.

30. Only WS 1933/34, SS 1934, SS 1935, and SS 1936 witnessed more rapid rates of decline; see table 6.

31. Bäumer, *Krisis*, p. 30.

32. Meissner, p. 121.

33. For the Weimar Republic, see Kater, *Studentenschaft*, pp. 60–61, 208 (table 2). In the summer semester of 1930, e.g., 60.7 percent of all German university students came from the lower middle class. For the Third Reich, see, e.g., Altstädter, p. 241, who points out that 52.4 percent of all students at Munich University in the winter semester 1935/36 came from the lower middle class. In the winter semester 1934/35, not less than

27.5 percent of all German students came from families of intermediate civil servants, the single most important group within the lower middle class. (Computed from data in Lorenz, I, pp. 363, 371.)

34. Kater, "Krisis," p. 231; Kater, *Studentenschaft*, p. 65; von Soden and Zipfel, p. 19.

35. Kater, *Studentenschaft*, p. 250 (note 52). Among high-ranking civil servants, on the other hand, this ratio was only 4 to 1.

36. Computed from data in Lorenz, I, p. 372.

37. Frick, p. 10.

38. See, e.g., Tritt, p. 1; McIntyre, p. 189.

39. The losses in male lives during the First World War had left Germany with a large surplus of unmarried women, estimated at approximately 2 million in 1933. See Kirkpatrick, pp. 117, 124; McIntyre, p. 185. That the Nazi regime did not wish to deny these women the right to earn a living was affirmed by Hitler himself in an interview on January 25, 1936; see Domarus, I, part 2, p. 567.

40. Bürkner, p. 23. Frobenius, p. 30, echoes Hitler's views. See also McIntyre, p. 185; Schorn, pp. 20–21; Vermehren-Göring, p. 76.

41. Frick, p. 10; Vogel, p. 6. See also McIntyre, pp. 185–86.

42. Siber, pp. 24–25, 27–28; McIntyre, p. 185. Characteristically, Hitler himself offered a somewhat different reason why he thought women made good teachers: "They alone are physically and psychologically fit to repeat the same things over and over again" (Hitler on April 12, 1942, as quoted in Picker, p. 274).

43. See table 8.

44. See table 8. On the popularity of medical studies among German women in the Weimar Republic, see Kater, "Krisis," pp. 213–15.

45. Male medical students increased their share of the entire male student population from 21.7 percent in 1933 to 27.7 percent in 1936 and 29.5 percent in 1939 (computed from data in Lorenz, I, pp. 148–51).

46. See table 9. For women's share of all medical students in 1914–1932, see Kater, "Krisis," p. 214.

47. Luetkens, p. 203; see also Kotschnig, p. 121.

48. Gaebel, p. 24.

49. Schoenbaum, p. 228. At the end of 1938, approximately three thousand medical doctors served in the SS.

50. See table 8; see also for subsequent figures on women students of medicine and law.

51. Computed from data in Lorenz, I, pp. 148–51.

52. See table 8.

53. The percentage of all male students in the law faculties declined from 22.6 percent in the summer semester of 1928 to 15.0 percent in the winter semester 1932/33 (computed from data in Lorenz, I, p. 148, and *Statistisches Handbuch*, p. 623).

54. Kater, *Studentenschaft*, pp. 68–69.

55. Salaries, e.g., remained low in spite of inflation, and the civil service lost a great deal of its traditional prestige. See Schoenbaum, pp. 220, 233; Grunberger, pp. 128ff.

56. See, e.g., Freisler's letter to national and local authorities on behalf of the Ministry of Justice, recommending the hiring of female law specialists; cited in Noakes and Pridham, p. 368.

57. See table 8. The absolute number of women students of law was 122 in the summer

semester of 1936, 68 in the summer semester of 1937, 42 in the summer semester of 1938, and 57 in the summer semester of 1939. See Lorenz, I, pp. 149–50.

58. See table 8.

59. Between 1933 and 1939, male students of natural sciences dropped from 11.1 percent to 9.5 percent of the male student population (computed from data in Lorenz, I, pp. 148–51).

60. See table 8. Between 1928 and 1933, e.g., the number of coeds in the faculties of natural sciences dropped from 20.9 percent to 13.6 percent of the total female student population.

61. See table 8.

62. Cron, p. 249; Altstädter, p. 250; Weyrather, p. 145. The categorization and terminology used here are basically those of Kater, *Studentenschaft*, pp. 60, 208 (footnotes 1–3). See also table 10.

63. Kater, "Reich Vocational Contest," p. 227 (footnote 18); Kater, *Studentenschaft*, pp. 6–61.

64. Cron, p. 252.

65. After 1933, e.g., the *Deutsche Hochschulführer* ceased to publish the occupation of the students' fathers.

66. These and following figures computed from data in Lorenz, I, pp. 363, 371.

67. See table 10; also Hervé, p. 17.

68. Cron, p. 252.

69. Both Kater, "Krisis," p. 231, and Kreutzberger, p. 70, point out that in the Weimar Republic a disproportionately high percentage of all women students came from the upper middle class. For a discussion of the "elitist background" of the pre-World War I generation of women students (i.e., "the first generation of [German] female academics"), see Jarausch, pp. 109–10.

70. Quoted from Kater, *Studentenschaft*, p. 61.

71. Quoted from ibid., p. 62.

72. On working students in the Weimar Republic, see Kater, "The Work Student."

73. Kater, "Krisis," pp. 208, 240–41.

74. It is also revealing that in the only known fictionalized account of the plight of a woman student in the Third Reich the heroine, "a coed of the year 1935," cannot afford rail travel, lives in an unheated room, etc., but fails even to consider looking for a part-time job; see Wirth-Stockhausen, "Barbara."

75. Kater, "Work Student," p. 89.

76. Kater, "Krisis," p. 243.

77. As in the case of a man in Tübingen who could not afford to send his daughter to a camp in Silesia, see the letter of the woman student in charge of "labor service" recruitment (*Vertrauensstudentin*) in Southwest Germany to a Professor Hennig in Tübingen, August 9, 1936, ARNW II *504.

78. Quote from Schoenbaum, p. 79.

CHAPTER 5

1. In Prussia, e.g., women had only been admitted to the universities as full-fledged students in 1908. See Jarausch, p. 37.

2. Evans, *Feminist Movement*, p. 254.

3. For critical treatments of these "Nazi feminists," see Kater, "Frauen," pp. 228ff.; Evans, *Feminist Movement*, p. 248; Opitz, pp. 260–62; Rupp, pp. 17–18.

4. Evans, *Feminist Movement*, p. 259.

5. Reichenau, "Die Begabte Frau," p. 18. On Reichenau, see Rupp, p. 22.

6. Lenz-von Borries, pp. 203–4; "Zur Frage," pp. 166–67; Becker.

7. Kühn, "Geistige Führung," pp. 211–13; Schorn, pp. 21–22.

8. Hoffa, pp. 204–5.

9. Sevin, pp. 973–74; Kranzhoff, p. 245.

10. Sevin, p. 973.

11. Kühn, "Natürlicher," p. 34.

12. Reichenau, "Die begabte Frau," p. 18.

13. Schlüter-Hermkes, pp. 217–18.

14. Bäumer, "30 Jahre," p. 584.

15. For more elaborate descriptions by Nazi women students of the "bluestocking" phenomenon of the Weimar years, see, e.g., Machwirth, "Die Nationalsozialistische Studentin"; Daniels, p. 79; Gaensecke, "Die Entwicklung." See also Stephenson, "Girls' Higher Education," p. 62.

16. Hertha von Ferber, "Studentinnen in Rittmarshausen," ANSt report of March 1934, ARNW II *526.

17. Kottenhoff, "Aufgaben und Ziele," p. 81. Similar argumentations in Wolff, pp. 103–5; Gesa, p. 56.

18. Kottenhoff, "Die Studentin in der ANSt," p. 59.

19. "Aufgaben und Ziele der ANSt"; Brettschneider; also Brettschneider's letter to the Nazi women student leader in Heidelberg, June 4, 1933, ARNW II *547.

CHAPTER 6

1. Faust, I, p. 37; Kater, "NSD-Studentenbund," p. 148; Steinberg, p. 452. On the NSDStB, see the studies of Dibner, Faust, Giles, and Kater.

2. Kater, "Krisis," p. 254; Faust, I, pp. 173–74; "Richtlinien für die ANSt," March 15, 1932, ARNW II *65 g604; L. Machwirth's introduction to a series of articles on the ANSt in *Der Student der Ostmark*, January 25, 1936.

3. Faust, I, p. 174; ANSt circular 2, June 5, 1931, ARNW II *a584.

4. Steinberg, p. 504.

5. ANSt "Bundesbrief Nr. 1," June 1933, ARNW I *80 g43.

6. Various reports of ANSt Freiburg and Karlsruhe, ARNW II *499; ANSt Dresden, ARNW II *501; and ANSt Göttingen, ARNW II *524.

7. ANSt "Bundesbrief Nr. 1," June 1933, ARNW I *80 g43.

8. Franze, pp. 291–92; Bleuel and Klinnert, p. 255.

9. Brettschneider's letter to the ANSt leader in Leipzig, September 28, 1933, ARNW II *545.

10. DSt Main Office for Women Students, circular G2 1933/34, November 1, 1933, ARNW I *80 g43.

11. Ibid., circular G4 1933/34, December 15, 1933, ARNW II *551.

12. Various reports of Main Office VI for the winter semester of 1933/34, ARNW II *524; Adam, p. 105.

13. Report of Main Office VI Leipzig, December 15, 1933, ARNW II *501.

14. DSt Main Office for Women Students, form letter, "An das Kulturministerium,"

November 23, 1933, ARNW II *530; correspondence between G. Brettschneider and the Bavarian minister of education, December 1933–January 1934, ARNW II *530.

15. In Frankfurt, e.g., the NSDStB leaders denied the ANSt the use of their office, typewriter, and telephone and claimed the right to approve ANSt articles prior to their publication. See the report of ANSt Frankfurt of October 30, 1933, ARNW II *499.

16. G. Brettschneider to the ANSt leader in Frankfurt, November 27, 1933, ARNW II *499.

17. Document entitled "Im Namen der Amtsleiterinnen des Hauptamtes VI," n.d., ARNW II *530.

18. DSt circular A5/1933–34, November 28, 1933, ARNW I *03 g64.

19. *DStZ*, February 3, 1934; Brettschneider's letter to the leader of Main Office VI in Leipzig, February 3, 1934, ARNW II *505.

20. Stitz, pp. 205, 234, 256.

21. Ibid., pp. 382–83; Kupisch, pp. 198–200.

22. Reich ANSt leader Machwirth to the ANSt leader in Göttingen, May 3, 1935, ARNW II *534.

23. Circulars to all regional ANSt leaders, July 16 and 30, 1933, ARNW II *536.

24. Various reports of regional ANSt leaders for 1933 and 1934, ARNW II *524 and II *526.

25. "Mitgliederstand des NSDStB," undated document in ARNW II *A17.

26. Circular of ANSt and Main Office VI in the Leipzig region, April 9, 1934, ARNW II *533.

27. Report of the ANSt leader in Bavaria, September 25, 1934, ARNW II *526.

28. Report of the ANSt leader in the Leipzig region, August 26, 1934, ARNW II *526; report of the ANSt leader in western Germany, n.d., ARNW II *526; various reports on the training camps in ARNW II *525 and 526.

29. DSt Main Office VI, circular DSt G3/34, May 18, 1934, ARNW I *80 g511.

30. Reports of ANSt/Main Office VI in Leipzig, August 18 and 26, 1934, and report of ANSt and Main Office VI in western Germany, n.d., all in ARNW II *526; Adam, p. 105.

31. Brettschneider to the ANSt leader in Freiburg, December 13, 1933, ARNW II *499.

32. Report of Main Office VI in Kiel to Brettschneider, May 31, 1934, ARNW II *542.

33. NSDStB circular St.F.5/34, September 28, 1934, ARNW II *511; Faust, II, pp. 128–29; Kreppel, pp. 43–44; Düning, p. 62; Rühle, II, p. 226; Franze, pp. 294ff.

34. Machwirth, "Kameradinnen"; Machwirth's letter to V. Hauswald in Leipzig, May 2, 1935, and to U. Seiger in Berlin, January 10, 1935, ARNW II *550.

35. Berndt, p. 267.

36. Lorenz, I, p. 53.

37. BDM *Gauverbandsführerin-Ost* in Berlin to Stäbel, November 25, 1933, ARNW I *80 g566.

38. Correspondence between Brettschneider and the ANSt leader in East Prussia, July 7 and 13, 1934, ARNW II *524; *DSt Nachrichtendienst*, vol. 7, no. A24, July 26, 1934, p. 4.

39. Bollmus, p. 245.

40. Kreppel, p. 44; Machwirth, "Kameradinnen"; report by the leader of Main Office VI in Leipzig, December 13, 1934, ARNW II *505.

41. *DSt Verordnungs- und Mitteilungsblatt*, August 23, 1934, pp. 1–2.

42. Derichsweiler's letter to Brettschneider, October 1, 1934, ARNW II *515; NSDStB circular St.F.15/34, December 12, 1934, ARNW II *f62; notice in DStZ of December 20, 1934.

43. "Arbeitsplan der ANSt"; ANSt circular 1/34, December 12, 1934, ARNW II *f62.

44. NSDStB Reich leadership circular of September 4, 1934, ARNW II *527.

45. See, e.g., the protocol of the NSDStB meeting in Frankfurt on May 11–12, 1935, ARNW II *f319.

46. Derichsweiler's letter to the NSDStB leader in Silesia, November 12, 1935, ARNW II *529.

47. *DSt Verordnungs- und Mitteilungsblatt*, vol. 2, October 15, 1935, p. 7.

48. *Nationalsozialistische Frauenschaft*, p. 16. On Scholtz-Klink and her empire, see Stephenson, *Nazi Organization of Women*. Scholtz-Klink herself has just recently published her own account of the role of women in the Third Reich; see her *Die Frau im Dritten Reich*.

49. Minutes of a "Meeting with Frau Scholtz-Klink on December 12, 1934," ARNW II *530.

50. "Vereinbarung zwischen ANSt und NS-Frauenschaft," ARNW II *551; ANSt circular 4/35, February 11, 1935, and 13/35, November 21, 1935, in ARNW II *551 and ARNW II *490 (a401), respectively.

51. DSt Main Office for Women Students, circular VI/H6/1935, March 1, 1935, ARNW I *80 g43.

52. The "agricultural service" was therefore often described as a "harvest aid" (*Erntehilfe*).

53. "Der Landdienst-Einsatz der Studenten in Ostpreussen," report of January 14, 1935, ARNW I *78 g316; "In Hessen."

54. DSt Office for Labor Service, section for "peasants' service," circular of December 13, 1934, ARNW I *78 g316; "Studentinnen im Landdienst"; DSt Office for Labor Service, section for "peasants' service," circular AD6 1934/35, January 30, 1935, ARNW I *78 g316.

55. "Arbeitsbericht des Landdienstes der Deutschen Studentenschaft: Sommereinsatz 1935," n.d., ARNW I *78 a372.

56. "Semesterbericht des Landdienstes der Deutschen Studentenschaft: Wintersemester 1935/36," n.d., ARNW I *78 a372.

57. ANSt circular 12/35, October 31, 1935, ARNW II *499 (a401); Adam, p. 105.

58. Report on the winter semester 1935/36 by the ANSt leader in Leipzig, n.d., ARNW II *538; report of the ANSt leader in Hamburg, April 17, 1936, ARNW II *531.

59. Report of ANSt Leipzig on the winter semester 1935/36, n.d., ARNW II *538.

60. Franze, pp. 323–24; Alpers.

61. Kühnl, p. 154.

62. Faust, II, p. 132; Franze, p. 315; Dibner, pp. 231–32; notice of Derichsweiler's resignation in *Der Frankfurter Student*, November 20, 1936. On the background of Scheel's appointment, see also Giles, "Rise," p. 174.

63. Ley's decree no. 8137, April 19, 1937, BA NS 38/17; Scheel, *Die Reichsstudentenführung*, p. 9; Franze, p. 316.

64. Scheel's letter to ANSt leader Inge Wolff, November 12, 1936, ARNW II *A17;

RSF "Chef-Befehl Nr. 1," November 16, 1936, and "Chef-Befehl Nr. 2," n.d., ARNW I *06 f56; *NS-Jahrbuch*, 1938, p. 243.

65. Giles, "Political Education," pp. 11ff.

66. REM circular Wi 740 II 9b, February 22, 1937, GLAK, 235, no. 4877.

67. Giles, *Political Education*, pp. 11ff.; "Die Arbeit einer ANSt-Zelle."

68. Giles, *Political Education*, pp. 11–12; *Verordnungsblatt des Reichsstudentenführers*, October 5, 1937, p. 117.

69. See, e.g., Brandenburg, pp. 180–81, 184–85.

70. RSF Office for Women Students, order Stn 8/37, March 15, 1937, ARNW II *a16; "Studentin und Bund Deutscher Mädchen [*sic*]"; "Zum Abkommen."

CHAPTER 7

1. See, e.g., Scholtz-Klink's remarks in her undated pamphlet "Der Deutsche Frauenarbeitsdienst," ARNW II *524.

2. Scheel, "Der NSD-Studentenbund," pp. 207–8; "Bericht über."

3. Giles, "Political Education," p. 14.

4. "Grundlegende Erkenntnisse"; Vogel, p. 10; Scheel, *Die Reichsstudentenführung*, p. 28.

5. DSt Main Office for Women Students, office for *Gemeinschaftspflege*, appendix to circular G2 1933/34 of November 1, 1933, ARNW I *80 g43.

6. *Die ANSt-Gruppe*, WS 1937/38, appendix, p. 11: "Abendausgestaltung: Frauenabend," ARNW II *515; ANSt *Schulungsbrief* "Die Germanische Frau," appendix, p. 32: "Abendausgestaltung," ARNW II *XV a499 (a401).

7. *Tage Studentischer Kunst*. The sorry state of cultural affairs in Nazi Germany as a whole was likewise covered up by means of "lavishly arranged celebrations" of individuals; see Fest, *Hitler*, p. 550. On women and cultural life in Nazi Germany in general, see Klinksiek, pp. 127ff.

8. Hitler, *Mein Kampf*, p. 414.

9. DSt Main Office VI, appendix to circular G2 1933/34, "Richtlinien des Amtes für Sport," November 1, 1933, ARNW I *80 g43; Bernett, pp. 110–11.

10. Lohlöffel, pp. 118–20; Frobenius, p. 19.

11. DSt Main Office VI, appendix to circular G2 1933/34, "Richtlinien des Amtes für Sport," November 1, 1933, ARNW I *80 g43; Lohlöffel, pp. 118–19; Plagemann; Dürselen.

12. Report of Else Reimann, "Die Bedeutung der Leibesübungen in der Erziehung der Studentinnen," n.d., ARNW II *516.

13. Report of Main Office VI at Bonn University, January 11, 1934, ARNW II *524, and other reports of Main Office VI for the winter semester 1933/34 in ARNW II *524.

14. DSt Main Office VI, circular G3/34, May 18, 1934, ARNW I *80 g511.

15. Report of the deputy ANSt leader in Göttingen, August 23, 1934, ARNW II *534.

16. Report of Main Office VI in Leipzig, November 11, 1934, ARNW II *533.

17. DSt Main Office VI, circular VI H4/1935, February 21, 1935, ARNW I *80 g43.

18. See, e.g., Dürselen.

19. "Reichswettkämpfe der Studentinnen 1939."

20. Gaensecke, "Die Frau"; Lotze, "Studentin und Sozialismus."

21. Gaensecke, "Die Frau."

22. Kottenhoff, "Die Studentin in der ANSt."

23. *Deutsche Studentenschaft: Verordnungs- und Mitteilungsblatt*, no. 10, August 1, 1935, pp. 11–12; Franze, pp. 198–200.

24. Undated report, "Im Namen der Amtsleiterinnen," ARNW II *530; Vehlow, p. 150.

25. DSt Main Office for Women Students, appendix to circular G3 1933/34, December 15, 1933, ARNW II *551.

26. DSt Main Offices I and VI, collective circular W20/1934, June 28, 1934, ARNW I *01 g57.

27. See table 4.

28. Report of Main Office VI at TH Dresden, June 30, 1935, ARNW II *535.

29. *Deutsche Studentenschaft: Verordnungs- und Mitteilungsblatt*, no. 10, August 1, 1935, p. 6; report on the faculty work of Main Office VI at Munich University, February 2, 1936, ARNW II *535.

30. Pamphlet of Main Office VI in Königsberg, August 24, 1935, ARNW II *499.

31. Goese.

32. "Die Medizinstudentin im BDM"; Newitt, p. 73.

33. Agreement between the BDM and the RSF Office for Women Students, May 26, 1937, ARNW I *80 g587; *Verordnungsblatt des Reichsstudentenführers*, no. 12, June 10, 1937, p. 9; "Die Medizinstudentin im BDM"; Zörlein.

34. For a concise history of the RBWK of university students, see Kater, "Reich Vocational Contest."

35. Ibid., p. 229.

36. Kottenhoff, "Die geistige Bereitschaft," p. 8; Kottenhoff, "Mann und Frau," pp. 5–6.

37. DSt Main Office VI, circular VI H3/1936, February 12, 1936, ARNW II *550; "Auch die Studentinnen kämpfen mit."

38. ANSt leader Inge Wolff to the RBWK organizer in Königsberg, January 17, 1936, ARNW II *542; Karl, p. 85.

39. Karl, p. 85.

40. Undated report on the RBWK of women students in metropolitan Berlin, ARNW II *532.

41. Results quoted in Kater, "Reich Vocational Contest," p. 229.

42. Karl, p. 85.

43. Some 7 percent of all 7,797 women students in the winter semester 1935/36.

44. See table 7.

45. These measures included appointment of a special "section leader for the Reich Vocational Contest of women students" within Main Office VI; see the circular "An die Wettkampfleiter des RBWK," October 24, 1936, ARNW I *06 f67.

46. Kubach, *Studenten bauen auf! Der 2. Reichsberufswettkampf*, p. 14.

47. DSt office for the "Labor Service" for women, circular 6, August 6, 1936, ARNW II *541; Kottenhoff, "Mann und Frau."

48. Kottenhoff, "Die Studentin im Reichsberufswettkampf."

49. Axmann, pp. 359–60.

50. Kubach, *Studenten bauen auf! Der 2. Reichsberufswettkampf*, pp. 22, 52; Kottenhoff, "Die geistige Bereitschaft," p. 9.

51. "So denken die siegreichen Studentinnen"; Hackmann; "Empfang der Reichs-siegergruppe."

52. Claasen, p. 505.

53. Kottenhoff, "Die Studentin im Reichsberufswettkampf."

54. Kater, "Reich Vocational Contest," p. 231.

55. Ibid., p. 232.

56. Kottenhoff, "Die Studentin im Reichsberufswettkampf."

57. Kater, "Reich Vocational Contest," p. 229.

58. Kubach, *Studenten bauen auf! Der 3. Reichsberufswettkampf*, pp. 27, 71.

59. Kubach, *Studenten bauen auf! Der 4. Reichsberufswettkampf*, p. 17.

60. Reports of ANSt in Munich/Upper Bavaria, March 4, 1939, ANSt Halle, February 27, 1939, and ANSt Würzburg, February 10, 1939, ARNW II *540.

61. Kubach, *Studenten bauen auf! Der 4. Reichsberufswettkampf*, pp. 16, 68–69; "Studentinnen geben Rechenschaft."

62. Wünsche, "Die Reichssiegerarbeit," pp. 534–38; Wünsche, "Mutterschaft und Frauenarbeit," pp. 8–9.

63. Kater, "Reich Vocational Contest," p. 236.

64. Kottenhoff, "Querschnitt," p. 6.

65. See, e.g., Kühnl, pp. 84–86; Schoenbaum, pp. 55ff.

66. Kühnl, pp. 85–86.

67. Schoenbaum, pp. 53ff.

68. Kater, "Reich Vocational Contest," p. 227 (also footnote on p. 18).

69. See, e.g., Schoenbaum, p. 59.

70. See, e.g., Kottenhoff, "Die Studentin in der ANSt," p. 58.

71. Kottenhoff, "Bekenntnis," p. 3.

72. Hell.

73. See, e.g., the report of Main Office VI in Leipzig, July 25, 1934, ARNW II *501; "Unsere Studentinnen bescheren"; ANSt circular 3/34, December 15, 1934, ARNW II *499 (a401); Hell; Hein; "Die Arbeit der Studentinnen in der NSV."

74. "Richtlinien Nr. 2 für die Mitarbeit der Studentinnen in der NS Volkswohlfahrt," February 18, 1935, ARNW I *80 g43; ANSt circular 3/34, December 15, 1934, ARNW II *499 (a401).

75. Report of Main Office VI in Western Germany, n.d., ARNW II *526; report on the WHW work in Königsberg, February 26, 1935, ARNW I *80 g564; report of the Office for Women Students in East Prussia, February 24, 1939, and at Münster University, both for WS 1938/39, ARNW II *540.

76. ANSt leader in Silesia to Machwirth, June 28, 1935, ARNW II *499 (a401).

77. Reports of the ANSt leader in region IV [the Leipzig area] on the summer semester 1934, August 26, 1934, ARNW II *526; report on the WHW work of women students at Cologne University, February 14, 1935, ARNW II *534.

78. Schoenbaum, pp. 75–76.

79. Ibid., p. 78.

80. See, e.g., Prenzel; Miedzinski, "Landdienst und Fabrikdienst," p. 107; "Fabrikdienst der Studentinnen."

81. "Erfahrungen der Studentinnen im Fabrikeinsatz," p. 32; protocol of the NSDStB *Reichstagung* in Frankfurt, May 11–12, 1935, II/3, ARNW II *f319; "Zum Fabrikdienst der Königsberger Studentinnen"; Lotze, "Studentinnen arbeiten in Betrieben"; Rothe, "Studentin im Fabrikdienst," p. 559; Oehring, p. 79; "Die Arbeit des Frauenamtes."

82. Rothe, "Studentin im Fabrikdienst," p. 559; report, "Arbeiterinnen und Studentinnen," n.d., ARNW II *524.

83. ANSt circular 14/35, "Fabrikdienst der ANSt," December 13, 1935, and ANSt circular 3/36, "Fabrikdienst der Studentinnen," May 12, 1936, both in ARNW II *499 (a401); undated copy of an agreement between Derichsweiler and Scholtz-Klink, ARNW IV-I *24/3; Lübben, p. 688.

84. DSt Main Office VI, circular VI/H3-1936, May 13, 1936, ARNW I *80 g43; "Einsatz im Jahre 1936," undated report in ARNW II *548.

85. Inge Wolff to woman student A. Habenhorst, June 9, 1937, ARNW I *80 g548 (g552).

86. "Auszug aus dem Bericht über die Frauenarbeit im Sommer 1937," undated report in ARNW II *548.

87. Inge Wolff to Scholtz-Klink, June 22, 1937, ARNW I *80 g594; report of the firm *Maschinen für Waffenverpackung GmbH* in Lübeck to the RSF Office for Women Students, June 29, 1937, ARNW I *80 g594.

88. Ursula Marquardt to M. Betz, September 9, 1937, ARNW I *80 g548 (g552).

89. M. Betz to A. Schleicher, ANSt leader in Cologne, June 8, 1938, and to the ANSt leader in Heidelberg, July 5, 1938, both letters in ARNW I *80 g595.

90. Report of ANSt Münster, July 7, 1938, and of ANSt Leipzig, n.d., both in ARNW II *536; report of the RSF Office for Women Students in Erlangen, February 24, 1939, ARNW II *532.

91. Report "Studentischer Fabrikdienst," n.d., ARNW V *a556.

92. Various reports of the RSF Office for Women Students, ARNW II *540.

93. *Verordnungsblatt des Reichsstudentenführers*, no. 7, April 20, 1937, pp. 38, 41–42, and no. 8, May 1, 1937, p. 47; "Studentin und Erntehilfe."

94. "Studentin im Einsatz," *Die ANSt-Gruppe*, summer semester 1938, no. 3, ARNW II *f147; Miedzinski, "Landdienst und Fabrikdienst," pp. 105ff.

95. DSt Office for Labor Service, section for "peasants' service," circular 2, December 18, 1935, ARNW I *78 a372.

96. Mertesdorf; Wiedmann.

97. See, e.g., "Arbeitsbericht des Landdienstes der Deutschen Studentenschaft: Sommereinsatz 1935," n.d., ARNW I *78 a372.

98. "Arbeitsbericht des Landdienstes der Deutschen Studentenschaft: Sommereinsatz 1935/36," n.d., ARNW I *78 a372.

99. "Die Ernte rief"; Mertesdorf; Grüntzig, p. 219; DSt Office for Labor Service, section for "peasants' service," circular 2, December 18, 1935, ARNW I *78 a372.

100. Mertesdorf; "Die Arbeit der Studentinnen," pp. 33–34.

101. See, e.g., Carr, pp. 53ff.

102. Himmler's letter to Scheel, n.d., ARNW I *07 f321.

103. Schoenbaum, p. 167.

104. Appeal to women students to participate in the "agricultural service," signed by Inge Wolff, *DB*, January 27, 1937.

105. "Studentin und Erntehilfe."

106. *Die ANSt-Gruppe*, June 30, 1939, pp. 5ff.

107. "Auf Erntearbeit in Ostpreussen, Briefe von Studentinnen der Albertus-Universität in Königsberg," n.d., ARNW II *545.

108. Miedzinski, "Man ruft uns"; Falkenberg; "Hilfe, die sich selbst lohnt."

109. Grüntzig, p. 219.

110. See, e.g., the report "Das feine Fräulein aus der Stadt," *NSK*, August 20, 1937.

111. "Aufruf des Reichsstudentenführers."

112. ANSt report from the region Munich/Upper Bavaria, March 4, 1939, ARNW II *540; report from ANSt Münster, July 7, 1938, ARNW II *536; report of the RSF Office for Women Students in Erlangen, February 25, 1939, ARNW II *532.

113. Report of the ANSt leader in Breslau, June 29, 1938, ARNW I *80 g595.

114. Reports of the RSF Office for Women Students in East Prussia, February 24, 1939, of ANSt Breslau, February 19, 1939, of ANSt Bonn, February 23, 1939, and of the RSF Office for Women Students in Würzburg, February 10, 1939, all in ARNW II *540.

115. Report of the student leader in Bonn to Scheel, June 28, 1939, ARNW I *07 f321.

116. Compulsory military service was introduced on March 16, 1935; see, e.g., Broszat, *Staat*, p. 313.

117. See, e.g., the opinion of Rosenberg, cited in Mosse, *Nazi Culture*, p. 40.

118. Kottenhoff, "Aufgaben und Ziele," p. 87.

119. Konietzko; protocol of a meeting of ANSt Dresden, July 6, 1934, ARNW II *501.

120. Rothe, "Studentin im Frauendienst."

121. Quotes from the minutes of a speech by the Reich Leader for "women's service," n.d., ARNW II *548; Rothe, "Studentin im Frauendienst."

122. DSt Main Office VI, circular G2 1933/34, October 28, 1933, appendix with instructions for the "women's service," ARNW I *80 g43.

123. Ibid.; see also Betz, "Einsatz der Studentinnen," pp. 103–5; Käte Ramlow's undated report, "Referat über Frauendienst," ARNW I *06 a490; Riemer and Fout, p. 112.

124. See, e.g., the letter of ANSt Freiburg's leader to Brettschneider, December 1, 1933, and the reply of December 4, 1933, ARNW II *499. See also G. Rothe's letters to TeNo Berlin, October 19, 1933, ARNW II *524, and to the dean of the medical faculty in Göttingen, November 6, 1933, ARNW II *546.

125. Report of Main Office VI in Heidelberg, n.d., ARNW II *544; report of TeNo Leipzig, "Kursus für Studentinnen der Universität," n.d., ARNW II *524.

126. DSt Main Office VI, circular DSt G3/34, May 18, 1934, ARNW I *80 g511.

127. DSt Main Office VI, office for the "women's service" circular 5, n.d., ARNW I *80 g43; Betz, "Studentin mit Stahlhelm."

128. "Studentin in der Bewegung."

129. Grimme, pp. 34–36.

130. Report of the office for "women's service" in Heidelberg, February 2, 1936, ARNW II *544.

131. *DSt Verordnungs- und Mitteilungsblatt*, November 1, 1935, p. 12, and April 1, 1936, pp. 6–7; "Die Medizinstudentin im Luftschutzdienst"; Betz, "Einsatz der Studentinnen"; report of the office for "women's service" in Heidelberg, n.d., ARNW II *544.

132. See, e.g., the confidential report "Arbeitsbericht über die bisherige Frauendienstarbeit im Amt Studentinnen," March 8, 1938, ARNW II *548; "Frauendienst."

133. "Studentin im Luftschutz," poem in a report by Marianne Fiedler (student in Leipzig), n.d., ARNW II *519. A rough translation would read:

Brave girls display their skill
Fighting fire with water and sand;
Gas masks hide their faces,
Steel helmets are strapped on tightly. . .
The coeds calmly do their duty,
Oblivious of the noise all around.

134. Altstädter, p. 241.

135. See table 10.

136. See, e.g., Kühnl, pp. 119ff.

137. Hamilton, p. 425, thus uses the term "avuncular" to describe the attitude of bourgeois newspapers towards National Socialism.

138. That upper-middle-class daughters tended to share their parents' political views is not at all surprising. Writing about the attitude of Germans towards Nazism, Hamilton, p. 437, emphasizes that "political outlooks are learned from one's parents—in most cases. . .from the father. . . .The children. . .tend to locate themselves in a like-minded [political] milieu [etc.]."

CHAPTER 8

1. See the figures in Milward, p. 47.

2. We refer to the studies of Georg, Pfahlmann, and Homze. On the use of female labor, see Winkler; Gersdorff; Rupp, pp. 74ff.; and McIntyre, pp. 209ff.

3. REM circular WA 401/39g RV, January 10, 1940, BA R21/26.

4. An SD report of November 20, 1943, in IZG MA 441/8, is characteristic in this respect; see also Stephenson, "Girls' Higher Education," pp. 55, 57–58; Kottenhoff, "Akademische Frauenberufe."

5. See table 11. The situation at Tübingen University is described in Adam, p. 189.

6. Ludwig, pp. 290, 298; Giles, "Rise," p. 178.

7. Lorenz, II, pp. 73, 75.

8. "Die Reichsvermittlungsstelle"; McIntyre, p. 209.

9. REM circular E III a 2614 WJ, January 19, 1940, GLAK 235/4877; Klecker, p. 502.

10. REM circular of February 14, 1942, GLAK 235/4877 (also in BA R21/452); REM circular of July 6, 1943, BA R21 Rep/938.

11. "Studenten heiraten"; report of ANSt Frankfurt, July 29, 1940, ARNW II *533.

12. The Langemarck Foundation provided young Nazis between the ages of seventeen and twenty-four who did not have a formal secondary school training with the opportunity to prepare themselves for academic studies, obtain the "academic maturity" (Hochschulreife) certificate, and take up university studies; see, e.g., Schoenbaum, pp. 262–63.

13. Gmelin; Hilger, pp. 12–13; Verordnungsblatt des Reichsstudentenführers, July 20, 1944, "Amt Studentinnen," pp. 8–9.

14. Dammer-Kottenhoff, "Die Neugründung"; undated report, "Die Kriegsarbeit des deutschen Studententums im Dezember 1942 und im Januar 1943," HIS, reel 20, folder 375, frame 225.

15. REM circular WJ 651, April 24, 1944, GLAK 235/5110. On the KHD, see Winkler, pp. 130ff.; Kleiber, pp. 213–14.

16. *Reichsstudentenwerk: Bericht über die Arbeit im Kriege*, p. 66.

17. See, e.g., the report of ANSt Frankfurt, July 29, 1940, ARNW II *533.

18. See Bajohr, pp. 267ff.

19. Hess to all NSDAP district leaders, March 17, 1941, and his order no. A10/41 of the same date, ARNW II *543; Steinert, pp. 196–97; Domarus, II, part 2, pp. 707–8; Focke and Reimer, p. 163; Winkler, pp. 108–10; Rupp, pp. 108–9; Bajohr, pp. 271–72.

20. See, e.g., Hitler's speech of May 4, 1941, in Domarus, II, part 2, pp. 707–8.

21. SD reports of February 16 and July 16, 1942, IZG MA441/6.

22. See table 12.

23. Gersdorff, p. 47; Grunberger, p. 256.

24. REM circular WA 1960, December 30, 1944, appendix, "Die Massnahmen...," BA R21/29.

25. Steinert, pp. 355–56; Focke and Reimer, pp. 164–65.

26. See table 12.

27. SD report of February 16, 1942, IZG MA441/6.

28. Gersdorff, p. 53; Focke and Reimer, p. 162; Winkler, p. 92; Rupp, p. 169; Bajohr, p. 256.

29. "Studenten heiraten"; report of ANSt Frankfurt, July 29, 1940, ARNW II *533.

30. See table 1.

31. The figures that follow apply to the *Altreich*, i.e., Germany within the borders imposed by the Versailles Treaty, not to the so-called *Grossdeutschland*, which included Hitler's territorial conquests such as Austria and the Sudeten area.

32. See table 13.

33. See table 12.

34. *Reichsstudentenwerk: Bericht über die Arbeit im Kriege*, pp. 31–32; Stephenson, "Girls' Higher Education," p. 56.

35. Eisenlohr, pp. 583–85.

36. Lorenz, II, appendix, "Entwicklung," pp. 8–19 (percentages computed); Ludwig, pp. 290–91.

37. See table 14. Also Raiser, p. 89; Ludwig, pp. 290, 292.

38. Lorenz, II, appendix, "Entwicklung," pp. 16, 19.

39. Ibid., pp. 8–19.

CHAPTER 9

1. See, e.g., Kottenhoff, "Jahr der Pflicht."

2. ANSt reports for the second trimester 1940, ARNW II *533. That membership in the ANSt teams was not compulsory is confirmed in *Verordnungsblatt des Reichsstudentenführers*, July 20, 1944, "Amt Studentinnen"; see also Kalb, "Die Arbeitsgemeinschaft," p. 114.

3. Report of ANSt Halle for the second trimester 1940, n.d., ARNW II *533.

4. Letter of K. Schüddekopf to the author of this study, August 27, 1975.

5. *Mitteilungsblatt der Hochschulgruppe des NSDStB Universität Frankfurt a.M.*, copy in ARNW I *20 g612.

6. Report of ANSt in the Cologne/Aachen region for the second trimester 1940, n.d., ARNW II *533.

7. Kalb, "Die Arbeitsgemeinschaft," p. 115.

8. Betz, "Eine Ausstellung"; Goldmann; "Reichswettkämpfe der Studentinnen"; "Reichswettkämpfe deutscher Studentinnen," pp. 6–7; Söllinger, pp. 72–73; Kottenhoff, "Studentinnen vor der Öffentlichkeit."

9. *Verordnungsblatt des Reichsstudentenführers*, February 5, 1940, "Amt Studentinnen"; Kalb, "Die Arbeitsgemeinschaft," p. 114.

10. Kalb, "Die Arbeitsgemeinschaft," p. 115.

11. *Verordnungsblatt des Reichsstudentenführers*, October 31, 1940, pp. 26–27.

12. See, e.g., the reports of ANSt in the Berlin region for the second trimester 1940, July 5, 1940, and of ANSt in the Frankfurt region, September 19, 1940, both in ARNW II *533; SD report of November 24, 1939, "Unwürdige Haltung der jungen Studenten," IZG MA441/1; Boelcke, *Kriegspropaganda*, p. 241.

13. "Die Weiterarbeit der ANSt-Gruppen"; various ANSt reports for the second trimester 1940, ARNW II *533.

14. *Die ANSt-Gruppe*, February 15, 1940, p. 3. A similar point is made in the REM circular WA 401/39g RV, January 10, 1940, BA R21/26.

15. Quoted in Gersdorff, p. 352. See also Scholtz-Klink, *Die Frau*, pp. 384–85.

16. Kottenhoff, "Dank und Gelöbnis."

17. REM decree WJ 4410, November 15, 1939, BA R21/453.

18. The precise figures were: winter semester 1941, 694 (3.7%); summer semester 1941, 733 (3.6%); winter semester 1941/42, 697 (3.1%); summer semester 1942, 936 (3.3%); winter semester 1942/43, 1,056 (3.2%); summer semester 1943, 1,342 (3.4%); winter semester 1943/44, 2,334 (5.5%). These figures are for all institutions of higher learning in *Grossdeutschland* (source: Lorenz, II, appendix, "Entwicklung," pp. 6–7).

19. *Verordnungsblatt des Reichsstudentenführers*, February 5, 1940, "Reichsreferentin für Studentinnen."

20. Report, "Kriegseinsatz der Studenten von Kriegsbeginn an bis 16.12.42," December 17, 1942, BA NS/26/375; *Reichsstudentenführung: Studentischer Kriegspropagandaeinsatz*, pp. 5–6; "Aufruf von Reichsminister Rust an die deutschen Studenten und Studentinnen," n.d., BA R21/453.

21. K. Schüddekopf in a letter to the author of this study, August 27, 1975.

22. *Reichsstudentenführung: Studentischer Kriegspropagandaeinsatz*, pp. 5–6.

23. "England Material," n.d., NAW T-81, 257, frame 5048447ff.

24. Report, "Kriegseinsatz der Studenten von Kriegsbeginn an bis 16.12.42," December 17, 1942, BA NS/26/375.

25. K. Schüddekopf in a letter to the author of this study, August 27, 1975. That not very many women could have participated is suggested by the small numbers of exclusively female "war propaganda service" groups; see "Semesterbericht" of ANSt Düsseldorf, July 18, 1940, ARNW II *533.

26. Kottenhoff, "Kriegsarbeit"; Dola; Kalb, "Die Arbeitsgemeinschaft," p. 115.

27. Dola; Leven, pp. 114–15; Buschatzki; Reise; report of ANSt in the Munich/Upper Bavaria region, September 5, 1940, ARNW II *533.

28. Report of ANSt Berlin, September 17, 1940, ARNW II *533; Buresch-Riebe, pp. 90–91; "Kriegseinsatz der Studenten von Kriegsbeginn an bis 16.12.42," December 17, 1942, BA NS/26/375; Kalb, "Die Arbeitsgemeinschaft," p. 115.

29. Kottenhoff's appeal in *DB*, July 3, 1940; REM circular WJ 2080 (b), October 3, 1940, BA R21/453; sample of a *Kriegsdienstpass* in BA R21/453.

30. "Kriegseinsatz der Studenten von Kriegsbeginn an bis 16.12.42," December 17, 1942, BA NS/26/375; Buresch-Riebe, p. 70; Kottenhoff, "Kriegsarbeit."

31. Report of the ANSt in the Cologne/Aachen region for the second trimester 1940, ARNW II *533.

32. Report of the Office for Women Students at Cologne University for the second trimester 1940, n.d., ARNW II *533.

33. Report of ANSt Frankfurt for the second trimester 1940, September 19, 1940, ARNW II *533.

34. Reports of ANSt Berlin, August 5 and September 17, 1940, ARNW II *533.

35. RSF *K-Befehl* 31/40, in *Verordnungsblatt des Reichsstudentenführers*, May 20, 1940, p. 31.

36. "Erfahrungen," pp. 32–33.

37. Miedzinski, "Geschenk"; Buresch-Riebe, p. 70.

38. "Erfahrungen," pp. 32-33.

39. Various ANSt reports in ARNW II *533.

40. Hohn, p. 107.

41. Report of the RSF in the Hamburg region, n.d., ARNW V *a556.

42. Ibid.

43. Broszat, *Der Staat Hitlers*, p. 395. See Koehl's monograph for a detailed study of the office of the RKF.

44. Koehl, p. 53; Broszat, *Zweihundert Jahre*, p. 223.

45. The areas earmarked for German settlement were those Polish territories which were considered "ancient German land" and which were therefore annexed to Germany, and not the "government general" of Poland, which remained outside the Reich as a sort of Polish reservation; see Wiesner, p. 5.

46. Broszat, *Zweihundert Jahre*, p. 225; Koehl, pp. 47–48.

47. Höhne, p. 287; Broszat, *Zweihundert Jahre*, p. 227; Wunderlich, pp. 189ff.; Koehl, p. 87.

48. Wiesner, p. 5.

49. Dörken, p. 154.

50. "Studentinnen bei der Siedlerbetreuung," pp. 85, 90.

51. Kalb, "Facheinsatz," pp. 19–20.

52. Dörken, p. 157.

53. Ibid., p. 156.

54. Ibid., pp. 156–57.

55. Siebert.

56. Kalb, "Facheinsatz," p. 21; "Studentinnen bei der Siedlerbetreuung," p. 85.

57. "Studentinnen bei der Siedlerbetreuung," pp. 82, 84–85.

58. Kalb, "Facheinsatz," pp. 20–21.

59. "Studentinnen bei der Siedlerbetreuung," pp. 84–85.

60. Kalb, "Facheinsatz," p. 21; Kalb, "Wir dienen."

61. Kalb, "Facheinsatz," p. 21.

62. "Studentinnen bei der Siedlerbetreuung," pp. 94–95.

63. Ibid., pp. 95–96.

64. Ibid., pp. 112–13.

65. Ibid., p. 86.

66. Computed from the figures in table 13.

67. "Studentinnen bei der Siedlerbetreuung," pp. 82–83.

68. Report of the Cologne Office for Women Students for the second trimester 1940, n.d., ARNW II *533.

69. Hiegemann; "Studentinnen bei der Siedlerbetreuung," p. 85.

70. RSF "executive assistant" (*Stabsführer*) Thomas' circular of December 1, 1942, ARNW I *01 a594.

71. SD reports of March 3, 1941, IZG MA441/1; SD report of October 23, 1941, BA R21 Rep/922; Boelcke, *Kriegspropaganda*, p. 633; Bleuel, pp. 304, 312.

72. RSF "executive assistant" Thomas' circular of December 1, 1942, ARNW I *01 a594.

73. Ibid.

74. RSF circular St.6/41, May 9, 1941, ARNW 3 *00 g614.

CHAPTER 10

1. Hitler in the fall of 1938, as quoted in Fest, *Hitler*, p. 592.

2. Domarus, I, part 2, p. 674.

3. Hess' order A 10/41, March 17, 1941, ARNW I *00 g614.

4. RSF order St.5/41, May 9, 1941, ARNW I *00 g614.

5. REM circular WJ 2112, June 19, 1941, BA R21/453.

6. Appeal by RSF deputy leader Gmelin to all German students, June 11, 1941, ARNW I *00 g614.

7. Decree Va 5213/177 of the Reich labor minister quoted in "Einsatz in der Rüstungsindustrie," pp. 2–3; REM circulars WJ 2112, June 19, 1941, BA R21/453, and WJ 3230RV, November 15, 1941, BA R21/453.

8. REM circular WJ 3230 RV, November 15, 1941, BA R21/453.

9. Decree Va 5213/177 of the Reich labor minister quoted in "Einsatz in der Rüstungsindustrie," pp. 3–7.

10. *Mitteilungsblatt der Hochschulgruppe Frankfurt*, p. 17.

11. NSDStB leader in the Brandenburg region, circular of June 21, 1941, ARNW I *00 g614.

12. SD report, "Zur Hochschullage im Sommersemester 1941," July 10, 1941, pp. 12–15, IZG MA441/4; see also Giles, "National Socialist Students' Association," pp. 258–59.

13. RSF "executive assistant" Thomas' circular of July 3, 1941, ARNW I *00 g614.

14. REM circular WJ 3270/42, November 10, 1942, BA R21 Rep/938.

15. See, e.g., Bollmus, p. 245.

16. "Aufruf des Reichsstudentenführers."

17. "Erfahrungen," p. 32.

18. Mickwitz, p. 270; "Zehn Stunden"; "Ich helfe."

19. Report on the "war service" of male and female students in Sorau, September 19, 1941, ARNW I *00 g614.

20. Domarus, II, part 2, p. 767.

21. "Aufruf des Reichsstudentenführers."

22. R. Kalb to the Hamburg region RSF office, May 29, 1941; "Bericht über die Hamburger Studentinnen," report by one A. von Conrad in Metz, both in ARNW V* a540.

23. "Aufruf des Reichsstudentenführers"; "Kriegshilfsdienst," p. 51; Gersdorff, pp. 354–55.

24. Milward, p. 113; Gersdorff, p. 54; Broszat, *Der Staat Hitlers*, p. 378; Speer, pp. 293–94.

25. Speer, pp. 294–95; Noakes and Pridham, p. 647; Broszat, *Der Staat Hitlers*, p. 378.

26. Milward, p. 47. For an excellent treatment of women's work during the Second World War, see Bajohr, pp. 251ff.

27. Fest, *Hitler*, pp. 643, 703.

28. On the *Kinderlandverschickung*, see Focke and Reimer, pp. 55ff.

29. Letter from the REM to the GBA, reference WJ 1180/864, May 19, 1942, BA R21 Rep/938.

30. GBA report, "Ferieneinsatz von Studenten und Studentinnen," June 12, 1942, ARNW V *4 a587.

31. RSF "war service department" (*Einsatzleitung*), "Merkblatt," n.d., ARNW V *4 a587.

32. See, e.g., the references to the poor performance of women students in the *Kriegseinsatz* in RSF "executive assistant" circular M.8, December 1, 1942, HIS, 120, folder 375, frame 225. Sophie Scholl of the White Rose student resistance group in Munich was one of the reluctant participants in the "armament service" in August–September 1942; see Vinke, p. 113.

33. RSF "war service department" circular "Disziplinare Behandlung von Studenten und Studentinnen die ihrer Einsatzpflicht nicht nachgekommen sind," n.d., BA R21 Rep/938.

34. GBA report, "Ferieneinsatz von Studenten und Studentinnen," June 12, 1942, ARNW V *4 a587.

35. Seidel, p. 41.

36. Scheel's telegram to Rust of October 13, 1942, BA R21 Rep/938.

37. Gersdorff, p. 55; Speer, p. 335.

38. Milward, pp. 47, 113; Bajohr, pp. 288ff.

39. Moltmann, pp. 321–22; Bajohr, pp. 288–89.

40. Steinert, pp. 355–56; Winkler, pp. 135–36; Bleuel, pp. 95–96.

41. Gersdorff, p. 47; Grunberger, p. 256; Focke and Reimer, p. 165.

42. See table 13.

43. REM to Lammers, October 9, 1943, as quoted in Gersdorff, pp. 415ff., gives March 16, 1943, as the date of Hitler's statement; a letter from Göring to Hierl on April 29, 1943, BA R21 Rep/938, gives March 22, 1943.

44. REM circular WJ 900/43 Va(b), March 22, 1943, and circular WJ 1310 Va(a), July 20, 1943, BA R21/453; see also Adam, pp. 194–95.

45. REM circular WJ 1904 (a), July 20, 1943, BA R21/453.

46. *Verordnungsblatt des Reichsstudentenführers*, July 20, 1944, "Amt Studentinnen," p. 3.

47. Ibid.

48. REM circular WA 1960, December 30, 1944, appendix, "Die Massnahmen...," p. 23, BA R21/29; Steinert, pp. 355–56.

49. See table 12.

50. GBA circular, "Meldung von Männer und Frauen," May 4, 1943, BA R21/453.

51. RSF leader in the Baden/Alsace region to the regional DAF office, letter of January 24, 1944, GLAK 235/5110.

52. *Verordnungsblatt des Reichsstudentenführers*, July 20, 1944, "Amt Studentinnen," p. 18.

53. Giles, "National Socialist Students' Association," p. 280.

54. REM to the rector of Berlin University, letter of February 29, 1944, BA R21/453.

55. I refer to the studies of Petry, Stern, Vinke, Scholl, and others. For a new look at youth resistance in the Third Reich, see Horn. Of particular interest are the interviews with Inge Aicher-Scholl in Reuter and Poneleit, pp. 171ff., and Vinke, pp. 177ff.

56. Petry, p. 36.

57. Wüst, rector of Munich University, to Rust, letter of February 23, 1943, BA R21 Rep/922.

58. Ibid.; also Wüst's letter to Rust of June 23, 1944, BA R21 Rep/922; testimony of K. Schüddekopf in a letter of August 27, 1975, to the author of this study.

59. Petry, pp. 50–52, 99, 101, 170–72; see also the letter of the dean of the medical faculty at Berlin University to the university rector, March 3, 1943, and the letter of Wüst, rector of Munich University, to the REM, February 23, 1943, BA R21 Rep/922.

60. These and following details of the events of January–February 1943 in Munich are taken from Petry, passim. Vinke, p. 129, offers a slightly different version of the incident of January 13, 1943.

61. Cited in ibid., p. 156. To her parents Sophie Scholl made a similar remark: "This [her execution] will make waves." Quoted in ibid., p. 164.

62. Elling, pp. 61–62; Hochmuth and Meyer, pp. 387–418; *Das Permanente Kolonialinstitut*, pp. 147ff.; Giles, "National Socialist Students' Association," pp. 286ff.

63. "Rundbrief Nr. 1: Die Aktion Scholl ruft Sie," Munich, April 1943, and accompanying letter from the head of the SIPO and the SD in Frankfurt to the REM, November 1943, BA R21 Rep/922.

64. REM to Lammers, letter of October 9, 1943, quoted in Gersdorff, pp. 415ff.

65. Göring's letter to Hierl, April 29, 1943, BA R21 Rep/938.

66. REM to Sauckel, letter of November 2, 1943, quoted in Gersdorff, p. 419.

67. REM circular WJ 651, April 24, 1944, GLAK 235/5110.

68. See table 12.

69. See table 13.

70. Boelcke, *Deutschlands Rüstung*, p. 398.

71. REM circular WA 1960, December 29, 1944, appendix, "Die Massnahmen...," 1, BA R21/29; Bajohr, p. 295.

72. See, e.g., Rust's letter to Goebbels, August 3, 1944, quoted in Gersdorff, pp. 430–33.

73. REM circular WA 1960, December 30, 1944, appendix, "Die Massnahmen...," 1, BA R21/29.

74. Rust's letter to Goebbels, n.d., quoted in Gersdorff, pp. 433–34.

75. REM circular RV 391/44, September 1, 1944, BA R21/453.

76. REM circular WA 1960, December 30, 1944, appendix, "Die Massnahmen...," 2, BA R21/29; "Aus dem Reich: Vom totalen Kriegseinsatz."

77. REM circular WA 1220 RV(a), October 12, 1944, BA R21/29; Adam, pp. 198ff.

78. REM circular WJ 1812/44 RV, November 25, 1944, BA R21/453.

79. REM circular WJ 1960, December 30, 1944, appendix, "Die Massnahmen...," 2–3, BA R21/29.

80. Ibid., p. 6.

81. Ringer, *Education*, pp. 25–27.

82. See table 13.

83. Winkler, p. 125.

84. On education and social mobility, see Ringer, *Education*, pp. 28–29.

85. Winkler, p. 124.

86. Duverger's ideas in this respect are set forth in his *The Political Role of Women*; see also Tiger, pp. 85–86, for a similar view.

87. See Marwick, 1970.

88. Rupp, p. 176.

89. In 1960, 1965, and 1970, women accounted for 20, 24, and 30.7 percent, respectively, of all university students in West Germany. With a female representation of about 25 percent in 1960, 26.1 percent in 1965, 35.6 percent in 1970, and 48.2 percent in 1975, the situation at the East German universities was somewhat more impressive. See Quetsch, p. 16; Pross, pp. 11, 66; Hervé, p. 20; Helwig, pp. 72–73; Speigner, p. 204. On the problem of the limited academic opportunities for women in the Federal German Republic, see also Dahrendorff, pp. 72, 104.

Glossary of Frequently Used German Terms

Abiturientin. Female high school graduate.

Arbeitsdienst. "Labor service," a six-month service in a labor camp, compulsory for prospective women university students from 1934 to 1944.

Arbeitseinsatz. "Labor mobilization," the compulsory labor draft of German women during World War II.

Arbeitsgemeinschaft. "Working community," a term often used to denote teams of female students involved in actions such as the "faculty work."

Fabrikdienst. "Factory service," the voluntary mobilization of women university students during their holidays for work in factories.

Fachschaftsarbeit. "Faculty work," extracurricular projects for women students, related to their future professional work.

Frauendienst. "Women's service," the compulsory paramilitary training of women university students.

Frauenstudium. Women's higher education; female academic aspirations.

Kriegsdienst or *Kriegseinsatz*. "War service," the mobilization of women students for all kinds of aid/actions during World War II.

Landdienst. "Agricultural service," the voluntary mobilization of women students for work on farms, mostly during the harvest season.

Machtergreifung. Hitler's advent to power, i.e., his appointment as German chancellor on January 30, 1933. Literally, "grabbing of power."

Männerbund. "Male league," a term used to denote the male-exclusionist character of the Nazi party.

Osteinsatz. "Service in the east," the voluntary involvement of women university students in the "resettlement" of ethnic Germans in occupied Poland.

Pflichtsport. "Compulsory sports," compulsory extracurricular physical exercises for women students.

Reichsberufswettkampf. "Reich Vocational Contest," a competition whereby teams of students used their academic skills to work on projects deemed relevant for the entire German nation.

Reichsführung. "Reich leadership," i.e., the national leadership of Nazi organizations such as the NSDStB and the ANSt.

Reichsleitung. See *Reichsführung.*

Reichsstudentenführung. "Reich Student Leadership," the name of the Nazi organization for university students following the merger of the DSt and the NSDStB in late 1936.

Rüstungseinsatz. "Armament action," the compulsory mobilization of women students for militarily important work in factories during World War II.

Volksgemeinschaft. "Racial community," a Nazi term which denotes the racially homogeneous community of all Germans.

Wehrmacht. The German army, as it was called in the Third Reich.

Bibliography

UNPUBLISHED ARCHIVAL SOURCES

Archives of the Former RSF and of the NSDStB (*Archiv der ehemaligen RSF und des NSDStB*). Würzburg, Germany [ARNW]. Department (*Abteilung*) I, records of the DSt and the RSF.
———. Department II, records of the NSDStB, including the ANSt.
———. Department IV, records of the Würzburg NSDStB and the RSF.
———. Department V, records of individual student federations such as the Hamburg DSt.
Archives of the Institute for Contemporary History (*Institut für Zeitgeschichte*). Munich, Germany [IZG] Department MA 441, SD reports "Meldungen aus dem Reich."
Federal Archives (*Bundesarchiv*). Koblenz, Germany [BA]. Department R 21, records of the REM.
———. Department NS, records of the NSDAP.
———. Department Zsg, press clippings.
General State Archives (*Generallandesarchiv*) of Baden. Karlsruhe, Germany [GLAK].
———. Department 235, records of the Baden universities.
Hoover Institution on War, Revolution, and Peace. Stanford, California [HIS]. Microfilms of the NSDAP *Hauptarchiv*, reels 13 (*Reichsfrauenführung*) and 20 (*NSDStB*).
National Archives. Washington, D.C. [NAW]. Captured German records microfilmed at Alexandria, Virginia, series T–74, T–81, T–405.

CORRESPONDENCE AND INTERVIEWS

Gerlach, Lydia, interview in Würzburg, May 14, 1975.
Herding, Pia, interview in San Francisco, August 26, 1975.
Schüddekopf, Katharina, letters of July 28 and August 27, 1975.

PUBLISHED SOURCES AND LITERATURE

Adam, Uwe Dietrich. *Hochschule und Nationalsozialismus: Die Universität Tübingen im Dritten Reich*. Tübingen, 1977.

Der Alltägliche Faschismus: Frauen im Dritten Reich. Berlin and Bonn, 1981.

Alpers, Käte. "Studentinnen-Arbeit in unserem Gau," *Niedersächsische Hochschul-Zeitung*, November 1936.

Alstädter, Wilfried. "Sippe und berufliche Herkunft der Studierenden an der Universität München im Winterhalbjahr 1935/36," *Bavaria, Statistisches Landesamt: Zeitschrift des Bayerischen Statistischen Landesamtes* 69, 1937, pp. 237–62.

"Die Arbeit der Studentinnen," *Die Studentische Kameradschaft*, no. 6, February 1938, pp. 31–34.

"Die Arbeit der Studentinnen in der NSV und im Winterhilfswerk," *DB*, December 23, 1936.

"Die Arbeit des Frauenamtes der DAF ist Sozialismus der Tat," *Aufklärungs- und Rednerinformationsmaterial der Reichspropagandaleitung der NSDAP und des Propagandaamtes der Deutschen Arbeitsfront*, no. 21, September 1935, entry "Frau."

"Die Arbeit einer ANSt-Zelle," *Der Student der Ostmark*, November 10, 1936.

"Arbeitsdienst und Studentin," *DStZ*, July 12, 1934.

"Arbeitsplan der ANSt für das Wintersemester 1934/35." *Freiburger Studenten-Zeitung*, February 5, 1935.

"Auch die Studentinnen kämpfen mit," *DB*, June 15, 1937.

"Aufgaben und Ziele der ANSt," *Der Frankfurter Student*, June 15, 1935, p. 6.

"Aufruf des Reichsstudentenführers," *DB*, July 11, 1942.

"Aus dem Reich: Vom totalen Kriegseinsatz." *DB*, September 1944, p. 8.

"Auslesewirkung der Frauenberufe," *Die Frau* 43, December 1935, pp. 189–90.

Axmann, Artur. *Der Reichsberufswettkampf*. Berlin, 1938.

Bäumer, Gertrud. "30 Jahre Frauenstudium," *Die Frau* 45, 1937/38, pp. 579–84.

———. *Krisis des Frauenstudiums: Die Frau im neuen Lebensraum*. Leipzig, 1932.

Baeumler, Alfred. *Männerbund und Wissenschaft*. Berlin, 1934.

Bajohr, Stefan. *Die Hälfte der Fabrik: Geschichte der Frauenarbeit in Deutschland 1914 bis 1945*. Marburg, 1979.

Beard, Charles A. "Education Under the Nazis," *Foreign Affairs* 14, April 1936, pp. 437–52.

Becker, Gisela. "Beruf der Frau," *DStZ*, December 2, 1933.

Benz, Wolfgang. "Vom freiwilligen Arbeitsdienst zur Arbeitsdienstpflicht," *VZG* 16, October 1968, pp. 317–46.

"Bericht über die Schulungsarbeit der Studentinnen im Sommersemester," *StPD*, no. 15, April 16, 1938.

Berndt, Alfred-Ingemar (ed.). *Das Archiv: Nachschlagwerk für Politik, Wirtschaft, Kultur*. Berlin, 1933.

Bernett, Hajo. "Die Indoktrination des Deutschen Hochschulsports nach 1933," in Hajo Bernett (ed.), *Untersuchungen zur Zeitgeschichte des Sports*, pp. 83–114. Schorndorf, 1973.

"Berufsmöglichkeiten für Akademikerinnen," *Student in Würzburg* 19, May 1938, p. 10.

Betz, Mathilde. "Eine Ausstellung in Darmstadt: Aus der Arbeit der deutschen Studentin," *DB*, July 26, 1941.

――――. "Einsatz der Studentinnen im Frauendienst," in *Deutsches Frauenschaffen: Jahrbuch der Reichsfrauenführung 1939*, pp. 103–5. Dortmund, 1939.

――――. "Studentin mit Stahlhelm," *DB*, April 20, 1937.

Beyer, Karl. *Die Ebenbürtigkeit der Frau im Nationalsozialistischen Deutschland: Ihre erzieherische Aufgabe*. Leipzig, 1933.

Bleuel, Hans-Peter. *Strength Through Joy: Sex and Society in Nazi Germany*. London and Sydney, 1976. (Originally published in 1972 in Berne as *Das Saubere Reich: Theorie und Praxis des sittlichen Lebens im Dritten Reich*.)

Bleuel, Hans-Peter, and Klinnert, Ernst. *Deutsche Studenten auf dem Weg ins Dritte Reich: Ideologien—Programme—Aktionen, 1918–1935*. Gütersloh, 1967.

Bloch, Ernst. *Vom Hasard zur Katastrophe: Politische Aufsätze 1934–39*. Frankfurt, 1972.

Blüher, Hans. *Die Rolle der Erotik in der männlichen Gesellschaft: Eine Theorie der menschlichen Staatsbildung nach Wesen und Wert*. New edition, Stuttgart, 1962 (first published in 1917).

Boberach, Heinz (ed.). *Meldungen aus dem Reich: Auswahl aus den geheimen Lageberichten des Sicherheitsdienstes der SS 1939–1944*. Neuwied and Berlin, 1965.

Boedeker, Elisabeth, et al. *25 Jahre Frauenstudium in Deutschland: Verzeichnis der Doktorarbeiten von Frauen 1908–1933*. 4 vols. Hannover, 1935–1937.

Boelcke, Willi A. (ed.). *Deutschlands Rüstung im zweiten Weltkrieg: Hitlers Konferenzen mit Albert Speer 1942–1945*. Frankfurt, 1969.

――――. (ed.). *Kriegspropaganda 1939–1941: Geheime Ministerkonferenzen im Reichspropagandaministerium*. Stuttgart, 1966.

Böttcher, Ilse. "Eine Studentin findet Kameradschaft der Arbeit," *Der Aktivist*, February 15, 1934.

Boje, Walter A. "Frauen in Zukunft nicht mehr zu den juristischen und tierärztlichen Staatsprüfungen zugelassen?" *Die Frau* 42, January 1935, pp. 231–34.

Bollmus, Reinhard. *Das Amt Rosenberg und seine Gegner: Studien zum Machtkampf im nationalsozialistischen Herrschaftssystem*. Stuttgart, 1970.

Bossmann, D. (ed.). *"Was Ich über Adolf Hitler gehört habe": Folgen eines Tabus: Auszüge aus Schüleraufsätzen von heute*. Frankfurt, 1977.

Brandenburg, Hans-Christian. *Die Geschichte der HJ: Wege und Irrwege einer Generation*. Cologne, 1968.

Breit, Ernst. *Das Jungmädel im Arbeitsdienst*. Kevelaer, 1935.

Brettschneider, Gisela. "Kameradinnen!" *DStZ*, June 1933.

Bridenthal, Renate. "Beyond *Kinder, Küche, Kirche*: Weimar Women at Work," *CEH* 6, June 1973, pp. 148–66.

Broszat, Martin. *Der Staat Hitlers: Grundlegung und Entwicklung seiner inneren Verfassung*. 2nd ed. Munich, 1971.

――――. *Zweihundert Jahre deutscher Polenpolitik*. Munich, 1963.

Brünneck, Wiltraut von. "Die Aufgaben der Frau im Recht." *Frauenkultur*, November 1937, pp. 9–10.

Budde, Gertrud. "Eindrücke einer Studentin von der gegenwärtigen Lage des Frauenstudiums," *Deutsche Mädchenbildung* 11, 1935, pp. 128–35.

Burghardt, Christine. *Die Deutsche Frau: Küchenmagd—Tuchtsau—Leibeigene im III. Reich: Geschichte oder Gegenwart?* Münster, 1978.

Bürkner, Trude. *Der Bund Deutscher Mädel in der Hitlerjugend*. Berlin, 1937.

Bullock, Allan. *Hitler: A Study in Tyranny*. London, 1962.

Bumm, Ernst. *Über das Frauenstudium: Rede zur Gedächtnisfeier des Stifters der Berliner Universität König Friedrich Wilhelms III in der Aula am 3. August 1917, gehalten von Ernst Bumm*. Berlin, 1917.

Buresch-Riebe, Ilse. *Frauenleistung im Kriege*. Berlin, 1941.

Burgdörfer, Friedrich. *Kinder des Vertrauens: Bevölkerungspolitische Erfolge und Aufgaben im Grossdeutschen Reich*. Berlin, 1942.

————. *Volk ohne Jugend: Geburtenschwund und Überalterung des deutschen Vokskörpers: Ein Problem der Volkswirtschaft, der Sozialpolitik, der Nationalen Zukunft*. Berlin, 1932.

Buschatzki. "Soldate als Gäste unserer Studentinnen," *DB*, March 18, 1941, appendix, "Student im Bereich Süd."

Carr, William. *Arms, Autarky, and Aggression: A Study in German Foreign Policy, 1933–1939*. London, 1972.

Charlier, J. M., and de Launay, J. *Hitler et les Femmes*. Brussels, 1979.

Claasen, Eva. "Wer ist die Beste? Vom ethischen und praktischen Wert des Reichsberufswettkampfes," *NS-Frauenwarte* 7, February 1938, pp. 504–5.

Coler, Luise, and Pfannstiehl, Emmy (eds.). *Frau und Mutter*. Düsseldorf, 1940.

Cron, Helmut. "Die Studentin: Soziales Herkommen und Berufswahl," *Die Frau* 45, 1937/38, pp. 240–52.

Dahrendorff, Ralf. *Society and Democracy in Germany*. Garden City, N.Y., 1969.

Dammer-Kottenhoff, Anna. "Die Neugründung der Hochschulgemeinschaft deutscher Frauen," *DB*, November 28, 1942.

Daniels, Felicitas. "Eine Studentin spricht," in *Deutsches Frauenschaffen: Jahrbuch der Reichsfrauenführung 1936*, p. 79. Dortmund, 1936.

Daübler-Gmelin, Herta. *Frauenarbeitslosigkeit oder Reserve zurück an den Herd*. Reinbek bei Hamburg, 1977.

Der Deutsche Hochschulführer: Lebens- und Studienverhältnisse an den deutschen Hochschulen. Vols. 1933–1943. Berlin, 1933–1943.

Deutsche Hochschulstatistik. Vols. 1928–1935. Berlin, 1928–1935.

Deutsches Frauenschaffen: Jahrbuch der Reichsfrauenführung. Vols. 1936–1941. Dortmund, 1936–1941. (From 1940: *Deutsches Frauenschaffen im Kriege*.)

Dibner, Ursula Ruth. "The History of the National Socialist German Student League." Ph.D. diss. Michigan, 1969.

Dienstvorschrift für die Arbeit der Studentenführer im Kriege. Munich, 1940.

Dörken, Ursula. "Studentischer Lehrereinsatz im östlichen Warthegau," in Hans Ochsenius (ed.), *Hamburger Studentenbuch*, pp. 154–58. Hamburg, 1941.

"Dola." "Die Hochschulgemeinschaft deutscher Frauen," *DB*, March 11, 1941.

Domarus, Max (ed.). *Hitler: Reden und Proklamationen, 1932–1945*. 2 vols. Munich, 1962–1963.

Dreissig, Wilhelmine. "Die Abiturientinnen im Frauenarbeitsdienst," *Wissen und Dienst* 9, April 23, 1936, p. 11.

————. "Der Ausgleichsdienst der Abiturientinnen," *Wissen und Dienst* 9, January 27, 1936, p. 8.

————. "Frauenarbeitsdienst und Frauenstudium," *Wissen und Dienst* 9, August 19, 1936, pp. 10–11.

Düning, Hans-Joachim. *Der SA-Student im Kampf um die Hochschule (1925–1935)*. Weimar, 1936.

Dürselen, Hedwig. "Die Frau und der Wettkampfsport," *Der Student der Ostmark*, April 15, 1939.

Duverger, Maurice. *The Political Role of Women*. Paris, 1955.

Eben-Servaes, Ilse. "Die Rechtswahrerin (Juristin)," in *Die Akademischen Berufe*, pp. 5–11. Berlin, 1938.

Eilers, Rolf. *Die Nationalsozialistische Schulpolitik: Eine Studie zur Funktion der Erziehung im totalitären Staat*. Cologne and Opladen, 1963.

"Einführung pflichtmässiger Fabrikdienstes für Studentinnen," *DB*, March 10, 1940.

"Einsatz in der Rüstungsindustrie," appendix to *Verordnungsblatt des Reichsstudentenführers*, June 15, 1941.

Eisenlohr, F. "Das Chemiestudium der Frau," *Der Student im Osten* 26, April 1941, pp. 583–85.

Elling, Hanna. *Frauen im Deutschen Widerstand 1933–45*. Frankfurt, 1978.

"Empfang der Reichssiegergruppe Juristinnen durch die Reichsfrauenführerin und den Reichsrechtsführer," *DB*, June 15, 1937.

"Erfahrungen der Studentinnen im Fabrikeinsatz," *Monatshefte für NS-Sozialpolitik* 9, 1942, pp. 32–36.

"Die Ernte rief—Wir kamen!" *DB*, July 4, 1939.

Evans, Richard J. *The Feminist Movement in Germany, 1894–1933*. Beverly Hills, Calif., 1976.

———. "German Women and the Triumph of Hitler," article accepted for demand publication, abstract printed in *JMH* 48, March 1976.

"Fabrikdienst der Studentinnen: Wir wollen helfen…doch ohne Sensation!" *DB*, November 20, 1935.

Falkenberg, Waltraut. "Kameradin im Landdienst," *DB*, January 22, 1937.

Faust, Anselm. *Der Nationalsozialistische Deutsche Studentenbund: Studenten und Nationalsozialismus in der Weimarer Republik*. 2 vols. Düsseldorf, 1973.

Feickert, Andreas. *Studenten greifen an: Nationalsozialistische Hochschulrevolution*. Hamburg, 1934.

Fest, Joachim. *The Face of the Third Reich: Portraits of the Nazi Leadership*. New York, 1970.

———. *Hitler*. New York, 1973.

Focke, Harald, and Reimer, Uwe. *Alltag unterm Hakenkreuz: Wie die Nazis das Leben der Deutschen veränderten*. Reinbek bei Hamburg, 1979.

"Förderung von Studentinnen," in *Reichsstudentenwerk: Kurzbericht aus der Arbeit des Jahres 1935*. Berlin, n.d. (unpaginated pamphlet).

"Förderung von Studentinnen," *Umschau der Studentenwerke: Versuche, Ratschläge, 1934*, no. 12, October 1934 (unpaginated).

Franze, Manfred. *Die Erlanger Studentenschaft, 1918–1945*. Würzburg, 1972.

"Frauendienst," *DB*, June 14, 1938.

"Frauenstudium," appendix to *Ich studiere: Ein Überblick über die Arbeit des deutschen Studententums*. Munich, 1940.

"Frauenstudium aussichtreich!" *Der Student der Ostmark*, December 10, 1938.

Frick, Wilhelm. *Die deutsche Frau im nationalsozialistischen Staate*. Langensalza, 1934.

Friedrich, Theodor. *Formenwandel von Frauenwesen und Frauenbildung*. Leipzig, 1934.

Frobenius, Else. *Die Frau im Dritten Reich: Eine Schrift für das Deutsche Volk*. Berlin, 1933.

Gaebel, Käthe. "Die Aussichten der Frau in akademischen Berufen," in Hans Sikorski (ed.), *Wohin? Ein Ratgeber zur Berufswahl der Abiturienten*, pp. 20–27. Berlin and Leipzig, 1933.

Gaensecke, Ruth. "Die Entwicklung des Frauenstudiums und seine Aufgabe im heutigen Staat," *Volk im Werden* 3, 1935, pp. 112–16.

———. "Die Frau auf der Hochschule—ihr Einsatz im Volk," *DStZ*, May 31, 1934.

Garraty, John A. "The New Deal, National Socialism, and the Great Depression," *AHR* 78, October 1973, pp. 907–44.

Georg, Enno. *Die wirtschaftlichen Unternehmungen der SS*. Stuttgart, 1963.

Gersdorff, Ursula von. *Frauen im Kriegsdienst, 1914–1945*. Stuttgart, 1969.

Gerstein, Hannelore. *Studierende Mädchen: Zum Problem des vorzeitigen Abgangs von der Universität*. Munich, 1965.

Gesa. "Studentin—Kameradin: Zur Stellung der Studentin an der neuen deutschen Hochschule," *NSK*, no. 152, July 5, 1937, appendix, "Die Deutsche Frau."

Giles, Geoffrey J. "The National Socialist Students' Association in Hamburg, 1926–1945." Ph.D. diss., Cambridge University, 1975.

———. "Political Education in the NSD-Studentenbund 1933–1945." Typewritten manuscript.

———. "The Rise of the National Socialist Students' Association and the Failure of Political Education in the Third Reich," in Peter D. Stachura (ed.), *The Shaping of the Nazi State*, pp. 160–85. London and New York, 1978.

Glaser, Hermann. *Eros in der Politik: Eine sozialpathologische Untersuchung*. Cologne, 1967.

———. *Spiesser-Ideologie: Von der Zerstörung des deutschen Geistes im 19. und 20. Jahrhundert*. Freiburg im Breisgau, 1964.

Gmelin, Ulrich. "Vorstudienausbildung für Frauen," *DB*, September 19, 1942.

Goese, J. "Studentinnen im Krankendienst," *DB*, April 1, 1936.

Goldmann, Gerda. "Der Anstieg im Leistungssport der Studentinnen," *DB*, July 26, 1941.

Grimme, Hugo. *Der Reichsluftschutzbund: Ziele, Leistungen, und Organisation*. Berlin, 1935.

Grotjahn, A. *Der Geburtenrückgang und seine Bekämpfung durch eine Elternschaftsversicherung*. Dresden, n.d.

Grün, Richard. "Frauenerziehung, die Schicksalfrage des deutschen Volkes," *Deutsches Bildungswesen*, March 1934, pp. 151–54.

Grüntzig, Christa. "Landdienst in der Ostmark," *Die Frau* 43, January 1936, pp. 219–23.

Grunberger, Richard. *The 12-Year Reich: A Social History of Nazi Germany, 1933–1945*. New York, 1971.

"Grundlegende Erkenntnisse aus den Lagern der ANSt: Um die Einheit des geistigen und kulturellen Frauenschaffens," *DB*, April 25, 1939.

Hackmann, Erdmuth. "Studentinnen siegen im RBWK," *Berliner Börsen-Zeitung*, May 10, 1937.

Hamilton, Richard F. *Who Voted for Hitler?* Princeton, 1982.

Hartnacke, Wilhelm. *Bildungswahn—Volkstod! Vortrag, gehalten am 17. Februar 1932 im Auditorium Maximum der Universität München für die Deutsche Gesellschaft für Rassenhygiene*. Munich, 1932.

Hartshorne, Edward Yarnell. *The German Universities and National Socialism*. Cambridge, Mass., 1937.

————. *German Youth and the Nazi Dream of Victory*. New York and Toronto, 1941.

————. "Numerical Changes in the German Student Body," *Nature*, July 23, 1938, pp. 175–76.

Hein, Margarethe. "NSV-Arbeit der Studentinnen," *Niedersächsische Hochschulzeitung*, December 18, 1935.

Hell, K. "Die Studentin in der NS-Volkswohlfahrt," *Der Heidelberger Student*, February 27, 1934.

Helwig, Gisela. *Zwischen Familie und Beruf: Die Stellung der Frau in beiden deutschen Staaten*. Cologne, 1974.

Hervé, Florence. *Studentinnen in der BRD: Eine Soziologische Untersuchung*. Cologne, 1973.

Heuss, Theodor. *Hitlers Weg: Eine Schrift aus dem Jahre 1932*. Tübingen, 1968.

Heyl, John D. "Hitler's Economic Thought: A Reappraisal," *CEH* 6, March 1973, pp. 83–96.

Hiegemann, Friedrich. "Lehrereinsatz der Studentinnen im Osten," *DB*, March 7, 1942.

Hilberg, Raul. *The Destruction of the European Jews*. Chicago, 1961.

"Hilfe, die sich selbst lohnt: Studentinnen im Fabrik-, Land- und NSV-Dienst," *StPD*, no. 35, September 3, 1938.

Hilger, Marie-Luise. "Ein neuer Weg zum Frauenstudium: Vorstudienausbildung für Frauen durch die Reichsstudentenführung," *Frauenkultur*, Winter 1943/44, pp. 12–13.

Hillgruber, Andreas. *Hitlers Strategie: Politik und Kriegsführung, 1940–1941*. Frankfurt, 1965.

Hitler, Adolf. *Mein Kampf*. Sentry Edition, Boston, 1943.

Hochmuth, Ursel, and Meyer, Gertrud. *Streiflichter aus dem Hamburger Widerstand, 1933–1945: Berichte und Dokumente*. Frankfurt, 1969.

"Die Hochschulförderung der Studentin," in *Reichsstudentenwerk: Kurzberichte aus der Arbeit des Jahres 1937*, pp. 16–17, Berlin, n.d.

Höhne, Heinz. *The Order of the Death's Head: The Story of Hitler's SS*. London, 1972.

Hörster-Philipps, Ulrike (ed.). *Wer war Hitler wirklich? Grosskapital und Faschismus, 1918–1945, Dokumente*. Cologne, 1978.

Hoffa, Lizzie. "Das Frauenstudium," *Ärztliche Mitteilungen* 43, 1933, pp. 203–5.

Hohn, Marianne. "Studentischer Fabrikdienst," in Hans Ochsenius (ed.), *Hamburger Studentenbuch 1941*, pp. 107–10. Hamburg, 1941.

Homze, Edward L. *Foreign Labour in Nazi Germany*. Princeton, 1957.

Horn, Daniel. "Youth Resistance in the Third Reich: A Social Portrait," *JSH* 7, Fall 1973, pp. 26–50.

Huber, Engelbert. *Das ist Nationalsozialismus: Organisation und Weltanschauung der NSDAP*. Stuttgart, 1933.

"Ich helfe Stukas bauen: Als Einsatzstudentin bei Junkers," *DB*, August 23, 1941.

"In Hessen," *Der Deutsche Student*, February 1935, pp. 111–12.

Jacobsen, Hans-Adolf. *Die nationalsozialistische Aussenpolitik, 1933–1938*. Frankfurt and Berlin, 1968.

Janssen, Karl-Heinz. "Bleibt uns Hitler nicht erspart? Der NS-Diktator auf der Bestseller-Liste," *Die Zeit*, July 27, 1973.

Jarausch, Konrad H. *Students, Society, and Politics in Imperial Germany: The Rise of Academic Illiberalism*. Princeton, 1982.

Kalb, Renate. "Die Arbeitsgemeinschaft nationalsozialistischer Studentinnen: Aufgaben und Ziele," *Die Ärztin* 17, 1941, pp. 113–16.

————. "Facheinsatz Ost 1940 der deutschen Studentinnen," *Die Ärztin* 17, 1941, pp. 19–21.

————. "Wir dienen dem Osten," *Frauenkultur, 1940*, no. 10, October 1940, p. 9.

Karl, Liselotte. "Erlanger Studentinnen im Gauentscheid des Reichsberufswettkampfes in Nürnberg," *Erlanger Hochschul-Blätter, 1935/36*, no. 17, April 1936, pp. 85–86.

Kater, Michael H. "Ansätze zu einer Soziologie der SA bis zur Röhm-Krise," in Ulrich Engelhardt et al. (eds.), *Soziale Bewegung und Politische Verfassung: Beiträge zur Geschichte der modernen Welt*, pp. 798–831. Stuttgart, 1976.

————. "Frauen in der NS-Bewegung," *VZG* 31, April 1983.

————. "Krisis des Frauenstudiums in der Weimarer Republik," *VSWG* 59, 1972, pp. 207–55.

————. "Der NSD-Studentenbund von 1926 bis 1928: Randgruppe zwischen Hitler und Strasser," *VZG*, no. 2, 1974, pp. 148–90.

————. "The Reich Vocational Contest and Students of Higher Learning in Nazi Germany," *CEH* 7, September 1974, pp. 225–61.

————. *Studentenschaft und Rechtsradikalismus in Deutschland, 1928–1933: Eine sozialgeschichtliche Studie zur Bildungskrise in der Weimarer Republik.* Hamburg, 1975.

————. "The Work Student: A Socio-Economic Phenomenon of Early Weimar Germany," *JCH* 10, January 1975, pp. 71–94.

————. "Zum gegenseitigen Verhältnis von SA und SS in der Sozialgeschichte des Nationalsozialismus von 1925–1939," *VSWG* 62, 1975, pp. 339–79.

————. "Zur Soziographie der frühen NSDAP," *VZG* 19, 1971, pp. 124–59.

Kirkpatrick, Clifford. *Nazi Germany, Its Women and Family Life.* Indianapolis and New York, 1938.

Klaus, Martin. *Mädchen im Dritten Reich: Der Bund Deutscher Mädel (BDM)*, Cologne, 1983.

Klecker, Erika. "Frauenvorbildung und Frauenstudium an den deutschen Universitäten," *Die Ärztin* 17, 1941, pp. 499–505.

Kleiber, Lore. " 'Wo Ihr seid, da soll die Sonne Scheinen'—Der Frauenarbeitsdienst am Ende der Weimarer Republik und im Nationalsozialismus," in *Mutterkreuz und Arbeitsbuch: Zur Geschichte der Frauen in der Weimarer Republik und im Nationalsozialismus*, pp. 188–214. Frankfurt, 1981.

Klinksiek, Dorothee. *Die Frau im NS-Staat.* Stuttgart, 1982.

Knodel, John E. *The Decline of Fertility in Germany, 1871–1939.* Princeton, 1974.

Köberle, Sophie. "Aus Erziehungswesen und Erziehungswissenschaft: Stimmen zur Frauenfrage," *Deutsches Bildungswesen*, March 1934, pp. 176–81.

Koehl, Robert L. *RKFDV. German Resettlement and Population Policy, 1939–1945.* Cambridge, Mass., 1957.

Köhler, Henning. *Arbeitsdienst in Deutschland: Pläne und Verwirklichungsformen bis zur Einführung der Arbeitsdienstpflicht im Jahre 1935.* Berlin, 1967.

Konietzko, Hilde. "Frauendienst ist der Wehrdienst der deutschen Studentin," *Der Student der Ostmark*, January 25, 1936, special issue: "10 Jahre NSD-Studentenbund, 1926–1936."

Koonz, Claudia. "Mothers in the Fatherland: Women in Nazi Germany," in Renate

Bridenthal and Claudia Koonz (eds.), *Becoming Visible: Women in European History*, pp. 445–73. Boston, 1977.
———. "Nazi Women Before 1933: Rebels Against Emancipation," *Social Science Quarterly*, March 1976, pp. 553–63.
Korherr, Richard. "Geburtenrückgang," *Süddeutsche Monatshefte*, December 1927.
Kotschnig, Walter M. *Unemployment in the Learned Professions: An International Study of Occupational and Educational Planning*. London, 1937.
Kottenhoff, Anna. "Akademische Frauenberufe," *DB*, November 29, 1941.
———. "Aufgaben und Ziele der Studentinnenarbeit," in *Deutsches Frauenschaffen...1937*, pp. 81–88. Dortmund, 1937.
———. "Bekenntnis zur Hochschule," *Frauenkultur*, November 1937, pp. 2–3.
———. "Dank und Gelöbnis der deutschen Studentin," *DB*, April 22, 1941.
———. "Fragen des Frauenstudiums," *Die Frau* 46, 1939, pp. 456–60.
———. "Die geistige Bereitschaft der Frau an der Hochschule: Erkenntnisse aus dem Reichsberufswettkampf der deutschen Studenten," *Frauenkultur*, August 1937, pp. 8–9.
———. "Jahr der Pflicht: Aus der Kriegsarbeit der deutschen Studentinnen," *DB*, December 17, 1940.
———. "Kriegsarbeit neben dem Studium," *DB*, December 17, 1940.
———. "Mann und Frau in geistiger Zusammenarbeit: Erkenntnisse aus dem Reichsberufswettkampf der Studentinnen," *NSK*, no. 89, April 19, 1937, Appendix, "Die Deutsche Frau."
———. "Querschnitt durch den Reichsberufswettkampf der deutschen Studentin," *Frauenkultur*, July 1938, pp. 6–7.
———. "Die Studentin im Reichsberufswettkampf: Aufgaben und Themenstellung," *StPD*, no. 36, November 6, 1937.
———. "Die Studentin in der ANSt: Bericht anlässlich des Deutschen Studententages 1933 [*sic.*; actually 1939] in Würzburg," *Der Student der Ostmark*, July 5, 1939.
———. "Studentinnen vor der Öffentlichkeit!" *DB*, July 26, 1941.
———. "Wert und Bedeutung des Frauenstudiums," *NS-Monatshefte* 13, 1942, pp. 133–40.
———. "Zur Lage der deutschen Frau," *Die Frau* 44, September 1937, pp. 689–90.
Kranzhoff, Maria. "Zur Frage des Frauenstudiums," *Stimmen der Zeit*, ser. 3, vol. 124, 1933, pp. 243–50.
Kreppel, Otto. *Nationalsozialistisches Studententum und Studentenrecht*. Königsberg, 1932.
Kreutzberger, Wolfgang. *Studenten und Politik, 1918–1933: Der Fall Freiburg im Breisgau*. Göttingen, 1972.
"Kriegshilfsdienst," *Die Fachgruppe*, no. 6, February 1942, pp. 51–52.
Kubach, Fritz. *Studenten bauen auf! Der 2. Reichsberufswettkampf der deutschen Studenten, 1936/37*. Berlin, n.d.
———. *Studenten bauen auf! Der 3. Reichsberufswettkampf der deutschen Studenten, 1937/38: Ein Rechenschaftsbericht*. Berlin, n.d.
———. *Studenten bauen auf! Der 4. Reichsberufswettkampf der deutschen Studenten, 1938/39: Ein Rechenschaftsbericht*. Munich, n.d.
Kuczynski, Robert René. *"Living Space" and Population Problems*. Oxford, 1939.
Kühn, Lenore. "Geistige Führung im Frauentum," *Die Frau* 41, January 1934, pp. 210–13.

————. "Natürlicher Aristokratismus," in Irmgard Reichenau (ed.), *Deutsche Frauen an Adolf Hitler*, pp. 28–39. Leipzig, 1933.

Kühnl, Reinhard. *Formen bürgerlicher Herrschaft: Liberalismus—Faschismus*. Reinbek bei Hamburg, 1971.

Kupisch, Karl. *Studenten entdecken die Bibel: Die Geschichte der Deutschen Christlichen Studentenvereinigung (DCVSF)*. Hamburg, 1964.

Kutzleb, Hjalmar. "Über das Bildungsideal der Frau," *Volk im Werden*, no. 2, 1933, pp. 41ff.

Lange, Georg. "Die weibliche Begabung und die neue Schule," *Deutsche Mädchenbildung*, no. 6, 1933.

Langer, Walter C. *The Mind of Adolf Hitler: The Secret Wartime Report*. New York, 1973.

Leers, Johannes von. "Unsere Kameradinnen oder unsere 'Gäste'?" *DStZ*, November 25, 1933.

Lenz-von Borries, Kara. "Frauenstudium und Auslese," *Die Frau* 41, January 1934, pp. 202–4.

Leven, Eva. "Lazarettendienst Winter 1940," in Hans Ochsenius (ed.), *Hamburger Studentenbuch 1941*, pp. 114–15. Hamburg, 1941.

Loewenberg, Peter. "The Psychohistorical Origins of the Nazi Youth Cohort," *AHR* 76, December 1971, pp. 1475–1502.

Lohlöffel, Edith von. "Leitsätze für die körperliche Erziehung der Studentinnen an deutschen Hochschulen," *Die Ärztin* 10, 1934, pp. 118–21.

Lorenz, Charlotte. *Zehn-Jahres-Statistik des Hochschulbesuchs und der Abschlussprüfungen*. 2 vols. Berlin, 1943.

Lotze, Elisabeth. "Studentinnen arbeiten in Betrieben," *Der Heidelberger Student*, May 22, 1935.

————. "Studentin und Sozialismus," *Der Heidelberger Student*, January 24, 1934.

Ludwig, Karl-Heinz. *Technik und Ingenieure im Dritten Reich*. Düsseldorf, 1974.

Lübben, Rosemarie. "Studentischer Einsatz in den Fabriken," *Die Frau* 43, August 1936, pp. 688–89.

Luetkens, Charlotte. "Enrolments at German Universities Since 1933," *Sociological Review* 31, January 1939, pp. 194–209.

Machwirth, Liselotte. "Kameradinnen!" *DStZ*, December 13, 1934.

————. "Die nationalsozialistische Studentin," *VB*, November 30, 1935.

Marwick, Arthur. *Britain in the Century of Total War: War, Peace, and Social Change, 1900–1967*. Harmondsworth, 1970.

Maschmann, Melita. *Fazit: Kein Rechtfertigungsversuch*. Stuttgart, 1963.

Mason, T. W. *Arbeiterklasse und Volksgemeinschaft: Dokumente und Materialien zur deutschen Arbeiterpolitik, 1936–1939*. Opladen, 1975.

————. "Labour in the Third Reich, 1933–1939," *Past and Present*, no. 33, April 1966, pp. 112–41.

————. "Women in Germany, 1925–1940: Family, Welfare, and Work, Part I," *History Workshop: A Journal of Socialist Historians* 1, Spring 1976, pp. 74–113.

McIntyre-Stephenson, Jill. "Women and the Professions in Germany, 1930–1940," in Anthony Nicholls and Erich Matthias (eds.), *German Democracy and the Triumph of Hitler: Essays in Recent German History*, pp. 175–213. New York, 1971.

"Die Medizinstudentin im BDM," *StPD*, no. 17, June 19, 1937.

"Die Medizinstudentin im Luftschutzdienst," *Die Frau* 44, December 1936, p. 182.

Meissner, Gertrud. "Die Entwicklung des Frauenstudiums in jüngster Zeit," *Deutsche Mädchenbildung* 11, 1935, pp. 116–27.

Merkl, Peter H. *Political Violence Under the Swastika: 581 Early Nazis.* Princeton, 1975.

Mertesdorf, Maria. "Aufgaben der Studentin im Landdienst," *Der Frankfurter Student,* February 17, 1936.

Mickwitz, L. von. "Aus dem Rüstungseinsatz der Studentinnen," *Nachrichten des deutschen auslandswissenschaftlichen Instituts,* no. 2/3, November 1941, p. 270.

Miedzinski, Herta. "Das Geschenk der 650,000 Arbeitsstunden: Von dem Fabrikeinsatz der deutschen Studentinnen," *DB,* December 17, 1940.

———. "Landdienst und Fabrikdienst als praktische Frauenarbeit an der Hochschule," in *Deutsches Frauenschaffen...1939,* pp. 105–8. Dortmund, 1939.

———. "Man ruft uns! Wir packen an! Die Studentin in der Landhilfe,"*NS-Frauenwarte* 7, September 1938, pp. 134–35.

Mierendorff, Carl. "Gesicht und Charakter der nationalsozialistischen Bewegung," *Die Gesellschaft* 30, 1930, pp. 489–504.

Milward, Alan S. *The German Economy at War.* London, 1965.

Mitteilungsblatt der Hochschulgruppe des N.S.D.St.B., Universität Frankfurt a.M. Frankfurt, 1941.

Moltmann, Günter. "Goebbels' Speech on Total War, February 18, 1943," in Hajo Holborn (ed.), *Republic to Reich: The Making of the Nazi Revolution, Ten Essays,* pp. 298–342. New York, 1973.

Mosse, George L. *The Crisis of German Ideology: Intellectual Origins of the Third Reich.* New York, 1964.

———. *Nazi Culture: Intellectual, Cultural, and Social Life in the Third Reich.* New York, 1968.

Mutterkreuz und Arbeitsbuch: Zur Geschichte der Frauen in der Weimarer Republik und im Nationalsozialismus. Frankfurt, 1981.

Nationalsozialistische Frauenschaft. Berlin, 1937.

Nemse. "Die Frauenfrage vom eugenischen Standpunkt aus betrachtet," *Deutsches Ärzteblatt,* no. 4, 1933.

Newitt, Hillary. *Women Must choose: The Position of Women in Europe To-day.* London, 1937.

Nitsch, Wolfgang et al. *Hochschule in der Demokratie: Kritische Beiträge zur Erbschaft und Reform der deutschen Universität.* Berlin, 1965.

Noakes, Jeremy, and Pridham, Geoffrey (eds.). *Documents on Nazism, 1919–1945.* New York, 1975.

Oehring, Jutta. "Studentinnen im Fabrikdienst: Brief einer Studentin aus einer Fabrik," *Die Erziehung* 11, 1936, pp. 79–83.

Opitz, Reinhard. *Der Deutsche Sozialliberalismus, 1917–1933.* Cologne, 1973.

Paatero, Salme. "Der Einfluss der Studien und der geistigen Berufsarbeit auf die Frau mit besonderer Berücksichtigung der Mutterschaft," *Acta Societatis Medicorum Fennicae "Duodecim,"* ser. B, vol. 30, 1941, pp. 1–35.

Pauwels, Jacques R. "Women and University Studies in the Third Reich, 1933–1945." Ph.D. diss., York University, Toronto, 1976.

Payne, Robert. *The Life and Death of Adolf Hitler.* New York and Washington, D.C., 1973.

Das Permanente Kolonialinstitut: 50 Jahre Hamburger Universität. Hamburg, 1969.

Petry, Christian. *Studenten aufs Schafott: Die Weisse Rose und ihr Scheitern.* Munich, 1968.

Petzina, Dieter. *Autarkiepolitik im Dritten Reich: Der nationalsozialistische Vierjahresplan.* Stuttgart, 1968.

Pfahlmann, H. *Fremdarbeiter und Kriegsgefangene in der deutschen Kriegswirtschaft, 1939–1945.* Darmstadt, 1968.

Picker, Henry (ed.). *Hitlers Tischgespräche im Führerhauptquartier, 1941–1942.* 2nd ed. Stuttgart, 1965.

Plagemann, Rita. "Studentin und Sport," *Der Heidelberger Student*, December 12, 1933.

Prenzel, Christa. "Studentin im Fabrikdienst," *StPD*, no. 118, May 21, 1939.

Pross, Helge. *Über die Bildungschancen von Mädchen in der Bundesrepublik.* Frankfurt, 1969.

Puckett, Hugh Wiley. *Germany's Women Go Forward.* New edition. New York, 1967.

Quetsch, Cäcilie. *Die zahlenmässige Entwicklung des Hochschulbesuches in den letzten fünfzig Jahren.* Berlin, 1960.

Raiser, Edith. "Die Studentin an der Technischen Hochschule," in *Studentisches Jahrbuch der Technischen Hochschule Darmstadt*, pp. 89–92. Darmstadt, 1943.

Reichenau, Irmgard. "Die begabte Frau," in Irmgard Reichenau (ed.), *Deutsche Frauen an Adolf Hitler*, pp. 13–27. Leipzig, 1933.

Reichsstudentenführung: Studentischer Kriegspropagandaeinsatz: Grundbefehl. Munich, 1939.

Reichsstudentenwerk: Bericht über die Arbeit im Kriege. Berlin, 1941.

Reichsstudentenwerk: Kurzbericht aus der Arbeit des Jahres—. Vols. 1935–1939. Berlin-Charlottenburg, 1935–1939.

"Die Reichsvermittlungsstelle für Frauenberufe ist für Akademikerinnen tätig geworden," *DB*, January 16, 1940.

"Reichswettkämpfe der Studentinnen 1939," *DB*, August 15, 1939.

"Reichswettkämpfe deutscher Studentinnen im Kriege," *Frauenkultur*, September 1941, pp. 6–7.

Reise, L. "Soldatendienst der Reichsstudentenführung," *Die Fachgruppe*, no. 5, July 1941, p. 7.

Reuter, Angelika, and Poneleit, Barbara. *Seit 1848, Frauen im Widerstand: Frauen im Faschismus, 1933–1945.* N.p., 1977.

Riemer, Eleanor S., and Fout, John C. (eds.). *European Women: A Documentary History, 1789–1945.* New York, 1980.

Ringer, Fritz K. *The Decline of the German Mandarins: The German Academic Community, 1890–1933.* Cambridge, Mass., 1969.

———. *Education and Society in Modern Europe.* Bloomington and London, 1979.

Rompel, Josef. *Die Frau im Lebensraume des Mannes: Emanzipation und Volkswohl.* Darmstadt and Leipzig, 1932.

Rosenberg, Alfred. *Der Mythus des 20. Jahrhunderts: Eine Wertung der seelisch-geistigen Gestaltungskämpfe unserer Zeit.* 41st and 42nd eds. Munich, 1934.

Rosten, Curt. *Das ABC des Nationalsozialismus.* 3rd ed. Berlin, 1933.

Rothe, Gisela. "Studentin im Fabrikdienst," *Der Deutsche Student*, September 1935, pp. 559–61.

———. "Studentin im Frauendienst," *Der Aktivist*, December 21, 1934.

Rühle, Gerd (ed.). *Das Dritte Reich: Dokumentarische Darstellung des Aufbaues der Nation.* 6 vols. Berlin, 1934–1939.

Ruge, Arnold. *Das Wesen der Universitäten und das Studium der Frauen: Ein Beitrag zur modernen Kulturbewegung.* Leipzig, 1912.

Ruoff, Wilhelm. *Lage und Ziele der akademischen Jugend.* Leipzig, 1933.

Rupp, Leila. *Mobilizing Women for War: German and American Propaganda, 1939–1945.* Princeton, 1978.

Salomon, Alice. "Hochschule und Frauenbewegung," in Michael Doeberl (ed.), *Das Akademische Deutschland*, vol. 3, pp. 419–24. Berlin, 1930.

Schairer, Reinhold. *Die Akademische Berufsnot.* Jena, 1932.

Scheel, Gustav Adolf. "Der NSD-Studentenbund," in Rudolf Benze and Gustav Gräfer (eds.), *Erziehungsmächte und Erziehungshoheit im Grossdeutschen Reich als gestaltende Kräfte im Leben des Deutschen*, pp. 187–211. Leipzig, 1940.

―――. *Die Reichsstudentenführung.* Berlin, 1938.

Schleunes, Karl A. *The Twisted Road to Auschwitz: Nazi Policy towards German Jews, 1933–1939.* Urbana, Ill., 1970.

Schlömer, Hans. "Die Ära der Gleichschaltung: Das Deutsche Studentenwerk im Dritten Reich," in *Deutsches Studentenwerk, 1921–1961: Festschrift zum vierzigjährigen Bestehen*, pp. 63–79. Bonn, 1961.

Schlüter-Hermkes, Maria. "Die Selbstbehauptung der Frau an der deutschen Hochschule," *Die Frau* 41, January 1934, pp. 214–18.

Schoenbaum, David. *Hitler's Social Revolution: Class and Status in Nazi Germany, 1933–1939.* New York, 1966.

Scholl, Inge. *Students Against Tyranny: The Resistance of the White Rose, Munich, 1942–1943.* Middletown, Conn., 1970.

Scholtz-Klink, Gertrud. *Die Frau im Dritten Reich.* Tübingen, 1978.

―――. "Studentinnen und Berufseinsatz," *StPD*, no. 1, March 3, 1937.

Schorn, Maria. "Frauenstudium in der Zukunft," in Auguste Reber-Gruber (ed.), *Weibliche Erziehung im NSLB*, pp. 15–22. Leipzig and Berlin, 1934.

Schuster, Otto. "Die Frauenfrage an den Hochschulen," *Wissen und Dienst, 1935*, no. 1, January 1935.

Seggel, Sophie. "Vom FAD—dem weiblichen Arbeitsdienst," *Die Frau* 43, January 4, 1936, pp. 216–18.

Seidel, Gerhard. "Der studentische Kriegseinsatz," in *Der Deutsche Hochschulführer, 1943*, pp. 39–41.

Seipp. "Arbeitsdienst und Hochschule," in Hermann Müller-Brandenburg (ed.), *Jahrbuch des Reichsarbeitsdienstes, 1937/38*, pp. 28–33. Berlin, 1937.

Sevin, Barbara. "Die Deutsche Studentin," *Reichsverband Deutscher Offizieren* 13, November 25, 1934, pp. 973–74.

Shirer, William L. *The Rise and Fall of the Third Reich: A History of Nazi Germany.* New York, 1967.

Siber, Paula. *Die Frauenfrage und ihre Lösung durch den Nationalsozialismus.* Wolfenbüttel and Berlin, 1933.

Siebert, Margret. "Studentinnen beim 'Medizinischen Facheinsatz Ost' vom Sommer 1940," *Die Ärztin* 17, 1941, pp. 312–15.

Sikorski, Hans. *Der Lebensraum der akademischen Berufe.* Dresden, 1930.

"So denken die siegreichen Studentinnen," *NSK*, no. 100, May 3, 1937.

Soden, Kristine von, and Zipfel, Gaby (eds.). *70 Jahre Frauenstudium: Frauen in der Wissenschaft.* Cologne, 1979.

Söllinger, Ernst. "Die Reichswettkämpfe der Studentinnen 1941 in Darmstadt," in *Stu-*

dentisches Jahrbuch der Technischen Hochschule Darmstadt, 1943, pp. 69–75. Darmstadt, 1943.

Speer, Albert. *Inside the Third Reich*. New York, 1970.

Speigner, Wulfram. ''Bildung für die Frauen und Mädchen,'' in Herta Kuhrig and Wulfram Speigner (eds.), *Wie Emanzipiert sind die Frauen in der DDR? Beruf—Bildung—Familie*. Cologne, 1979.

Statistisches Handbuch für Deutschland, 1928–1944. Munich, 1949.

Statistisches Jahrbuch für das Deutsche Reich. Berlin, 1917–1941/42.

Steakley, James D. *The Homosexual Emancipation Movement in Germany*. New York, 1975.

Steinberg, Michael Stephen. ''Sabres, Books, and Brownshirts: The Radicalization of the German Student, 1918–1935.'' Ph.D. diss., Johns Hopkins University, 1971.

Steinert, Marlis G. *Hitlers Krieg und die Deutschen: Stimmung und Haltung der deutschen Bevölkerung im zweiten Weltkrieg*. Düsseldorf and Vienna, 1970.

Stephenson, Jill. ''Girls' Higher Education in Germany in the 1930's,'' *JCH* 10, January 1975, pp. 41–69.

———. *The Nazi Organisation of Women*. Totowa, N.J., 1981.

———. ''The Nazi Organisation of Women 1933–1939,'' in Peter D. Stachura (ed.), *The Shaping of the Nazi State*, pp. 186–209. London and New York, 1978.

———. *Women in Nazi Society*. London, 1975.

Stern, J. P. ''The White Rose,'' *German Life and Letters: A Quarterly Review* 11, 1957/58, pp. 81–101.

Stierlin, Helm. *Adolf Hitler: Familienperspektiven*. Frankfurt, 1975.

Stitz, Peter. *Der CV 1919–1938: Der Hochschulpolitische Weg des Cartellverbandes der katholischen deutschen Studentenverbindungen (CV) vom Ende des 1. Weltkrieges bis zur Vernichtung durch den Nationalsozialismus*. Munich, 1970.

''Studenten heiraten,'' *DB*, July 1944.

''Studentin in der Bewegung,'' *Der Heidelberger Student*, December 9, 1935.

''Studentinnen bei der Siedlerbetreuung und im Kindergarteneinsatz,'' *Die Fachgruppe*, no. 4, April 1941, pp. 82–121.

''Studentinnen geben Rechenschaft,'' *DB*, February 6, 1940.

''Studentinnen im Landdienst,'' *Der Student der Ostmark*, December 4, 1935.

''Studentinnen und Berufseinsatz,'' *StPD*, no. 1, March 3, 1937.

''Studentin und Bund Deutscher Mädchen [*sic*],'' *NSK*, no. 46, February 25, 1937.

''Studentin und Erntehilfe,'' *StPD*, no. 9, April 28, 1937.

''Die Studentin von heute: Sechs Monate Arbeitsdienst und dann zur Hochschule,'' *DB*, November 16, 1937.

Tage Studentischer Kunst, 9.–12.2.1939. Munich, 1940.

Thalmann, Rita. *Etre Femme sous le IIIe Reich*. Paris, 1982.

Tiger, Lionel. *Men in Groups*. New York, 1970.

Tormin, Helmut. ''Die Zukunft des Frauenarbeitsdientes,'' *Soziale Praxis: Zentralblatt für Sozialpolitik und Wohlfahrtspflege* 44, September 5, 1935, pp. 1026–36.

Tournier, Michele. ''Women and Access to University in France and Germany (1861–1967),'' *Comparative Education* 9, October 1973, pp. 107–17.

Tritt, Hans. ''Vom Wert des Frauenstudiums,'' *Nachrichtenblatt für Studium und Beruf*, no. 2, 1939/40, pp. 1–6.

''Unsere Studentinnen bescheren Freiburger Kinder,'' *Freiburger Studentenzeitung*, January 14, 1936.

Bibliography 197

Vehlow, Sybille. "Geschichte der Königsberger ANSt von 1932 bis 1935," *Der Student der Ostmark*, January 25, 1936, special issue: "Zehn Jahre NSD-Studentenbund 1926–1936."

Vermehren-Göring, Beatrice. "Die Frau im akademischen Beruf," in *Deutsches Frauen-schaffen...1936*, pp. 76–78.

"Verstand bei Mann und Frau," *VB*, October 2, 1926.

Viereck, Peter. *Metapolitics: The Roots of the Nazi Mind*. Rev. and enlarged ed. New York, 1965.

Vinke, Hermann. *Das kurze Leben der Sophie Scholl*. Ravensburg, 1980.

Vogel, Georg. *Die Deutsche Frau, [Volume] III: Im Weltkriege und im Dritten Reich*. Breslau, n.d.

"Die Volksnähe deutsche Kriegsstudentin," *NS-Frauenwarte* 10, 1941/42, p. 87.

Waite, Robert L. *The Psychopathic God: Adolf Hitler*. New York, 1977.

Weinberg, Gerhardt L. *The Foreign Policy of Hitler's Germany: Diplomatic Revolution in Europe, 1933–36*. Chicago and London, 1970.

"Die Weiterarbeit der ANSt-Gruppen," *DB*, October 17, 1939.

Weyrather, Irmgard. "Numerus Clausus für Frauen—Studentinnen im Nationalsozialismus," in *Mutterkreuz und Arbeitsbuch: Zur Geschichte der Frauen in der Weimarer Republik und im Nationalsozialismus*, pp. 131–62. Frankfurt, 1981.

Wiedmann, Berthold. "Der Landdienst als kulturpolitische Aufgabe," *Freiburger Studentenzeitung*, June 4, 1936.

Wiesner, Rudolf. "Deutscher Einsatz im befreiten Osten," *Die Fachgruppe*, no. 1, April 1940, pp. 5–7.

Winkler, Dörte. *Frauenarbeit im "Dritten Reich."* Hamburg, 1977.

Winslow, W. Thacher. *Youth, a World Problem: A Study in World Perspective of Youth Conditions, Movements, and Programs*. Washington, D.C., 1937.

Wirth-Stockhausen, Julia. "Barbara: Eindrücke aus dem Leben einer Studentin unserer Tage," *Die Frau* 46, 1938–1939, pp. 118–29.

———. "Mutige Männer—anmutige Frauen!" *DB*, August 9, 1941.

Wolff, Inge. "Die Stellung der Studentin im Dritten Reich," in *Wille und Weg der Nationalsozialistischen Studenten: Bericht von der ersten Reichsarbeitstagung des NSD-Studentenbundes und der Deutschen Studentenschaft, Heidelberg, 22. bis 25. Juni, 1937*. Marburg, 1937, pp. 103–9.

Wünsche, Ilse. "Mutterschaft und Frauenarbeit im Tabakgewerbe: Reichssiegerarbeit der Sparte 'Deutsches Frauenschaffen' im Reichsberufswettkampf der deutschen Studenten 1938/39," *Frauenkultur, 1939*, no. 6, June 1939, pp. 8–9.

———. "Die Reichssiegerarbeit der Studentinnen 'Mutterschaft und Frauenarbeit im Tabakgewerbe' (Universität Heidelberg)," *Die Frau* 46, 1939, pp. 534–39.

Wunderlich, Frieda. *Farm Labor in Germany, 1910–1945: Its Historical Development Within the Framework of Agricultural and Social Policy*. Princeton, 1961.

"Zehn Stunden...Notiert von einer Studentin im Fabrikdienst," *DB*, October 18, 1941.

Zörlein, Maria. "Medizinstudentinnen!" in *Freiburger Studentenbuch, Sommersemester 1939*, p. 79. Freiburg im Breisgau, 1939.

"Zum Abkommen mit dem BDM: Mädel an der Hochschule," *DB*, March 9, 1937.

"Zum Fabrikdienst der Königsberger Studentinnen," *Der Student der Ostmark*, June 21, 1935.

"Zur Frage des Frauenstudiums und der verheirateten Akademikerin," *Die Ärztin* 9, August 1933, pp. 165–68.

NEWSPAPERS, JOURNALS, AND PERIODICALS

Die Ärztin

Der Aktivist: Das Blatt des Berliner Studenten und Arbeiters

Die ANSt-Gruppe: ANSt-Gruppen-Schulung

Die Bewegung: Zentralorgan des N.S.D. Studentenbundes [in this study usually abbreviated as *DB*]

Deutsche Frauenkultur

Deutsche Mädchenbildung

Der Deutsche Student: Zeitschrift der Deutschen Studentenschaft

Die Deutsche Studentenschaft: Nachrichtendienst

Deutsche Studentenschaft: Verordnungs- und mitteilungsblatt

Deutsche Studenten-Zeitung: Kampfblatt der Deutschen Studenten [*DStZ*]

Erlanger Hochschul-Blätter

Die Fachgruppe: Organ des Amtes Wissenschaft und Facherziehung und Mitteilungsblatt der Reichsfachgruppen der Reichsstudentenführung

Der Frankfurter Student

Die Frau: Organ des Bundes Deutscher Frauenvereine

Frauenkultur

Freiburger Studentenzeitung

Hansische Hochschul-Zeitung

Der Heidelberger Student

Hochschulblatt Grenzland Sachsen

Keesing's Contemporary Archives

Nationalsozialistische Frauenwarte: Zeitschrift der N.S. Frauenschaft

Nationalsozialistische Partei-Korrespondenz [*NSK*]

Niedersächsische Hochschulzeitung

Der Student der Ostmark

Der Student in Würzburg

Studenten-Pressedienst: Amtlicher Pressedienst des Reichsstudentenführers [*StPD*]

Die Studentische Kameradschaft

Verordnungsblatt des Reichsstudentenführers: Befehle des Reichsstudentenführers und Anordnungen der Amtsleiter der Reichsstudentenführung

Verordnungs- und Mitteilungsblatt des nationalsozialistischen deutschen Studentenbundes der NSDAP

Völkischer Beobachter [*VB*]

Index

About the Author

JACQUES R. PAUWELS is a Postdoctoral Fellow of the Social Sciences and Humanities Research Council of Canada and is currently engaged in the study of Public Administration at the University of Toronto, Canada. His published articles have appeared in *Der Convent, Akademische Monatsschrift* and *Huguenot Trails*, and he has contributed to Kay Goodman and Ruth H. Sander's *Women and German Studies: An Interdisciplinary and Comparative Approach.*